INTELLIGENCE AND RACE

Douglas Lee Eckberg

INTELLIGENCE AND RACE

The Origins and Dimensions
of the IQ Controversy

PRAEGER

PRAEGER SPECIAL STUDIES • PRAEGER SCIENTIFIC

Library of Congress Cataloging in Publication Data

Eckberg, Douglas Lee.
    Intelligence and race.

    Bibliography: p.
    Includes index.
    1. Intellect. 2. Intelligence tests. 3. Race.
I. Title.
BF432.A1E24   153.9'2   79-19795
ISBN 0- 03-052556-X

Published in 1979 by Praeger Publishers
A Division of Holt, Rinehart and Winston/CBS, Inc.
383 Madison Avenue, New York, New York 10017 U.S.A.

© 1979 by Douglas Lee Eckberg

9 038 987654321

Printed in the United States of America

ACKNOWLEDGMENTS

I am indebted to a number of people. No work is the product of a single person's labor, and this work is no exception. While it is not possible to acknowledge the sources of all the support I have received, a small number of people especially stand out for mention.

First, I thank my wife, Rose-Ellen May Eckberg, for the varieties of aid she has given me. Along with the emotional support one commonly mentions, she gave me both needed editorial and organizational assistance and real material support. When I was too tired to organize or rewrite materials, she took over the arduous task of completing such work by herself. It was her work that allowed this book to be published at this early date.

I also thank the members of my doctoral committee at the University of Texas at Austin (S. Dale McLemore, Joe R. Feagin, John Sibley Butler, Frank D. Bean, O. Eugene Jensen, and Walter Firey), whose support, encouragement, and advice were crucial in the development of this work. Among other things, their help allowed this work to become more than just a dissertation. I am especially indebted to Dale McLemore for his ability to grasp the core of an argument incisively and to see its strengths and weaknesses. Further, to the extent that this book maintains organizational clarity, the credit lies with Dr. McLemore.

I am also indebted to Louis A. Zurcher, Jr., for his general encouragement as both professor and dean, and for the role he and other members of the Graduate School of the University of Texas at Austin played in allowing me to receive a fellowship in the W. H. Webb Chair in History and Ideas, and to become a fellow of the Graduate School. Such awards allowed me the time to complete this work.

Turning from organizational to personal contacts, I owe intellectual debts to four people in particular. First is David Roth, who not only introduced me to the literature on the IQ controversy but also worked with me in the development of the major points of the thesis presented here. It was Dave's sociological position on intelligence and testing that set me to this task. Second is Jerry Hirsch, for his biological and historical insight and firm support. Dr. Hirsch's work restored my faith in the thesis of this book when I was floundering with the issue of the genetic causation of traits. Just as important, his correspondence (and later, his personal contact) served to shore up flagging confidence several times. Third is John Garcia, whose special insight into the structure of behavior helped me to make a case against the idea of a general intelligence. Finally, Lester Hill, Jr., has been more of a help than he can possibly know. Sharing an office, and ideas, with him for three years was a rare and welcome experience. His theoretical sophistication and sociological excitement are contagious.

It must be noted that, while the above people contributed to the development of this work, all errors of fact and interpretation are my own.

FOREWORD
by John Garcia

Since Aristotle, fire was considered an element of matter not only by the alchemists but by most chemists as well. All flammable substances were assumed to possess an inherent caloric stuff that was given off during combustion, oxidation, or respiration and that, ultimately, would be absorbed by the surrounding air. When saturated with this stuff, air would smother fire and would no longer support breathing animals. Fire was a phenomenological reality radiating heat and light and giving off gas and smoke that rose with a force sufficient to lift balloons into the skies. It demanded explanation. Some things burned brightly, others burned indifferently, and some things did not burn at all. What could be more natural than to infer that things contained varying amounts of a common substance capable of producing this entity called fire? In keeping with scientific tradition, a label was derived from the Greek term phlogistos (flammable) and employed by Robert Boyle (1627-91) and George E. Stahl (1660-1734). Thus christened, phlogiston was universally accepted and reified to begin a life of its own in the annals of science.

By the eighteenth century, a mass of empirical evidence contradicted the phlogiston theory. The Arabs pointed out that substances gained weight during burning, indicating that nothing was released; quite the contrary, something was gained. By 1775 Pierre Bayen converted mercuric oxide into metal and air by heating it and correctly concluded that the addition of air to the mercury (during oxidation) caused the increased weight of the mercuric oxide. But such evidence only forced the phlogistonists to invent prima facie proofs and tortuous explanations. Among the most curious of these assumptions was the alleged diminution of gravity by phlogistic action and the postulation of a negative weight for phlogiston, put forth about 1780.

One popular concept of the development of science holds that theories are not overthrown by new evidence but by persuasive new theories; however, this was not so for phlogiston theory. By 1738 Daniel Bernoulli already had postulated molecular action in his kinetic theory of heat and pressure, offering an elegant alternative to the theory that heat was an element of matter. But nearly a half century passed before Antoine Lavoisier, in 1783, sounded the death knell for phlogiston with these words:

Chemists have made of phlogiston a vague principle which is not rigorously defined, and which consequently adapts

itself to all explanations into which it may be introduced.
Sometimes this principle is heavy, and sometimes it is
not; sometimes it is free fire, sometimes it is fire combined with the earthy element; sometimes it passes through
the pores of vessels, and sometimes they are impenetrable
for it. It explains at once causticity and non-causticity,
transparency and opacity, colours and the absence of
colours. It is a veritable Proteus which changes its form
at every instance. *

Even then not all were convinced; Joseph Priestley went to his grave
in 1804 still believing in phlogiston.

Douglas Lee Eckberg reveals the similar protean nature of the
hypothetical construct "intelligence" in this comprehensive study,
Intelligence and Race. It is a phenomonological reality that, on the
average, some ethnic and socioeconomical classes of humans do better on selected tasks than some other classes do, but the explanation
that these differences in performance are due to differences in an inherent common stuff possessed in varying amounts by the various
classes of humans is by no means clear. Echoes of Lavoisier's
charges against the phlogistonists abound in Eckberg's early chapters.
When pressed for a definition of intelligence, mental testers often
take refuge behind a trivial form of operationism based on P. W.
Bridgeman's (1927) Logic of Modern Physics. Bridgeman said, "A
concept is synonomous with the corresponding set of operations" (p.
5). But the mental testers keep changing the operations, adapting the
concepts to fit all situations. Thus, intelligence is whatever the intelligence test measures; intelligence is the "first principle component of an infinitely large number of highly diverse tasks"; intelligence
is indexed by "the speed of learning and the complexity of what can be
learned"; intelligence does not simply index "the rate of learning of
certain types of more or less universally available information."†
Eckberg lays bare the contradictions in the various definitions of intelligence concealed in the operations of face validity, construct validity, factor analysis, and heritability statistics. Bridgeman warns:

---

*A. Wolf, A History of Science, Technology and Philosophy in
the 18th Century (London: George Allen and Unwin, 1962), p. 345.
    † The last three definitions are from A. R. Jensen, "Intelligence
and Learning," in Melbourne Studies in Education 1978, ed. Stephen
Murray-Smith (Melbourne: Melbourne University Press), pp. 112,
118, 124.

We must demand that the set of operations equivalent to
any concept be a unique set, for otherwise there are possibilities of ambiguity in practical applications we cannot
admit. . . . To adopt the operational point of view involves
much more than a mere restriction of the sense in which we
understand "concepts" but means a far reaching change in
all our habits of thought, in that we shall no longer permit
ourselves to use as tools in our thinking concepts of which
we cannot give an adequate account of in terms of operations. [Pp. 6, 31]

A stricter adherence to operationism might have spared us the
contradictions apparent in the writings of the hereditarians. Arthur
R. Jensen (1969a) says, "There is no answer [to] the question of what
intelligence really is" (pp. 5-6), but of course he believes that intelligence really exists polygenetically in the chromosomes. Hans J.
Eysenck (1962) complains that "intelligence tests are not based on any
very sound scientific principles"(p. 8), while Richard J. Herrnstein
(1971) proclaims that the measurement of intelligence is psychology's
"most telling accomplishment to date" (p. 45). What a stunning in-
dictment!
    But nothing in the history of chemistry, alchemy, or even sor-
cery prepares us for Eckberg's study. Racial intelligence literature
is marked with banal observations, meticulous analyses, bizarre assumptions, and gothic finaglings. My favorite character is Samuel
George Morton, as described by Stephen J. Gould (1978); this necro-
mancer collected over a thousand skulls between 1830 and 1851. Determined to replace the idle speculations on race with some hard facts,
he classified his grim collection into numerous races and divined their
racial intelligence, morality, and cultural capacity by pouring white
mustard seeds into their empty braincases; later he switched to lead
bb shot, a technological advance that gave him a more reliable measure. Culling out the skulls that contradicted his conclusions, he established the familiar hierarchy of prejudice: Europeans were viewed
as the epitome of mankind, the Hottentots as the nearest approxima-
tion to animals. Apparently chiding those fieldworkers who wasted
time talking and working with American Indians instead of pouring
shot into their skulls, he said, "The benevolent mind may regret the
inaptitude of the Indian for civilization, but objective evidence has established it none the less and sentimentality must yield to fact" (Gould
1978, p. 505). When Dr. Morton died the New York Tribune proclaimed that "probably no scientific man in America enjoyed a higher
reputation among the scholars of the world" (Gould 1978, p. 503).
    Surely no roguish alchemist selling his royal patrons a fraudulent
recipe for turning base metal to gold ever matched the bizarre accom-

plishments of Sir Cyril Burt recounted by Oliver Gillie (1976). Sir Cyril conjured up subjects and data as needed to support his conclusions that intelligence was mainly (85 percent) genetically determined, whatever that may mean. Gillie details the failure of his intense search for Sir Cyril's two collaborators, Miss Margaret Howard and Miss J. Conway. * Apparently they sprang full-grown from Sir Cyril's brow. These phantoms allegedly assisted Burt with the research that won him knightly spurs in Great Britain and the Thorndike Prize in the United States. Arthur R. Jensen (1969a) described the research as the "most satisfactory attempt to estimate the influence of heredity upon intelligence" and Hans J. Eysenck (1971) praised the "outstanding quality of design and statistical treatment of the studies."† Another missing lady—M. G. O'Conner, claimed by Sir Cyril to be an Irish student assistant—could not be located anywhere in Great Britain or Ireland. According to Gillie, Burt claimed that this leprechaun demonstrated that the ability of London schoolchildren had declined between 1914 and 1965. Burt used her data in his attack on the comprehensive (nonselective) schools in 1969. Exactly how Burt could argue that the school environment can depress the ability that he believed to be largely fixed by heredity is not clear. In any case, Gillie concludes that, even if the missing ladies did exist, "the evidence suggests they were not the ladies that Sir Cyril said they were and they could not have done all the things he said they did."‡ Gillie closes his letter with this remark:

> The time has now come for us to ask why Burt's work
> was looked at so uncritically by psychologists and others
> for such a long time. The answer might tell us something
> important about the role that power, charisma and wishful
> thinking can play in bolstering support for scientific
> theory. **

The wishful thinking is quite clear. The educational establishment wished to have an efficient device to sort out children for various tracks of education: Laborer, tradesman, technician, professional, merchant, chief. They wished the capacity for education to be a fixed immutable quantity so that children could be assigned early to their

---

*See Oliver Gillie, "Burt's Missing Ladies," Science 204 (1979): 1035-9, for the latest report of this intrigue. As far as we know, Burt never invented men, only women and children.

   † Ibid., p. 1038.
   ‡ Ibid., p. 1037.
   **Ibid., p. 1039.

appropriate educational tracks without need for untidy track switching later on down the line. Since there were some practical difficulties in assigning the master's child to a labor track and his servant's child to a professional track, the educational establishment wished that the capacity of the children would match the socioeconomic status of their parents. Cyril Burt gave them their wish and they knighted him.

The reader may be led by my Spanish surname and Hispanic heritage to suspect my somewhat impatient view of intelligence testing (Garcia 1977). However, Douglas Lee Eckberg is an intelligent young Nordic American with an impeccable Scandinavian-German heritage, who was fathered by a career army officer and reared in the southwestern United States. He treats the literature with a cool even-handed style and views the entire controversy from a detached sociological perspective.

Eckberg examines the entire social context of the testing environment and its effect upon the "objective" deliberations of mental testers. He reviews the political convictions and the social origins of the mental tester and the confrontations between the professional testers and the apprehensive young testees. When the testees are from a lower socioeconomic class or another ethnic group, the politically conservative tester is apt to perceive the testees as inherently inferior to his own social class. Another tester, bent on social reform, sees the testees as culturally deprived and in need of his remedial skills. To the objective eye, the testees are merely different from the tester. The perceptual and cognitive distortions of the tester are "natural," which is to say that the distortions are "advantageous to the economic and social survival" of the tester. As Albert Szent-Györgyi so eloquently put it: "The brain is not an organ of thinking, but an organ of survival like claws and fangs. It is made in such a way as to make us accept as truth that which is only advantage."*

It is obvious even to Jensen (1969a) that the intelligence test measures some things that the testee had learned before he came into the test situation. If all the testees come from the same socioeconomic class and ethnic group as the tester, it seems reasonable to assume that the individual differences in performance may be due to individual differences in their inherent ability to absorb information from a common culture. However, if the testees come from a variety of socioeconomic classes and ethnic groups, whose subcultures overlap to different degrees with that of the tester, we would expect individual differences in test performance even if all testees had exactly the same degree of inherent ability. This is the racial tester's dilem-

---

*A. Szent-Györgyi, "Science, Ethics and Politics," Science 125 (1957): 225-26.

ma: If we use a single test for all ethnic and socioeconomic groups, we cannot be sure all testees have had equivalent experience with the prerequisites of the test; if we use different tests for different groups we cannot be sure that the tests are equivalent measures of inherent ability. Human-testing methodology offers no empirical operations for resolving this dilemma. It offers many assumptions, however, and Eckberg examines these assumptions in detail.

The operations of conditioning and learning appear to offer an answer to the tester's dilemma. Simply start from scratch and teach the various ethnic and socioeconomic groups a series of associative tasks that are novel to all groups. Jensen (1969a) tried this, as had others before him. Learning performance on novel tasks proved to be virtually unrelated to intelligence as measured by IQ tests. At first, Jensen declared that these novel tasks required only a low-level, rote-memory ability and that a higher level of intelligence was required to handle meaningful material. But of course meaning depends upon prior experience as does IQ test performance, thus the correlation between learning of meaningful material and measured IQ is a spurious one dependent upon uncontrolled covariations in prior learning experience. Now, Jensen says that psychologists have known all along that learning ability is not the same as intelligence. He writes:

> For many years, definitions of intelligence usually included the "ability to learn". This would seem to accord with commonsense notions of intelligence and with simple observation. Is not the "bright" or high IQ pupil a "fast learner" and the "dull" or low IQ pupil a "slow learner"? Studies of learning ability in the experimental laboratory, however, apparently failed to uphold the commonsense connection between learning ability and IQ, and most psychologists dropped "ability to learn" from their definitions of intelligence. Ability to learn was still regarded as a mental ability, to be sure, but not the same ability as intelligence, at least as it is measured by IQ tests. *

Jensen's rationalizations would do credit to a phlogistonist. When prior experience is strictly controlled, the correlation between learning performance and measured intelligence approaches zero and differences between ethnic socioeconomic groups also approach zero.

---

*A. R. Jensen, "Intelligence and Learning," in <u>Melbourne Studies in Education 1978</u>, ed. Stephen Murray-Smith (Melbourne: Melbourne University Press).

Instead of concluding that the group differences in IQ depend upon differences in prior experiences of the various groups, he concludes that learning has nothing to do with intelligence, thus protecting his faith in the inherent nature of intelligence from empirical evidence. In the same way, the phlogistonists were able to protect their faith that an inherent element in flammable substances was the cause of fire, in the face of evidence showing that fire depended upon an environmental element, which proved to be free oxygen.

For most of us, intelligence is synonymous with the ability to learn, but it is probably a mistake to conceive of intelligence as a general capacity or general learning process, particularly if one wishes to make the genetic argument. Certainly, intelligence is not a general capacity of the vertebrate brain correlated with the volume of the braincase, as implied by Harry J. Jerison.* Nor does general intelligence depend upon the position of each species on that presumptive phylogenetic ladder rising to the primates and topped by man, as wishfully described by Jensen.† Phenomenologically, intelligence appears to be the capacity to acquire, store, and utilize information and, in its highest form, to transmit that information to others symbolically, as humans do linguistically. However, by this criterion, the human's closest rival appears to be the honeybee, not the anthropoid ape. According to the empirical evidence of the moment, the communication capacity of an ordinary honeybee far exceeds that of even those chimpanzees specially trained to communicate symbolically with man.‡

Learning capacity or intelligence is simply the behavioral component of adaptation. Its manifestation in the honeybee and man springs from different evolutionary origins, that is, it comes from different anatomical structures, from different genes. The superficial generality of intelligence arises out of the common evolutionary pressures faced by man and bee through convergent evolution. As a concrete example, take the problem of navigation or movement over long distances to seek advantages of food and climate. The most reliable signposts in the worldly environment are the sun, stars, and the geomagnetic field. These cues are used by bees, birds, and humans in intelligent ways, but each species employs a unique set of evolutionary

---

*H. J. Jerison, Evolution of the Brain and Intelligence (New York: Academic Press, 1973).

† A. R. Jensen, "Intelligence and Learning," in Melbourne Studies in Education 1978, ed. Stephen Murray-Smith (Melbourne: Melbourne University Press).

‡ J. L. Gould, "Honeybee Recruitment: The Dance-Language Controversy," Science 189 (1975): 685-93.

structures and each species learns its own navigational techniques. The generality of navigational behavior lies not in the animals but in the common environmental signposts of space and time.

The stuff that is measured by IQ tests is unique to humans and rises out of the social atmosphere nurturing the individual human mind. Any human infant raised to adulthood while isolated from all human society will be intellectually devastated forever. Any human infant transported to another culture will absorb the new culture as readily and completely as the original culture of his ancestors and he will flourish intellectually. As humans grow, absorb, and age in one culture, they lose the plastic ability to absorb another culture and, consequently, appear intellectually different.

Whenever a human group is isolated or even partially restricted by geographic, social, or biological barriers, that group will develop different phonemes, words, grammars, concepts, incentives, and values as a function of the degree of its segregation. This is the stuff from which intelligence tests and meaningful learning tasks are made. As far as we can tell, the development of this linguistic cultural stuff is the same intrinsic process for all human groups, however, the specific content is different. When one group is politically dominant over others, it is very apt to set up its own cultural content as a standard for all. Thus, in the United States the language of the dominant group became Standard Test English; Black English and Spanglish became "bad" English or "poor" grammar, reducing the measured IQ of minority schoolchildren and restricting them from academic tracks of privilege. Often the dominant class jealously guards its language and knowledge by segregation of schools to restrict competition from other groups. This is not new. In midsummer of the year 1612, Galileo explained why he did not always write in the "scholarly" Latin:

> I wrote in the colloquial tongue because I must have everyone able to read it, and for the same reason I wrote my last book in this language. I am induced to do this by seeing how many young men are sent through the universities at random to be made physicians, philosophers, and so on; thus many of them are committed to professions for which they are unsuited, while other men who would be fitted for these are taken up by family cares and other occupations remote from the literature. The latter are, as Ruzzante would say, furnished with "horse sense", but because they are unable to read things that are "Greek to them" they become convinced that in the "big books there are great new things of logic and philosophy and still more that is way over their heads."

Now I want them to see that just as nature has given
to them, as well as to philosophers, eyes with which to
see her works, so she has also given them brains
capable of penetrating and understanding them. *

John Garcia

Departments of Psychology,
Psychiatry, and the
Bio-behavioral Sciences,
University of California
Los Angeles, California

---

*Discoveries and Opinions of Galileo, translated with an Intro-
duction and Notes by Stillman Drake (Garden City, N.Y.: Doubleday,
1957), p. 84.

CONTENTS

LIST OF TABLES

LIST OF FIGURES

PART I

THE STATUS OF THE HEREDITARIAN POSITION IN THE IQ CONTROVERSY

1

INTRODUCTION

The thesis that racial and class differences in achievement are traceable to differences in the genetic makeup of social groups is an old one. During the first quarter of this century, it held the loyalty of the greater portion of the social scientific and biological communities. By the middle 1930s, however, it had died as a major thesis in Western science, for reasons that will be discussed later. While certain individuals continued to support the thesis after 1940, on the whole, it claimed few adherents and could be characterized as smoldering. As put by the social science historian George Ward Stocking (1960, chap. 1), social scientific conceptions of the place of race in social explanation could, by the late 1950s, best be described by the term agnostic. Further, it was but a short step from agnosticism to atheism.

Though it might only have smoldered, the issue of race never fully died. There existed currents in psychological thought and method that would act as catalysts for a reassertion of the old thesis, if only conditions became right. By the late 1960s conditions did become right. The growing dismay of many social scientists over their inability to readily change achievement patterns of the lower classes and nonwhites set the stage for the emergence of the belief that the failure of governmental programs lay in the targets of those programs —the poor and blacks themselves. This position, termed blaming the victim by some critics (for example, Ryan 1971), took many forms; but the form that caught the public eye, and that has had the greatest effect within social science itself, received emphasis in a long essay by Arthur R. Jensen in the Harvard Educational Review, in the winter of 1969.

Briefly, Jensen argued that poor and black people's scholastic deficits (and, by extension, their economic deficits) are not amenable to social amelioration of the usual kind. Put more bluntly, poor and black people are intellectually dull, and this dullness is a function of

3

genetic differences between groups, differences that are beyond the power of any straightforward environmental manipulations to rectify. Jensen developed a plausible genetic explanation of scholastic achievement, and then concluded by calling for a regimen of rote learning for individuals with low IQ scores. He also gave—although it was less central to his main argument, and curiously out of place in a discussion of individual differences in learning—a long aside on the educational deficits of blacks and a hint that a solution to the deficits is "eugenic foresight" (Jensen 1969a, p. 95).

Other writers soon joined Jensen. In Great Britain, his argument was repeated, basically intact, by Hans J. Eysenck (1971). In the United States, Richard J. Herrnstein (1971, 1973) used similar data and arguments in order to support the idea of the existence of a naturally stratified, meritocratic society. William Shockley (1972) used similar arguments in order to justify advocating the sterilization of dull people and (especially) blacks. *

Antagonistic response to Jensen's thesis was rapid, spurred by heavy reporting in the mass media; and the modern IQ controversy was born. In light of the well-known virulence of the attacks on inequalitarian theorists,† what is interesting is not the strength of the environmentalist response, but its weakness.‡ What emerged was a disagreement with Jensen's specific conclusion regarding innate black-white differences, but a general agreement with his argument as a whole. So striking, in fact, was this agreement with his general theme, at least early in the controversy, that when commenting on the

----

*Shockley (1972) showed an extreme racist nativism, in calling for the differential treatment of whites and blacks as groups, on the basis of average test-score differences. He wrote: "Nature has color-coded groups of individuals so that statistically reliable predictions of their adaptability to intellectually rewarding lives can be made and profitably be used by the pragmatic man in the street." (p. 307). Even many writers who found Jensen's arguments compelling found Shockley's objectionable.

† For a tracing of some of the problems faced by major hereditarian writers, see Jensen (1972, pp. 1-67), Herrnstein (1973, pp. 3-59), and Holden (1973). For some replies, see Hirsch (1975) and Purvin (1974).

‡ In this work, the terms environmentalist and hereditarian will be used to identify those individuals and loosely knit groups who can be characterized as anti-Jensen or pro-Jensen. As will become apparent, the IQ controversy does not rest simply on problems of genetic causation. Indeed, several of the most prominent environmentalists are active geneticists.

seven initial (invited) responses to his article Jensen boldly asserted (1969b):

> Seldom in my experience of reading the psychological literature have I seen the discussants of a supposedly "controversial" article (in the Editors' words) so much in agreement with all the main points of the article they were asked especially to criticize. On my main points the discussants agree with me at least as much as they agree among themselves, which is considerably. [Pp. 449–50]

Jensen's observation was largely correct, as was noted by other observers. One critic, while commenting on the Jensen paper, noted that Jensen's critics "would require even more space to critique than the original article itself" (Lewontin 1970a). Another commentator indicated that most reactions to the original article had been "wide-ranging and uncritical" and, on that basis, criticized the "scholarly incompetence" of much of the psychological community (Hirsch 1975, pp. 6–9). It is notable that neither of these two commentators is a psychometrician; both are geneticists. This fact will gain significance later.

Many of the early responses to Jensen attempted to explain his various lines of evidence in environmentalist terms. In effect, they tried to prove the null hypothesis, that no group differences in psychoneural functioning exist. These attacks were often quite speculative and addressed scattered elements of his argument without attacking the position as a whole. For example, where Jensen stated that intelligence was 80 percent genetically determined, critics attempted to demonstrate that it was only 40 or 45 or 60 percent determined (see, for example, Fehr 1969; Anandalkshmy and Adams 1969; Bodmer and Cavalli-Sforza 1970; Jencks 1972; Layzer 1974). Where Jensen stated that compensatory education had failed, critics responded that it had not in fact been tried (see, for example, Hunt 1969). Jensen successfully rejected these claims as ad hoc, and a review of the controversy published in 1974 concluded that the "environmentalist research programme" was then in a state of "degeneration" (Urbach 1974). *

---

*There are some severe problems with Urbach's analysis, which will not be dealt with here. However, his general observation, that the ad hoc arguments of most of Jensen's critics were not persuasive, is correct. The foundations of those criticisms will be analyzed later in this study.

This ad hoc nature of the responses to Jensen allowed a number of crucial elements in his argument to lie largely unexamined. Commonly, the heritability of the intelligence quotient (IQ) and the social deficits of blacks were the only topics to be discussed in any detail. When one realizes that the IQ controversy is not strictly a controversy over the biological versus the cultural determination of traits, but actually is a multifaceted argument, then this fact assumes some importance. Specifically, for one to assert that a preponderance of evidence supports the idea that one group is intellectually superior to another group, in any general sense, one must first take as given at least four prior assertions:

1. Paper-and-pencil tests constitute valid measures of human mental functioning.
2. This mental functioning can be characterized as metric-linear in structure, or at least approximately so, such that a single summary statistic (IQ) can stand for the congeries of elements that constitute the functioning.
3. Differences in this measured entity play important causal roles in educational and economic achievement.
4. Differences in this entity are largely hereditary. That is, they are both genetically inherited and beyond the power of environmental manipulation to modify beyond a relatively miniscule amount.

If one of the first three assertions is rejected, then the IQ controversy loses social significance. Further, all four assertions are open to considerable criticism, as this study will demonstrate. But early critics of the general hereditarian position did not challenge the four in any comprehensive manner. Instead, the measurement, structure, and social importance of intelligence were allowed to lie largely undiscussed. The issue of genetic determinism, while it did receive much scrutiny, was, for the most part, treated in a very narrow (and largely incorrect) manner. Specifically, many discussions here centered on the strength of heritability estimates (nature-nurture ratios) when inheritance was discussed, even though it has been known for some time (for example, Hogben 1939) that such ratios give very little information about either the genetic or the environmental determinants of traits.

THE PLACE OF ASSUMPTIONS
IN THE IQ CONTROVERSY

Because it may not be immediately apparent why the above assertions are crucial in the IQ controversy, a brief inspection of the hereditarian position in terms of its logical components will make this importance explicit. If some of the assertions seem not to be discussed much by opponents, it is because they have generally come to be implicitly accepted by both sides. Therefore, they have come to have the force of assumptions. Instead of openly standing as issues of debate, they are bypassed. It is only when they are once again made explicit, and are then examined, that a straightforward resolution of the controversy becomes likely.

The Measurement of Intelligence

Of all the issues that have come to be assumed by participants in the controversy, that of measurement may be the most important. This is so because the controversy developed around the fact that different groups have different average scores on standard intelligence tests. The scores are assumed to accurately represent the variable degree of intellectual ability for individuals (and, by extension, for groups), and this assumption is necessary. Otherwise, the controversy becomes nonempirical. Whatever the structure, or predictive validity, or genetic inheritance of IQ scores, if those scores are not representative of underlying psychoneural processes, then the hereditarian position can find neither confirmation nor disconfirmation by reference to them. Of course, the controversy could (and probably would) continue even if all those involved in it discounted the validity of scores, but it would continue as a purely speculative matter.

The position taken in this work is that the relationship between test scores and an underlying gradient of ability is characterized by contingency, or vagueness (as the term is used by Shwayder 1965); that is, the relationship cannot be specified. While it is commonly admitted that this is the case for individuals, a case for vagueness regarding group scores will be made later. This being so, attempts to use group scores in order to infer superiority and inferiority on any biological substrate considered to underlie the scores will be illusory. *

It should be stressed that not all environmentalists accept the validity of test scores. For example, those who accept one or an-

---

*It can legitimately be asked how we can determine the social importance, structure, and inheritance of intelligence if we deny the measurement of the phenomenon. As will become apparent later, there are many lines of evidence, besides test scores alone, that can be used to make our cases. Further, an analysis of test scores can be of interest if one wishes to critically examine the claims made about their, say, social importance.

other of the cultural-deprivation perspectives will often hold that test scores do not adequately represent the abilities of at least those at the bottom of the stratification hierarchy. This position is also held by those who stress the role of cultural bias in the development and standardization of tests (for example, Evans 1974, pp. 103-4). Yet many environmentalists tacitly assume the validity of tests for the same reasons that hereditarians do—some, because such an assumption allows then to consider their findings empirically justified. As a single example, the Marxist economists Samuel Bowles and Herbert Gintis (1974, 1976), more clearly than most observers, have noted the roles that undemonstrated assumptions play in the controversy, and their own work stresses the weak predictive ability of standard test scores for economic achievement. Yet these writers accept scores on the Armed Forces Qualification Test (AFQT) as measures of "adult cognitive achievement" (Bowles and Gintis 1974, pp. 18-19), apparently because such a position allows them to discount the importance of inherited intellectual differences. Other writers accept the biological validity of test scores simply because they were trained in a profession for which IQ, as a representation of a biological reality, is a major commitment. This will be discussed later.

The Structure of Intelligence

For the hereditarian position to stand, it must be possible to stratify people on a simple hierarchy of mental abilities. This point was acknowledged over half a century ago by one of the foremost advocates of general intelligence, Charles Spearman. Regarding the eugenics movement, Spearman (1914) wrote that "the eugenicists would be seriously hindered. Their efforts to better the race could be of slight avail, if they had to be dissipated in hunting after innumerable independent abilities" (pp. 220-21). Curiously, a large percentage of modern-day psychometricians appear to accept a multifactorial view of intelligence, at least for in-house discussions. Yet, when social pronouncements are made, single summary scores (IQs) are used in making group comparisons. The choice to be made seems to be between a monolithic view of intelligence, in which intelligence is considered to be what the tests are testing, and one or another particular view of intelligence. For example, there exists a two-factor view of intelligence, in which performance on any task is regarded as a joint function of a general factor and a factor specific to the task at hand (for example, Spearman 1927). There is also what Spearman termed the anarchic view of intelligence, in which performance is regarded as dependent on a wide array of shifting attributes that are quasi-independent. This is the position taken in this study. Finally, there are the positions that Spearman termed oligarchic, because they treat intelligence as consisting of a relatively limited set of factors or (sometimes) faculties.

The important point here is that, for any view but the monolithic, a notion of general inferiority-superiority is difficult to sustain. Jensen's work stresses the importance of a general factor, or g factor, in intelligence-test results, and thus supports such a notion; but even he recognizes the existence of multiple dimensions of mind, and this fact has been used in order to question the logical consistency of his position (for example, Lewontin 1970b). Whatever the legitimacy of this charge, it remains that the structure of intelligence deserves one's close inspection before one makes group comparisons in terms of this entity.

The Social Importance of Intelligence

It is logically possible for there to exist a unidimensional intelligence that appropriate tests accurately measure, without there likewise existing important social consequences of differences in this entity. In order to make the leap from intelligence differences to differential ranks in a socioeconomic hierarchy, one has first to posit the functional importance of the quality under investigation. Two examples should make this point clear.

First, fingerprint whorls are highly heritable physical characteristics, yet such configurations bear little relationship to success in any social sphere, with the possible exception of safecracking (where fingerprints can be used to track one down). Concerning behavioral phenomena, let us consider bipedalism. There exist individual differences in walking ability, many of which undoubtedly are genetically related. But a case for the social importance of walking ability, to this author's knowledge, has not been made by anyone. *
In any case, such public figures as a president of the United States (Franklin D. Roosevelt) and certain state governors (for example, George Wallace) have functioned while lacking walking ability.

With intelligence the case is quite different. The meritocratic position in social discussions (for example, Herrnstein 1973) requires that merit be a differentially distributed quality. In the context of the IQ controversy, merit means measured intelligence. So universal has been the tendency to equate IQ with merit that two critics (Bowles

---

*Indeed, when differences in this ability are publicly discussed, it is commonly in a context in which barriers to the self-mobility of those who lack walking ability are seen as unnecessary burdens, even as discriminatory. The prescription is always that such barriers be removed. There is a marked disjunction between the discussions about physical versus mental disabilities.

and Gintis 1974) have wondered aloud: Why, "amid a spirited liberal counterattack . . . is the validity of the genetic school's description of the social function of intelligence blandly accepted?" (p. 18). In light of this assumption, the social importance of measured intelligence requires investigation. The position held by this author, which will be confirmed later, is that the relationship between test scores and any of the commonly employed measures of achievement is small.

The Inheritance of Intelligence

If one accepts the three assumptions discussed above, one must go one step further before making claims about innate differences between individuals or groups. One must also assume that intelligence is genetically determined. By this it is not meant that one merely supposes a genetic component of intelligence. Rather, one must assume that intelligence is genetically inherited, and that, for all practical purposes, it is beyond the reach of change by pragmatic social intervention. This is a crucial distinction. On the one hand, if intelligence is not genetically inherited, then any charge of innate group differences will be unfounded. On the other hand, if intelligence is genetically inherited, but is also readily manipulable, then simple group comparisons will lack a necessary finality. This can occur for one of two reasons. First, group differences that appear may be functions of the environmental elements that affect intelligence. Second, even if real differences are found, it will be possible to manipulate them. In either case, the problem of group differences will be a moral and political one, rather than an empirical one.

TOWARD A SOCIOLOGY OF
HEREDITARIAN SOCIAL SCIENCE

From the foregoing discussion, it is evident that the status of each of the four assumptions is open to empirical and/or theoretical inquiry. In fact, it remains to be seen how strong is the hereditarian position when a piecemeal approach to criticism is abandoned for a full-scale analysis of the logical components of the hereditarian argument. However, a second issue also arises here. Given the above discussion, why have so many social and behavioral scientists apparently been so ready to accept such large portions of the Jensen argument without question? Clearly, something has acted to cause them to perceive the arguments in a selective manner.

That an individual can be selective in perception is a widely accepted fact. However, that the members of a scientific discipline (or disciplines) can be affected in large numbers is contrary to the majority position in the sociology of science. Generally, the development of knowledge within science is considered to be a cumulative process that is divorced from either the personal characteristics of individual practitioners or extrascientific processes. One of the most influential contemporary sociologists of science flatly states that the possibilities of a "sociology of the conceptual and theoretical contents of science are extremely limited" (Ben-David 1971, pp. 13-14). Nevertheless, there is evidence that insofar as issues of race and class are concerned, Ben-David is incorrect. For example, it has been shown that both political orientation and personal biography affect one's perception of issues of biology and social processes. Documentation of this point will set the stage for examination of the social determinants of that selective perception.

Social Influences on Perceptions
in Nature-Nurture Arguments

Historically, those social scientists taking the nature side in a nature-nurture dispute have tended to be politically right of the center, while those taking the nurture side have been to the left of the center. For example, Nicholas Pastore's (1949) study of earlier disputes found that only 2 of 24 major disputants did not fit this trend: Lewis Terman was a liberal (in the U.S. sense of the word) and a hereditarian, while J. B. Watson was a conservative and an environmentalist. However, in this century, a number of progressives, including several prominent socialists, were eugenicists (Pickens 1969). *

---

*Among those eugenicists who were also socialists were Karl Pearson, Jack London, Sidney and Beatrice Webb, and Harold Laski (Hofstadter 1959; Gossett 1963; Chase 1977). Besides being a socialist, Pearson was a free thinker, a feminist, and a member of the Men's and Women's Club, where sexual mores were widely discussed. He was also a close associate of Havelock Ellis and of Karl Marx's daughter Eleanor (MacKenzie and Barnes 1974, pp. 22-23). According to Pastore (1949, p. 41), he became increasingly conservative with time.

In like manner, recall that Herbert Spencer, whose beliefs on the nature of intelligence were later given form by Galton, believed in a laissez faire state. On the other hand, Galton advocated strong governmental intervention into the act of procreation. The liberal-conservative split can best be described as historically specific (Rosenberg 1964, 1966).

The relationship between elements in one's personal biography and one's conclusions about the sources of group differences in intelligence-test scores is also clear, but not absolute. For example, one multiple-correlational study (Sherwood and Nataupsky 1968) predicted with some success the conclusions of black-white intelligence research, on the basis of biographical characteristics. Measures used included age, place in the birth order, foreign- versus native-born grandparents, parents' education, urban versus rural childhood, and undergraduate achievement percentiles. The authors obtained a multiple correlation of 0.45 (R^2 = 0.20), which was statistically significant though small. Those who felt intelligence to be genetically inherited tended to be relatively younger and higher in birth order, with native-born grandparents, better-educated parents (though for the fathers this was curvilinear), nonurban childhoods, and higher undergraduate achievement records.

Following Jensen's article, R. W. Friedrichs (1973) polled a representative sample of the American Psychological Association, and found that slightly over two-thirds disagreed or tended to disagree with Jensen's thesis (this was similar to the findings in the study cited above). Those disagreeing tended to be younger than those agreeing (the opposite of the above findings). Those from the deep South tended to agree with the thesis, while those whose names were recognizably ethnically Jewish were less likely to agree than was the sample as a whole.

More recently, two sociologists (Lieberman and Reynolds 1975; Lieberman 1968) have shown a correlation of social factors with the belief in race as a biological reality. Briefly, those who argue that races are real, empirical entities tend to be first born or last born, male, born into a Catholic or conservative Protestant home, and born in a southern or border state. And all four of their grandparents tend to have been born within the United States. Those who deny the existence of race tend to be intermediate in birth order. They also tend to be female, to have a Jewish mother, and to have been born in the Third World. Their grandparents tend to have been born outside the United States, Canada, and northwestern Europe. The authors contend that where people with these "underdog" traits accept the existence of race, it is common that they have attended universities which support such a position (Lieberman and Reynolds 1975, p. 16).

As regards the IQ controversy, Jonathan Harwood (1976, 1977) has analyzed the political orientations of those who have taken strong stands, and he has repeated the findings of Pastore. This is shown in Table 1. At least according to Harwood, all the major environmentalists (that is, those who take an anti-Jensen stance) are reformers or radicals, while all those who are strongly pro-Jensen are conservatives. Harwood holds that political orientation is not

TABLE 1

The Political Orientations, Stance on Race-IQ, and Disciplines of
Major Disputants in the Modern IQ Controversy

Disputants	Political Views[a]	Stance[b]	Discipline
Pro-Jensen			
A. Jensen	Right (of center)	h	Psychology
H. Eysenck	Right	h	Psychology
R. Herrnstein	Right	h/e	Psychology
R. Cattell	Right	h	Psychology
D. Ingle	Right	h	Physiology
Anti-Jensen			
J. Hunt	Reformer	e	Psychology
M. Deutsch	Reformer	e	Psychology
E. Gordon	Reformer	e	Education
T. Dobzhansky	Reformer	h/e	Genetics
W. Bodmer	Reformer?	h/e	Population genetics
A. Montagu	Reformer	e	Anthropology
C. L. Brace	?	e	Anthropology
F. Livingston	?	e	Anthropology
J. Hirsch	Reformer	h/e	Behavior genetics
S. Rose	Radical	e	Neurobiology
R. Lewontin	Radical	h/e	Population genetics
L. Kamin	Radical	e	Psychology
B. Simon	Radical	e	Education
C. Jencks	Radical	h/e	Sociology
A. Halsey	Radical/ reformer	e	Sociology

[a]A question mark indicates the author did not have access to such information, or information was unclear.

[b]h = hereditarian, e = environmentalist, h/e = equivocal (often because genetic differences are seen as plausible but unproved and sometimes unlikely as well).

Source: Jonathon Harwood, "The Race-Intelligence Controversy: A Sociological Approach, II—'External' Factors," Social Studies of Science 7 (1977): 1-30. Copyright © 1977 by Sage Publications, London and Beverly Hills. Reprinted by permission.

TABLE 2

The Methodological Orientations of Participants in the IQ Controversy

Participants	Discipline	Methodological Orientation[a]	Revised Orientation[b]
Hereditarians			
A. R. Jensen	Psychology	Soft-hard[c]	
H. J. Eysenck	Psychology	Hard	
R. B. Cattell	Psychology	Hard	
Dwight Ingle	Physiology	—	Hard (physiological)
R. Herrnstein	Psychology	Hard	
Environmentalists			
A. H. Halsey	Sociology	—	
J. McV. Hunt	Psychology	Soft	
M. Deutsch	Psychology	Soft	
Edmund Gordon	Education	—	
Ashley Montagu	Anthropology	Soft	Soft-hard (some statistical)
Christopher Jencks	Sociology	—	Hard (quantitative-statistical)
Steven Rose	Neurobiology	—	Hard (neurobiological)
Richard Lewontin	Population genetics	—	Hard (quantitative-statistical)
Walter Bodmer	Population genetics	—	Hard (quantitative-statistical)
Jerry Hirsch	Behavior genetics	—	Hard (experimental)

[a]A dash indicates that Harwood had no information on this individual or that the individual is not a psychologist. Comparisons are limited to psychologists, with the exception of Montagu, an anthropologist.

[b]Revised orientations are offered by the present author. Here, people from disciplines outside psychology are included.

[c] Hard is defined by Harwood as "committed to 'scientific method,' experiment, quantification, reductionism, and a stress on precision and certainty." Soft is defined as "characterized by an attempt to 'understand every instance in all its individuality,' suspicion of fixed schemes of classification and general laws, distrust of statistical evidence, reliance on intuition, and on interest more in modifying or extending hypotheses than in disconfirming them."

Note: The concepts of hard and soft methodology are not very well articulated at this point, and it may be that a given writer will appear hard or soft depending on which of his or her works are cited, or on what is emphasized in a given work.

Source: Jonathan Harwood, "The Race-Intelligence Controversy: A Sociological Approach, I—Professional Factors," Social Studies of Science 6 (1976): 369-94. Copyright © 1976 by Sage Publications, London and Beverly Hills. Reprinted by permission.

the only factor that separates the pro- and anti-Jensen camps. His contention is that styles of thought also enter into the choice of position. For example, those who oppose the Jensen thesis tend to employ what Mannheim (1953) termed conservative thought, while those who support the thesis tend to be bourgeois liberal (Harwood 1976, p. 376; this argument comes originally from MacKenzie and Barnes 1974). Conservative thought should not be confused with right-of-center thought.

Basically, as presented by Harwood, the modes of thought can be contrasted along five dichotomies, in which the second part of each dichotomy is the conservative one: (1) rationalism versus intuition, (2) quantitative continuity versus qualitative discontinuity, (3) abstract-theoretical versus particular-concrete, (4) atomism-reductionism versus holism-emergence, and (5) static-ahistorical versus dynamic-historical (see Harwood 1976, pp. 376-82).

Methodologically, this means that hereditarians will tend to be hard, while environmentalists will be soft; and Harwood claims to have demonstrated this (see Table 2). Here, Harwood's arguments are not convincing; he has more clearly shown that hereditarians tend to be hard than that environmentalists tend to be soft, methodologically. This author has added to Harwood's table a column titled "Revised Orientation," in which the present author's perceptions of the methodological orientations of disputants are contrasted with the perceptions of Harwood. To the extent that these perceptions are valid, they indicate that environmentalists are a diverse group. Actually, what appears most strikingly is that hereditarians tend to be a more homogeneous group than are their opponents.

Harwood is on no firmer ground in his assessment that there exists a tendency for hereditarians to be bioscientists and for environmentalists to be social scientists. He feels that a small portion of the controversy seems to revolve around attempts by practitioners of the two loose communities to single out and defend domains of expertise. Thus, part of the debate is merely a boundary dispute. While several other writers have supported Harwood's contention on this point (for example, Pastore 1949, pp. 178-79; Halsey 1968), the idea of a boundary dispute finds too many exceptions to show much explanatory value. Rather, the contention of the present author is that strong hereditarians tend to be psychologists, while strong environmentalists tend to be from a variety of disciplines, including areas in biology. This idea will be developed more fully in Chapter 9. It should be noted that Harwood agrees on the relative weakness of a boundary-dispute explanation of the controversy.

Turning from the correlation of social factors with stands on various nature- nurture issues, there is evidence that majority positions on several of these issues have changed over time, with very little input of new information. For example, Provine (1973) has traced the history of scientific beliefs in race crossing, and found that majority opinion changed from being against interracial marriage to a general agnosticism regarding the possible results of such crosses, to a generally favorable view, without new information. In the period he covered, there simply was not a decisive study on race crossing. Essentially, the same change occurred concerning social scientific beliefs on race and intelligence (Cartwright and Burtis 1968).

On an individual level, Gerald Dworkin (1974) has demonstrated that papers presented by Jensen in 1967 and 1969 cited largely the same set of references, but that the 1967 paper was pretty straight-forward in its environmentalist position. Dworkin states that the major differences between the two papers had to do with the emphasis given to specified bits of information, and with the ways in which bits of information were employed. Hirsch (1967) has suggested that Jensen's switch came following a year he spent at Stanford University, where (according to Hirsch) he came under Shockley's influence. (For a different view of the social inputs to Jensen's position, see Harwood 1976.) But, be that as it may, there is no doubt that the positions of disputants rest on the same finite body of information, with the differences being largely those of selective emphasis and citation. *

---

*In fact, there is a growing body of evidence emerging that indicates that Jensen may have stacked evidence in his post-1967 work in a consistently hereditarian manner. For example, Hudson (1971) and Goldberger (1974b) have contrasted Jensen's treatment of, respectively, Turner's syndrome (a genetic disorder) and a classic study of adopted children (Burks 1928b), with the original texts. Textual analysis reveals that Jensen distorted the content of each work in arriving at his famous conclusion. Dever (1970) has castigated Jensen for distorting the content of a study in which he (Dever) participated. Most writers have not questioned Jensen's accuracy, especially insofar as he was one of the first writers to question the usefulness of the works of the late British psychometrician Cyril Burt (Jensen 1974; but see Hirsch, 1975, p. 7, n. 21). Martin Deutsch (1969) chided Jensen for 17 mostly unmentioned "errors" in early exchanges in the IQ controversy, but he was apparently embarrassed at his inability to document these. However, newer findings, along with Lewontin's incisive critiques (1970a, 1970b) of faults in Jensen's line of argumentation, lead one to suspect that Jensen has distorted other literature. Moreover, in Chapter 5 it will be shown that he has misled readers as to the nature of historical changes in IQ scores; in Chapter 3 it will be shown that he misrepresents the evidence from animal studies. These distortions have been uncovered despite the fact that the litera-

A Sociological Position on the IQ Controversy

The above studies support the idea that social factors affect the positions which scientists take, at least in what broadly can be termed nature-nurture disputes. Where specific beliefs have some social importance, social characteristics of investigators can help us predict their eventual judgments. This supports the idea of at least a social psychology of scientific beliefs. But can there also be a sociology of such beliefs?

While specific beliefs are individually held, the conceptual frameworks that support these beliefs are social constructions. More specifically, the parameters of scientific conceptualization are the nature of the empirical world, the cognitive matrixes we own by virture of our psychoneural makeup (that is, the way we are wired), and the interpretational categories we obtain by virtue of the cultural groups of which we are members. The interpretational parameters are sociological and can have important effects on perception and categorization.

However, perception and categorization are not all that occur within science. If knowledge can at all be considered socially constructed, then the manner in which social construction occurs must also be studied. For example, in the development of a unified position

---

ature on the IQ controversy is massive, and therefore, critical scutiny of a large number of claims is difficult.

Regarding other hereditarians, Goldberger (1974a, 1974b) has shown that both Herrnstein (1973) and Eysenck (1971) have made the identical distortions, in presenting the adopted-children's study mentioned above, that Jensen has made. Goldberger (1974b, p. 33) concludes that "Jensen's unreliable report of the Burks study has acquired a life of its own," and he broadly implies that Eysenck had not even read the study prior to borrowing Jensen's analysis.

However, stacking is not the same thing as falsifying. While Burt's work is now almost universally held to be unreliable, if not outright fraudulent (for example, Kamin 1974; Gillie 1976; Wade 1976), it is unlikely that any of Jensen's work is fraudulent. In fact, his stacking may be part of a process which is common in science. For example, several environmentalists (including Kamin) have also been shown to stack data (see Loehlin, Lindzey, and Spuhler 1975, pp. 292-99).

Gould (1978) has suggested that any unconscious manipulation of data and arguments may be common in scientific argumentation, and Hudson (1971) suggests that this may be most apparent when emotion-laden issues are at stake (see also Colman 1972).

in science, evidence must be acquired and marshaled. Specific interpretations must be made on given sets of data, and these interpretations must be defended against rival interpretations. Economic resources must be employed in the development of ongoing research. In a word, institutionalization is required. As put by Donald MacKenzie (1974) a discipline needs

> social support, finance and employment for its practitioners, recruits willing to enter it. It needs to develop means by which its practitioners can communicate with each other, and means by which recruits can be taught. In the absence of institutionalisation . . . there will be no coherent tradition, no systematic development of ideas. [P. 1]

Since a part of the process of institutionalization is the allocation of economic resources, and since these are controlled by major interest groups, macrosocial conditions are likely to affect ongoing research. Not only is the type of research likely to be affected but also its actual content; ideas which can find little support are unlikely to prove fruitful.

With respect to the modern IQ controversy, the question of interest is this: Why have the four issues discussed previously been treated as assumptions? This constitutes a more limited goal than does the analysis of the general process of institutionalization. If societal forces have entered into the development of psychological theory and methods, then we should be able to detect this in analyses of the works of the early leaders in the field, and in social and intellectual histories. We should then be able to determine whether the science has developed according to its own internal logic, or whether the social context of its development has affected its contents and conceptualizations. In the study that follows, it will be shown that the social context of the development of psychometric psychology did indeed affect that development, and that it did so in such a way as to cause the four issues to seem settled, for all practical purposes.

PLAN OF THE STUDY

What follows is twofold. First, the four assumptions in question will be treated as issues rather than as convenient assumptions. The empirical and theoretical bases of the issues will be investigated. This will demonstrate that the scientific belief that humanity is naturally stratified in terms of intellectual talent developed without any strong supporting evidence. Second, the development of psychometric psychology (and to a lesser extent, related sciences) will be traced, in order to uncover the sources of the presuppositional treatment of these issues. The assumptions of the ready measurement of intelligence, and of the generality, the importance, and the inheritance of it have interrelated histories that can indeed be investigated.

For purposes of this study, the two tasks are equally important. The historical analysis will demonstrate the arbitrariness of some modern conceptions of human ability, while the empirical analysis will demonstrate the overall weakness of those conceptions. Taken together, the two indicate that a different conception is possible and justifiable.

Part I of this study will investigate the theoretical and empirical status of the four assumptions, which will be treated separately in Chapters 2 through 5. Part II will investigate the development of those assumptions as standard aspects of psychometric research; in this way we will come to understand how they could remain unquestioned. To this end, Chapters 6 through 9 will detail the manner in which the pioneers of testing worked the assumptions into the fabric of psychological research, despite a lack of evidence as to their legitimacy. That is, where evidence appeared to indicate that the assumptions should not be maintained, the early testers worked in order to maintain their feeling that the assumptions should be held. Ultimately, their conceptions were passed on to their graduate students as issues which no longer required discussion. Finally, Chapter 10 will summarize the earlier chapters and will give clues as to where we may go from here.

2

THE MEASUREMENT
OF INTELLIGENCE

As mentioned in the preceding chapter, one must believe that
IQ scores are reasonable and accurate indexes of intellectual functioning, or the disputants in the current controversy lose their empirical bases. Since the controversy continues, it is evident that an
empirical status is generally granted to the scores. Now, for hereditarians it is absolutely essential for this to be the case, since their
arguments are based on test-score differences; they must assume that
score differences indicate differences in functioning. Thus Jensen
(1969a) holds that "probably the most important fact about intelligence
is that we can measure it" (pp. 5-6). So important is this reliance
on measurement that Jensen observes that we need not even argue
"the question to which there is no answer, the question of what intelligence really is." This point will become important below. Likewise, Herrnstein (1971) holds that the measurement of intelligence is
psychology's "most telling achievement to date" (p. 45). Few environmentalists have challenged him on this point, though to let it
pass is, in effect, to give away the first issue in the controversy.

Of course, not all environmentalists fully grant the legitimacy
of test scores for all portions of the population. The idea of test bias
is often used to discount the importance of group differences in test
scores (for example, Karier 1976). In a related manner, cultural
or linguistic deprivation is sometimes postulated as artificially lowering test scores (compare Bereiter and Engelmann 1966; Ginsburg
1972). What is crucial here is the fact that despite a willingness to
question the meanings of specific scores, IQ testing has seldom been
seen as a general theoretical problem. Rather, it is seen as a generally unproblematic procedure that, in some cases, misrepresents
a person's actual ability. Even among outspoken environmentalists,
the legitimacy of such scores for the determination of relative ability
is commonly accepted (for example, see Pettigrew 1964, chap. 5;
Scarr-Salapatek 1971a, 1971b; Jencks 1972, p. 52; Bowles and Gintis
1974, pp. 18-19).

This acceptance is relatively easy to understand considering that those who debate issues of intelligence within academia tend to be the very people who score high on standardized tests; otherwise, they simply would not be in academia (see Campbell 1971). In a larger context, tests are standard, respected features of contemporary U.S. culture.

Hardly anyone is not personally acquainted with such tests. Since World War I, mass testing has touched tens of millions of people in the United States alone. An entire industry has developed around testing as a professional activity; numerous versions of achievement, intelligence, attitude, and aptitude tests vie with one another on the open market; and many thousands of people are employed in one or another aspect of testing. If one attends graduate school, he or she has already had personal experience with IQ tests (probably either of the Stanford-Binet or Wechsler varieties), the National Merit Scholarship exams, the American College Test, the Scholastic Aptitude Test, and the Graduate Record Examination or one of the similar tests given for entrance to medical or law schools. The very designation IQ has entered the language and is universally recognized as indicating degrees of merit, ability, intelligence, knowledge, and so forth. In this regard, a large organization (Mensa) has been established, in which the sole criterion for membership is one's IQ score. So potent is the testing industry that it has been investigated by the U.S. Congress (American Psychologist 1965), an experience which did not noticeably affect it.

This major aspect of U.S. culture has grown up around the single activity that we call standardized testing. That much is well known. What is less well known, or at least less often considered, is that a commitment to this sort of activity developed in the absence of any a priori reason for supposing that activities in a test situation could be used to generalize about other sorts of activities in a meaningful way; the edifice grew, while its base remained relatively unexamined. Indeed, there are theoretical reasons to suppose that a strong relationship between test measurement and behavior in other fields need not obtain. For example, the behaviorist critique of attitude testing (for example, Tarter 1970) is built on the idea that operant contingencies are different in different sorts of situations. Therefore, evoked behaviors in different contexts should not correspond. Essentially the same relationship should hold for mental testing (for a behaviorist look at mental testing, see Bijou 1971).

The behavior-genetic criticism of mental testing is even more restrictive, limiting concordance in behavior to both environmental background and specific genotype. Finally, cognitive sociologists view tests as social interactions, the products of which bear a contingent, or vague, relationship to any postulated underlying ability (for example, Eckberg and Roth 1977).

The analysis that follows will examine the conception of IQ scores as measures of an underlying gradient of intellectual ability. First, the relationship between intelligence and operationalism will be discussed, as well as the assumptions embodied in the major forms of test validation. Following this, the nature of test construction will be discussed, and it will be shown that this necessarily entails a restriction of the degree to which testers can legitimately make inferences about the relative knowledge of test takers. The effects of cultural background, and of such individual characteristics as motivation, on test performance will be discussed, along with the effects of commonly employed test-management procedures. Finally, the results of an experiment using common test-construction procedures with rats will be presented. Overall, the discussions will cast serious doubt on the usefulness of test scores for any inferences about differential intelligence.

THE RELATIONSHIP BETWEEN INTELLIGENCE AND OPERATIONALISM

Intelligence is a hypothetical entity, the nature of which is inferred from what test takers know about the test items. But this knowledge of the test items is itself inferred on the basis of what test takers say about given items in terms of restrictive scoring formats and within the boundary of tester-test taker interaction. As will be shown, test takers can know quite a bit about test items, yet miss the items if their answers fail to correspond to those in the official scoring manuals. They can also miss items by the simple expedient of withdrawing from the interaction, by not trying on those items whose answers are not immediately apparent, by answering in the defensive monosyllables that are often taken to indicate a lack of knowledge, or by playing dumb. Thus, there are several leaps that must be made in inferring intelligence from test scores.

From its inception, testing has been guided by the general idea that there exists an underlying ability that clearly discriminates those whom we commonsensically refer to as dull from those who appear bright. Yet few attempts have ever been made to clearly elucidate the nature of this entity, or to show a necessary relationship between it and test performance. For example, the developer of the first successful mental tests, Alfred Binet, several times mentioned that he was not bound by a strict theory of intelligence; and U.S. popularizers of the tests, like Terman, praised him for this. What results is a situation in which a poorly conceived theoretical entity is measured by means of a set of procedures whose correspondence to that entity is not fully clear.

Various psychometric writers admit this fact, in principle. For example, concerning measurement, Eysenck (1962) states that "intelligence tests are not based on any very sound scientific principles" (p. 8). Others have admitted that "none of the existing scales are based on any recognized theory of intellectual development" (Warburton et al. 1972); and David Wechsler (1971) admits that even where theories are quite different, the general types of items used are limited, because statistical, rather than theoretical, requirements are considered of paramount importance. (For a review of this, see Block and Dworkin 1976.)

Because of this (and other reasons that will be presented in Chapters 6-8), the actual nature of the entity in question is never clearly spelled out. Yet it must be assumed to exist, or else the large-scale reliance on test scores would not occur. Therefore, in order to be able to make claims regarding the validity of test scores, it has become common to shunt aside questions of the meaning of intelligence, and to simply state that whatever intelligence is, it is what intelligence tests test (for example, Boring 1923). This tactic (considered old hat even in 1923) makes mental measurement an instance of the unbridled operationalism that was popular in the first quarter of this century (for example, Bridgeman 1927), but that has been largely discredited by modern philosophy of science. Thus, unlike conventional measurements in physical and biological science, IQ scores are purely instrumentally or operationally defined (see Layzer 1974, p. 1265). No attempt need be made to ground the scores in functional terms; hence Jensen's claim noted earlier in this chapter.

OPERATIONALISM AND VALIDITY
OF INTELLIGENCE TESTS

Because of this atheoretical operationalism, it is not clear just what a valid score is. For example, since the theoretical entity that is presumably measured is so little understood, it is not totally clear just what sorts of relationships would grant the measures construct validity.

Construct Validity

Two sorts of attempts at showing construct validity have come via the concepts of g and of heritability. Briefly, it is sometimes held that a high degree of heritability indicates that a real underlying phenomenon is being measured. However, there are problems with this line of reasoning. First, heritability says nothing about the kind of phenomenon being measured, so even if IQ were shown to have a very high degree of heritability, this would not enable us to say that intelligence is being measured. This line of evidence is not helpful here. Second, the actual degree of heritability of IQ is greatly disputed, with estimates ranging from near zero to near 100 percent (see Chapter 5). Third, even a very high degree of heritability can be a function of environmental variables or of artifacts of measurement. This being the case, even a high degree of heritability does not indicate that a real entity is being measured.

Somewhat the same thing has occurred with "g." It is often claimed (for example, Jensen 1969a) that the presence of a general factor, when test scores are factor analyzed, indicates the presence of a mental unity—Spearman's g factor (see Spearman 1904a, 1927). However, other researchers have been able to demonstrate that the presence of a general factor is sometimes an artifact of the factor-analysis procedures employed (for example, see Tryon 1932a, 1932b). Further, the procedures employed in the construction of tests guarantee that only those items that share variance will be maintained—that is, items that are quite similar to one another. Finally, the entire argument over the presence of a general factor rests on the assumption that correlation entails commonality (Block and Dworkin 1976), a statistical error that one often encounters in the social sciences. Other attempts at establishing construct validity have relied on the fact that test scores follow a normal distribution (for example, Jensen 1969a), and the fact that tests have a high degree of test-retest reliability, even though neither of these bears on the issue at hand (for example, see Lewontin 1970a; Evans 1969).

Face Validity

The issue of face validity is no more settled than is that of construct validity. IQ test questions tend to be of a multiple-choice, paper-and-pencil type, and a number of different types of questions are found on different tests. As will be shown later, researchers who have analyzed test items have often found themselves questioning why certain items were included in given tests, why directions were worded in a given way, and so forth. Further, various items can be answered in a number of rationally correct ways, even though only a very restricted set of answers is acceptable. Because of this, tests are not necessarily valid on their face, though items most often appear to be psychological in content.

Predictive Validity

Given the above, the primary validation procedure employed with tests is the prediction of a validity criterion—for example, scholastic attainment. Since from the inception of testing, it has been assumed that an underlying individual intelligence controls achievement, any correlation between test scores and other achievement is taken to validate the tests. Such a correlation satisfies common expectations regarding the role of intelligence in the social world. Later, it will be shown that no strong relationship in fact holds between test scores and future achievement, but here it need merely be shown that reliance on common expectations itself introduces important problems.

Three specific problems arise here. First, common expectations can be satisfied by far too many relationships. For example, the correlation between test scores and grade point average (GPA) reasonably can be attributed to many phenomena. As put by the philosophers Block and Dworkin (1976), "more than likely, many composites of qualities other than intelligence would satisfy those common expectations" (p. 425). For example, as will be shown in Chapter 4, apparently personality inventories successfully predict achievement. Further, if a given measure predicts achievement, one is not, on the basis of an assumption of intelligence, thereby freed from the obligation to investigate why such a prediction succeeds.

Second, many common expectations are simply incorrect (Block and Dworkin 1976, pp. 425-26). In the present case, if a real relationship between some kind of underlying intelligence and various kinds of achievement were complex, then a reliance on scales that were designed to correlate with school achievement—that is, scales for which school achievement was the validity criterion—would necessarily be overly restrictive. They would miss many manifestations of the postulated quality, and therefore not constitute valid measures of quality.

Third, operationalism commonly substitutes reliability for validity. But a quality which is "susceptible to very reliable reproduction" may not be the quality which one wishes to measure (Block and Dworkin 1976, p. 426). If one insists on modeling future research on this early quality, one will surely be led far astray from that with which one wishes to deal.

The general problem with measures which are purely operationally defined is that they are not clearly tied into theoretical frameworks within which they function in strictly specified manners. They admit too many general, rather than precise, expectations. A comparison of mental measurement with the measurement of temperature or electricity will demonstrate this.

On various occasions, Jensen (1969a, 1971) has referred to the development of the thermometer or electrical-measuring devices as exactly equivalent to the development of intelligence scales, because "if the measurements are reliable and reproducible, and the operations by which they are obtained can be objectively agreed upon, this is all that need be required for them to qualify as proper scientific data" (Jensen 1971, p. 11). Here we must first ignore three points:

he implies that the majority of the relevant scientific communities agree on the operations by which scores are to be generated (a complex issue); he uses the term <u>objectively</u> in an imprecise manner; and he uses the hedge term <u>scientific data</u> in place of the more direct <u>valid measurement</u> (all things are ultimately data). Stripping these points away, we are left with the assertion that one need not bother much with theoretical frameworks in the development of scientific measures.

In science, however, measures and theories of such phenomena as temperature and electricity have historically developed together (Kuhn 1961). This is not the case with intelligence testing. Recall Jensen's point quoted at the start of this chapter. It strains credulity to believe that he would hold there to be no point is asking the unanswerable questions about the real nature of electricity or temperature. Yet with intelligence this is just what he holds.

Returning to the problem of precision, the thermometer presents a classic example of the relationship between theory and measurement. As Block and Dworkin (1976, pp. 419-23) have shown in a similar critique of mental testing, the use of the thermometer had to wait for the development of a large body of other theoretical and experimental work concerning the meaning of degrees of heat, barometric pressure, coefficients of expansion of various liquids and solids, and so forth, before it could be usefully employed. Further, the sensation of heat had first to be seen as only vaguely related to the concept of heat before thermometers could gain wide acceptance, because so many objects that measure the same temperature feel differentially warm (for example, wood and steel). Common expectations had to be violated before a useful thermometer could be developed. Once these expectations were set aside, and a great deal of other research was performed, the thermometer could become a precise measurement tool, but not before. As put by Kuhn (1961), the "road from scientific law to scientific measurement can rarely be travelled in the reverse direction" (pp. 189-90).

Thus, the significance of a test score (or a collection of scores) is uncertain; test scores do not necessarily measure anything very important in human life. Further, it can be shown that score production is affected by a number of factors. Among these are the nature of test-construction procedures, testers' management techniques and interpretational repertoires, personal and group variations in interactional patterns, and the responses of testers to these variations. Each of these will be discussed in the following sections; the common theme will be that test scores are contingent phenomena, that they need not correspond to behavior in everyday life, and that changes in the above factors can lead to changes in the scores produced.

PROBLEMS IN THE
INTERPRETATION OF TEST SCORES

The paradigm of test-scale construction was provided by Binet and Theodore Simon (1905b) in the development of what was considered the first successful intelligence scale. Briefly, Binet and Simon employed a large number of items, most of which seemed to them to be psychological, or to tap what they considered "higher" mental processes (see Wolf 1973). Items were then forced into a scalar arrangement by means of two criteria. First, items which did not discriminate bright from dull children (or on which dull children did better than bright children) were considered bad items and were deleted (see Peterson 1925). The same procedure was used concerning the age of children. The items on each succeeding age scale were those which distinguished between children of different ages, and other items were discarded. (A more thorough look at this will appear in Chapter 6.)

An important point is that the general manner of test construction has not changed since the development of the 1905 scale, though the techniques themselves have become much more sophisticated (for example, Lord and Novick 1968). Still, items are included that correlate with one another. Further, new tests are considered valid to the extent that scores on them correlate with scores on old tests. This occurs whether one designs a totally new test or merely revises an existing test. When the Stanford-Binet was revised in 1937 and 1960, those items which correlated with mental age on the preceding form were included, and others were dropped (Anastasi 1968, p. 204).

An important determinant of the usual form of intelligence tests comes from reliability theory. To prevent test scores from varying widely from test to test, a large number of items are employed. This is a reliability criterion for test usefulness (Evans 1969, p. 217). A consequence of this is that only short-answer-type questions are employed, in order to keep the test from dragging on to the point where test takers are exhausted. But this means that one cannot test how well people will perform on problems which require long-term thought and complex repertoires of skills. More germane to this discussion, it also assumes that the items employed are, in general, good determinants of intellect, such that use of a large number of those items will lessen the impact of idiosyncratic answers to any given small set of items. But, as will be shown below, the validity of test items is precisely what is called into question when one investigates specific items.

However, if items are valid, they must meet certain other requirements. More important, they must be subject to interpretational closure. That is, an item must have a strictly limited number of possible correct answers. Otherwise, missing an item will not indicate a lack of intelligence, since a test taker might have a very good reason for choosing an incorrect answer. Since final test scores are merely the summation of item scores for that test—produced by one of a large variety of summary formulas—the final test score is valid only to the extent that individual items are valid. If individual items have questionable validity, then the question that can legitimately be asked is: What does measurement mean with respect to test scores? That is, what is the relationship between a score and relative brilliance?

The Problem of Item Closure

Consider the following hypothetical example. Guilford (1967, p. 42) presents us with four series of letters—PXNO, VRIM, AQES, and GUVC—with the request that we choose the series that does not fit with the others. According to Builford, the proper answer is AQES, since this is the only series with two vowels. This is true.

Now, what occurs when we apply different categorization schemes to these items? First, PXNO is the only series that ends in a vowel. Second, this same series of letters is the only one all of whose letters come from the second half of the alphabet; each of the other three series has two letters from the first half and two letters from the second half. Third, GUVC is the only series that does not contain within itself at least one legitimate English-language word or suffix, according to common standards of language usage. * Fourth, AQES is the only series that begins with a vowel. Fifth, if one lists the alphabet by integers, from A = 1 to Z = 26, GUVC is the only series in which the addition of integers yields a prime integer (53). This is also the only integer total that begins with an odd number. PXNO is the only series in which the addition of integers yields a number (69) which ends in an integer in the second half of the original ten integers. It is also the only series in which the addition of summary integers yields either a two-digit number or an odd number.

Some of these possible answers may appear unlikely, but they are rationally correct. Moreover, it is certain that other correct answers could be determined. In the context of mental testing, however, all but one of these answers would be considered incorrect, and would count against a person in the determination of one's final test

---

*The standard employed here is the New College Edition of the American Heritage Dictionary (1976), which contains the words no, rim, I, and a, and the suffix es, but which does not contain the slang term guv.

score. Further, the answer that is considered the correct one is correct from the standpoint of the test designer's sense of relevance; he or she determines what is a correct answer.

This critique may appear to be an attack on a straw man—surely, such items are not commonly employed in tests. However, studies by Eckberg and Roth (1977) and by Feinberg (1978) support it. Both studies analyze responses to individual test items, the former in terms of the kinds of responses given that were rationally justified by test takers, and the latter in terms of the kinds of processes that were required in order to complete an item correctly. The former study was limited to the Picture Completion Subtest of the Wechsler Intelligence Scale for Children (WISC), while the latter examined a large number of intelligence tests.

Briefly, Eckberg and Roth found that children who took tests could often give a large number of responses to test items that, while considered good responses in terms of the rational justifications employed by children in their regard, could not be given credit. No matter how good a tester considered a response, it could only be considered for credit if it closely matched the model answer given by the test maker in the scoring manual. Indeed, at least seven types of good misses were evident. First, on many items, more than one element was missing from a picture. Thus, children who noted that a man lacked eyelashes missed the item, because the proper answer was "eyebrows." Similarly, those who noted that a coat lacked a right breast pocket missed the item because the correct answer was "two buttonholes."

A second type of error developed because the test illustrations were poorly executed; a chicken's wing and a cow's udder were both taken to be missing at one time or another, because both were so poorly executed that children supposed them not to be shown at all. Third, the meaning of missing was ambiguous, because it was never clearly pointed out to children that the missing element was required to be a feature embedded in the objects shown. Several children missed items because they commented that the missing elements were objects which would regularly be associated with the picture shown, but which were not actually constituent parts of the picture. Thus, one child missed the item in which the coat lacked buttonholes, because he stated that the missing element was the man wearing the coat. This is interesting, because the coat was shown to be standing by itself, as if someone were wearing it. Likewise, in a picture of a rural home, in which a tree failed to cast a shadow despite a well-depicted sun, the answers "grass," "cars," and so forth were incorrect. Also incorrect was the answer that a hill in the background also failed to cast a shadow. A three-legged table was scored as incorrect when the child noted that paint was missing or dishes and food were missing.

A fourth type of good miss occurred because children taking the test and the test constructor differed on their interpretation of the items. One child noted that a well-dressed man lacked a sheriff's badge, when the correct response was <u>hatband</u>. When pressed on the reason for this response, the child responded that the man wore a broad-brimmed hat (like a cowboy hat), and wore a nameplate (this was the left breast pocket, represented by a sketched rectangle); therefore, the man was a sheriff and should have a star on his hat, as do sheriffs in cartoons. Another child noted that a one-hinged door lacked <u>the fish</u>. When the tester recovered from her shock at this response, she found that the child had interpreted the rough sketch of the door as representing an aquarium.

Fifth, on some items, the correct answer was an object which was not necessarily missing. On the already mentioned three-legged table, the missing leg was the one farthest from the viewer. One child, asked if the leg was missing, responded that one could not be expected to see it, because of the angle of view. Therefore, it might not actually be missing.

A sixth way of missing items which did not represent poor reasoning occurred where the item depicted objects not common to a child's cultural milieu. For example, one child missed the fact that a seven of spades lacked a spade, but later admitted that her family did not use playing cards.

A seventh way in which children missed items, but which did not necessarily reflect on any mental abilities, occurred where children, for various reasons, did not enjoy the test period and were obviously intent on getting through the test with as little involvement as possible. It has been noted that black children and lower-class children frequently attempt to avoid involvement (Labov 1972; Eisenberg 1966). More will be said about this later.

The comparatively broader study by Feinberg supports the conclusions of the above study. To quote from a summary of problems listed by Feinberg (1978):

> Many items had answers marked as right which might easily be understood as wrong. Others had marked as wrong answers which might easily be perceived as right. And in many cases, there seemed to be no readily identifiable criterion for giving credit for one response and not for another. In some instances the test-maker was making obvious assumptions that were not included in the question, but which were very important in arriving at the answer that the test approved as correct. In other instances the question called for one kind of response but the criterion for grading it

called for another one which was not communicated to
the subject in question. [Pp. 7-8]

In addition to these problems, Feinberg found numerous items that
required mere rote memorization (as in Jensen's "Level I" intelligence) and items that could be answered correctly only in a school
context—achievement-test items. These were in addition to the items
that showed clear cultural bias.

Feinberg's examination also covered the so-called culture-free
tests and found a set of specific problems. First, test instructions
were often ambiguous. In some cases, the types of items changed in
the middle of a test, but the instructions to the child did not. In addition, by eliminating verbal content and restricting performance to
abstract spatial representations, the tests appeared to lose any claim
to be measuring general intelligence. Two further points must be
made here. First, nonverbal tests seem to require considerable verbal interaction between the test giver and the test taker (Roth 1976),
a fact that makes the idea that such tests are not dependent on culturally mediated language use lose plausibility. Second, restriction
of tests to spatial representations does not make a test either culture
free or culturally fair. This point was made more forcefully by
Florence Goodenough (Goodenough and Harris 1950, p. 399), who,
after reviewing a quarter century of cross-cultural research using
her supposedly culture-free Draw-a-Man test, concluded that the
search for a culture-free test was "illusory."

Then what is the relationship between a test score and brightness? Even on the basis of the limited issue of item choice, it may
be characterized as uncertain. Items are constructed by test makers,
perhaps with the help of their graduate students. The large body of
items is then standardized by means of correlations generated when
a group of people of appropriate ages answers the items. Those
items that correlate well with appropriate criteria are kept, and others
are excluded. The standardization groups tend to be those who live
in communities near major universities, for obvious reasons. What
logically occurs is that those items on which a large portion of children share cultural categories with testers are retained. Those children who then organize their knowledge in different ways, or who
share a different body of knowledge, are penalized in the taking of the
tests. Some interesting findings regarding this fact will be presented
at the end of this chapter.

Problems of Test Management

If the meaning of test items is one problem in the use of tests,
the management of test takers is a second problem. At least since

the publication of the first major U.S. book on mental measurement
(Terman 1916), problems of test management have received wide discussion. However, this discussion has centered largely on common-
sense techniques for controlling test takers so that a good score can
be produced. From Terman (1916, pp. 121-34) to Wechsler (1949)
to Lee J. Cronbach (1969a), the hints given for the management of
tests have been of the wise-uncle variety. Repeatedly, one is told to
use tact and restraint in administering tests, though certain actions
are specifically forbidden; rapport and encouragement are always
stressed. Certain stereotyped phrases are recommended for use when
children do not perform as desired, or when children act upset (for
example, compare the strong similarities in the works of the three
abovementioned writers).

For a single, though telling, example of this tendency, note the
following advice to testers, taken from Wechsler (1949):

> Overactivity in young children is sometimes a particular
> problem. Here, judicious and tactful disregard is usually
> in order. Destruction of material, of course, cannot be
> permitted, but the child should be permitted to roam about
> the room to get acquainted with his surroundings as well as
> with the examiner. Children from undisciplined or undis-
> ciplining backgrounds sometimes try to take command of
> the situation. Here, again, some leeway is permissible,
> but the examiner should maintain [a] sufficient degree of
> control to permit correct administration of the test.
> [Pp. 21-22]

The fact that the advice contains so many nonspecifiable terms indicates how weak a guide for behavior it is. Yet this is treated as
though it were adequate to deal with the exigencies of the test. The
test is treated as though it were a generally unproblematic exercise
in which only a few problems might interfere with successful administration.

In contrast, those studies that have dealt with tests as social interactions have found the tests to be complex interactions, in which
the activities of the testers were constituent aspects of the ultimate
scores obtained. That is, testers are obligated to produce completed
IQ (or other) tests, but it is only by means of skillful management of
the multiform problematic situations that they face during the tests
that they are actually able to do this. Two analytically distinct, but
related, sorts of problems confront the tester: first, the abovementioned need for establishing rapport and second, control and interpretation of children's answers.

Rapport generally is considered to be a problem with children
who have a negative attitude to the test situation, but this is actually

only one of two problems. Negativism is widely acknowledged as a problem, especially with certain groups of children. Specifically, black and lower-class children tend to treat tests differently as compared with white middle-class children. This is depicted most dramatically in William Labov's (1972) microethnographic study of the testing of ghetto children (pp. 205-13).

What Labov found was that black children's test performance was a direct function of the tradition of hostility and distrust marking relations between the black community and those in positions of authority. In a test situation, Labov found that children withdrew from the interaction, answered in monosyllables, did not give any answers at all, if not forced to do so, and generally appeared sullen and dull. This tendency has been observed by others, most notably Ray C. Rist (1970), who noted it in a study of all-black classrooms. The image that comes across from such encounters is one of a dull child who is afraid to show his ignorance. Labov, however, was able to bring children out by changing the situation. He allowed the children to have friends present, provided potato chips, had the tester get down on the floor of the test room, and then had the tester introduce taboo words and topics—for example, "Is there anyone who says your momma drink pee?" (Labov 1972, p. 209).

The results of this manipulation were dramatic. Immediately, the children became skilled users of nonstandard English, were able to form complex puns and put-downs, and to form logically complex sentence patterns. The monosyllabic sullenness disappeared completely. (For another dramatic example, see Riessman 1974, pp. 206-7.) Rist's findings, while less spectacular, were equally noteworthy. He found that lower-class black children, though grossly discriminated against by schoolteachers (in favor of middle-class black children), and seldom addressed directly, except for reasons of control, did learn school material. In fact, they discussed course material among themselves, though they would not repeat it if the teacher asked for answers to questions. According to Rist, children learned the interaction patterns, which they would follow when confronted by the teacher, in their kindergarten year. In follow-up investigations, he recorded the entrenchment of negative interactions in the first and second grades.

The conclusions drawn from this is that the situation in which children find themselves affects the quality of interaction. To the extent that an IQ test can be considered an interaction, elements within it affect the performance of children. As mentioned above, this interaction may not only have to deal with negative attitudes; in the study by Eckberg and Roth, it was found that interest in the test could itself interfere with test completion. Those authors found that children who truly seemed to enjoy taking part in the WISC attempted to control the situation, and had constantly to be called down by testers.

Children tried to play with test materials, to cheat, to make nonsensical noises, and to tell long and involved stories that took attention away from what the testers perceived to be the task at hand, the completion of an IQ test. Dealing with involved children proved to be as great a challenge as dealing with withdrawn children; in some ways it was more of a problem, since with withdrawn children the test could be completed in short order. Unlike the case with the withdrawn children, some interested children took the test to be a serious episode, and some actually began crying when they missed questions. Management of such episodes was trying for both testers and children.

While the control of children was a serious problem, shaping and interpreting the answers was a chronic problem. Eckberg and Roth found that the asking of questions and the giving of answers could not be considered the simple input-output sequence that it is usually considered. Testers found that children's initial responses to test items often could not readily be scored as either correct or incorrect, because such responses were either ambiguous or not directed at test items. Testers were forced to shape children's answers to make them scorable, and only then could a score be assigned to them. On the Picture Completion Subtest, testers often had to narrow progressively the visual focus of the vague entity to which children referred, in order, finally, to make a decision as to whether children could be granted credit on an item. They had to do this without giving away the proper answer. A degree of looseness obtained here, because final answers that did not fully correspond to the model answer, were at times ultimately given credit for being close enough.

Because only a small range of responses to test items can be given credit, ultimate test scores appear to show little correspondence to other aspects of test-takers' knowledge. A long-term series of investigations by Cicourel et al. (1974) demonstrated just such a phenomenon. In particular, one study (Roth 1974) showed that the test scores children received gave little information regarding the child's store of culturally relevant knowledge. That is, children commonly knew a lot about test items that the tests were incapable of elucidating. Concerning objects, the children might or might not get the item right, but they would still know what the items were; they would know how such items were used and what the relationships of such items were with other items within their cultural milieu. These sorts of knowledge are important in the common course of managing one's life, yet tests missed them. The inference from this is that the picture of a child that emerges from a test depends on the type of information sought by the researcher. Along with the management problems mentioned above, this indicates that the management of the test situation necessarily introduces another level of contingency in the relationship between final scores and levels of ability (see also Mercer 1973, pp. 190-92).

Problems Related to the Variety of Human Differences

Yet another set of issues must be addressed in order to demonstrate the ambiguous nature of the score-intelligence nexus. This set has to do with test-performance differences based on group differences among test takers and differences in the management of tests due to superficial characteristics of test takers. Because tests have seldom been investigated in these terms, the following analysis must necessarily be based largely on nontest interactions.

Differences in Cognitive Characteristics

It has already been noted that different groups of children treat the test situation differently. The study by Eckberg and Roth, for example, mentioned differences in the degree of seriousness that children showed regarding the tests. More important here is the fact that such differences have a group base. For example, Eisenberg (1966) reported that he and his colleagues "had the repeated experience of finding middle class children intensely involved in test success, whereas lower class children seem mostly concerned with getting the test over with" (p. 507). Eisenberg explained this difference by means of the concept of "salience": lower-class children did not grant the examiner the right to question them and did not wish to show their proficiency. Recall, however, that in Labov's study, far from not wanting to show proficiency, children actively avoided giving responses. In the latter study, the situation of ghetto/middle-class hostility led to striking degrees of withdrawal from the interaction. The actual effect of such a difference on test scores requires study, but it is likely that a significant group difference could be based on such a fact alone.

This indicates that motivation affects test performance, where by motivation we mean both that some children are more enthusiastic about the tests than are other children and that the specific motivations driving children will vary. As an example of the first meaning of motivation, studies that have investigated middle-class/lower-class score differentials have found that practice on tests and the introduction of a reward (to increase motivation) can reduce the differences found (for example, Haggard 1954). This narrowing of gaps occurs when both middle-class and lower-class children are given practice and motivation. In a study not aimed at IQ test scores, another researcher found that working-class children scored much lower than did middle-class children on a scale that measured success striving in terms of need for achievement. However, when the children were paid ten dollars for their participation, the social-class differences in scores disappeared (Douvan 1956). In a study of children in Tanzania (Vernon 1969, pp. 107-10), it was found that the average gain on tests attributed to "practice effects" was 3.6 points, while the inclusion of various forms of coaching pushed the total gain to 6.4 points. Of more importance, though, is the fact that a special pep talk given between tests, in lieu of the coaching, led to score increases averaging 7.3 points. The pep talk was given by a Swahili-speaking person, and the author of the study attributed the gain to an increased motivation to perform for such a figure. In any event, the talk was more helpful than the coaching. Elsewhere, the race of the tester, expressions of approval and disapproval, and need were all shown to affect the learning of black children (Katz, Henchy, and Allen 1968).*

It appears that the specific form of motivation is also important in the generation of scores. For example, in a study reported by Eisenberg (1966, p. 508) a group of "moderately subnormal" children were taught a simple perceptual color discrimination. The correct answer was always rewarded, and the incorrect choice was never rewarded. Under these conditions, subjects went through hundreds of trials, never learning the discrimination. However, when, in addition to being rewarded for a proper choice, children were penalized for an improper choice, they readily learned the discrimination. Eisenberg concluded that the early failures were "embedded in the reward structure of the experiment, which would not ordinarily be thought of as part of the perceptual problem." Other motivation effects also appear to play roles in score determination. Such effects would explain why the race of the tester, the degree of approval granted to children, and need for approval all affected the outcome of black children's performance in learning trials. All of the above indicates that the goals of children enter into test performance in specific ways (see Greenfield 1971).

The degree to which the outcome of an ability test is contingent on the subject's response to that type of situation is shown most clearly in the literature on cultural differences and intelligence tests.

----

*Shuey (1966, pp. 507-8) mentioned that a review of the literature did not support the idea that differential motivation can explain at least black-white score differences. Yet three of the five sources she cited indicated that manipulation of motivation does have effects on test performance. Further, she omitted the Haggard (1954) study, probably because it did dealt with social class rather than race, and the Douvan (1956) study, probably because it did not deal specifically with IQ testing. The study by Katz, Henchy, and Allen (1968) was published after her work. Later, she listed eight different studies of aspirations that showed that blacks have levels of aspirations at least as high as those of whites. Yet none of those studies dealt at all with patterns of interactions in test situations. They simply did not deal with the issues at hand.

Recall Goodenough's repudiation of the Draw-a-Man test as a culture-free test (Goodenough and Harris 1950). Her repudiation was based on over two decades of research, which had demonstrated wide cultural differences in test performance, many of which simply could not be shown to have biological causes. This is part of a larger body of research that has shown important cultural differences in perception, language, learning patterns, and rules of classification (for a major review, see Cole and Scribner 1974). There is also a small body of literature that suggests that specific (nonintellective) group characteristics enter into the determination of test scores. Moreover, this literature suggests that the directions of such differences may be specific to the organization of the tests, and that they may be subject to manipulation (for example, Cohen 1969; Whimbey 1976; for a review, see Samuda 1975).*

The role of cultural differences in categorization is very important, because IQ tests are largely devoted to problems in which very specific forms of categorization are required. Cole and Scribner (1974, p. 122) have found that the basis of grouping is sensitive to children's familiarity with the materials presented, the content domain from which they are drawn, and the form in which they are presented. As an example, a study of the categorization criteria of Kenyan children (Fjellman 1971) found that rural children sorted animals on the basis of wild versus domesticated, while urban children sorted on the basis of color. In the IQ controversy, Jensen (1969a) has stated that middle-class children "rearrange input in such a way that the order of output in recall corresponds to the categories to which the objects may be assigned" (pp. 112-13), while children with low socioeconomic status may "show rather idiosyncratic pair-wise clusters that persist from trial to trial." Apropos of this discussion, it may be asked, "idiosyncratic" for whom? It is apparent that Jensen views possible divisional criteria as few in number; but as this chapter has stressed from the beginning, categorization schemes are almost unlimited in number. This point will bear repeating later.

---

*The effect of problem-solving style on the score of a standardized test is so important that at least one investigator claims to be able to raise a subject's IQ by teaching different modes of problem solving to the person (Whimbey 1976). He gives no data, but other writers indirectly bear him out. For example, Eysenck holds that error checking and persistence count in the production of scores (see Block and Dworkin 1976, pp. 449-57). Also, Bereiter and Engelmann (Bereiter 1976) have succeeded in raising IQ scores somewhat by teaching new problem-solving patterns.

It is apparent that both situational and cultural specificity affect performance. Such effects operate not only across vastly different cultures but also within the United States. For instance, one study comparing whites and blacks on standard verbal- and quantitative-ability tests found that the differences obtained were dependent on whether the tests were given in the normal paper-and-pencil manner, or were administered via a computer. In the normal format, the normal black-white differences obtained, but when the computer format was used, the verbal-test differences almost disappeared (Johnson and Mihal 1973). Why the specific results obtained is not clear. This specificity of response may explain why it is that on some tests (for example, the Progressive Matrixes), black-white IQ differences disappear in some situations but not in others (Semler and Iscoe 1966). Also, it may help to explain the findings of a variety of studies, which have shown that Middle Eastern Jews raised in their own homes score (on the average) 85 on IQ tests, while European Jews raised in their own homes average 105. When both are raised in Kibbutz nurseries, the average scores are 115 for both groups (Bloom 1969). The differences in cognitive organization need to be thoroughly investigated, because it appears that testers and teachers are commonly unaware of the social dynamics of such organization, even though they deal with children on a day-to-day basis (Dumont and Wax 1969; Rist 1970). The quote from Jensen (1969a, pp. 112-13) noted above demonstrates an example of just such a problem. The tester frequently imputes intelligence scores to personality "with little awareness of how much this behavior is a product of the particular relationship of the psychologist to the child, and of the testing situation as such" (Reissman 1974, p. 208).

Differential Treatment

What this suggests is that the specific management procedures employed will affect test outcomes. To the extent that such procedures vary according to the characteristics of the test taker, group differences (or just individual differences) are likely to occur. The complex interaction the test constitutes is most important here. The specific factors affecting interaction include, but are not limited to, the so-called self-fulfilling prophecy.

It is unfortunate that the idea of a self-fulfilling prophecy is tied in the public's mind so closely to the Rosenthal and Jacobson (1968) study Pygmalion in the Classroom. This study, which attempted to demonstrate that teachers unconsciously perform actions that lead to upward changes in the grades of children designated as high in academic potential, has almost universally come to be seen as poor in design and execution. Further, other investigators have not been able to repeat the results obtained with any degree of consistency (for a review, see Samuda 1975, pp. 496-97). Yet a sizable literature has grown that shows teachers' perceptions to have important effects on educational interactions. (For a major review of such studies, including the conditions under which teachers' perceptions do and do not seem important, see Persell 1977, pp. 123-34.)

A specific example of the role of adult management in the recorded characteristics of children comes, not from IQ testing, but from the Rist (1970) study of kindergarten children. It is this study that was referred to earlier in the comment that superficial characteristics of individuals can be acted upon differentially in order to produce the kinds of individual characteristics expected. In the classroom that Rist studied, teachers first categorized children according to "ideal types" of characteristics that they felt would be necessary in order to do well in school. These criteria tended to include physical appearance of children (including body odor, neatness of hair, and newness of clothes), the degree to which the children appeared to be leaders, the degree to which children spoke standard English, the relative wealth of children's parents, the education of children's parents, and the number of people in the children's families (all this was information available to the teachers).

Teachers made subjective evaluations of the children's chances of success based on these characteristics. They then acted differentially toward the children. Those thought to be fast learners were assigned seats near the front, were more often addressed, were worked with individually, were scolded less, and were allowed to address negative comments to the slow pupils. By the end of the school year, the interaction patterns had taken on castelike rigidity, and children tended to stay in the categories to which they were assigned over the next several grades (until the study was terminated).

One important finding of Rist's study (1970, pp. 426-30) was that children quickly learned differential interactional ploys they then used in the classrooms. Group hostility formed, and the fast learners began calling the slow learners dumb. The neglected group quickly withdrew from classroom participation and was often excluded by the teacher from whatever the subject at hand happened to be. In this manner, the styles of classroom participation for the children were set very early by the teachers themselves, though the teachers did not appear to be aware of this. They acted on a set of assumptions about the characteristics of the children, and the children came to match what had been expected of them.

As inferential leap is required in order to go from the Rist study (or those like it) to the problem of differential scores on IQ tests. However, it is not a large leap to the conclusion that treatment by testers can bring about large differences in children's behavior, or that testers would not be fully aware of the differences in their own actions. It is still less of a leap to the idea that the behavior patterns of different children can be determined by early interactional patterns to which they were exposed. Here, the Rist study and the Labov study (1972) dovetail neatly. We do know that children from different backgrounds have different conceptual styles, and at least one study (Cohen, Fraenkel, and Brewer 1968) has tied such differences to culture conflict. Briefly, middle-class children tend to be analytic in orientation, while the hard-core poor tend to be relational. These orientations are incompatible, and members of one group tend to misperceive the characteristics of the other. Interaction is affected, and cultural conflict is a normal outcome of interactions.

THE OUTCOME OF PSYCHOMETRIC PRACTICES: AN EXPERIMENT

If groups differ in a variety of ways, and if the ultimate selection of items for a test depends on the responses of subjects to the universe of possible items, then it follows that there may exist a bias in item selection. This bias may be related to the tendency for testers to employ items that mirror their own world views (Karier 1975); but it also may result from artifacts related to mathematical rules of item selection. A study has been performed to investigate this, with interesting results.

The study in question was performed by Harrington (1975), using different strains of rats as subjects and employing an extension of the Hebb-Williams Maze, the standard intelligence test for rats. Harrington argued that gene-environment interaction would lead to differential selection of items, if genetically different strains were employed in determining which items should be maintained. Specifically, since items commonly are included on final tests to the extent that the correlations between those items and the final score on the test as a whole are relatively high, then the presence of a large number of individuals from a genetically homogeneous group should lead to an ultimate selection of items for which item/test-score correlations were especially high for this select group. The expectation was that members of this group would then perform especially well on the final test.

To test this, Harrington employed a Latin-squares study in which six populations of rats were employed to select items from a 380-item universe for inclusion in six ultimate tests. The criterion for inclusion was this: The 50 items for which correlations with the final score were highest were included; the rest were discarded.

The six populations of rats were made up of varying numbers of members of six homogeneous lines of rats. In one population rats from a given strain would be highly represented; in others they would be represented in moderate numbers; in still others they might not be represented at all. Thus, for each population, different lines of rats were predominant.

Harrington ended with six different tests (that is, the items included in them were different). He then tested the various lines of rats on each of the tests and compared how well they did with each of the other lines. What he found was that the resulting rank order of the various lines of rats on the tests correlated with the level of representation of those lines in the item-selection population. The rank-order correlation was 0.562 ($z = 3.33$; $p < 0.001$). The findings strongly supported the idea that gene-environment interaction could lead to test bias, even where initial items appeared on their face to be fair. Thus, common standardization procedures led to favorable scores for whatever lines were overrepresented in the selection population.

Moreover, Harrington was adamant that the application of his findings to the testing of humans was direct (as opposed to being merely analogical), because what he had tested was the effect of normal psychometric methods. As he put it, "the experiment was an empirical test of common psychometric assumptions and procedures. Generalisation is therefore to those assumptions and procedures" (Harrington 1975, p. 709).

To the extent that these were the same assumptions and procedures that are employed in selecting items for testing humans, the same findings should in principle obtain. Further, it is commonly admitted that tests tend to be standardized on the basis of characteristics of Anglo-American populations.

The argument employed here is important for two reasons. First of all, it calls into question the basis for the argument that low-IQ minorities are necessarily dumber than others in a population. According to Harrington's results, numerical minorities necessarily should score lower. Moreover, though his study employed genetically different groups, he admitted, correctly, that the same results should follow for groups from different environmental (that is, cultural) backgrounds. Therefore, the less a group resembled the majority group in a population, the lower should be its average score. Second, and more to the point of this chapter, Harrington's study indicates the uniqueness of the genotype-environment-item interaction, thus supporting the argument that a specific performance does not give important information about any general characteristics. Thus, it calls into question the meaning of test scores.

SUMMARY

The general argument of this chapter has been that no clear relationship exists between IQ test scores and an underlying intelligence. The chapter has purposely not focused on the problem of the cultural bias apparent in many U.S. tests of intelligence, in order that the more general fact (of which the bias is a specific example) be considered. Where examples of the specificity of score differences were employed, they were used in order to make the general argument (though the specific arguments are themselves important and will be considered briefly).

The argument has relied on several points. First, the underlying entity (intelligence) is not specifically defined. Thus, it is not certain to what behaviors it would correspond. Second, intelligence tests are therefore strictly operationally developed. Because of this, it is not certain what meaning one should attach to a score. Third, it is known that the performance of people in the test situation is strongly dependent on a number of factors, including cognitive orientation, motivation, and a number of other very specific factors. Fourth, since tests are social situations, such socially relevant factors as the management techniques used by testers are important factors in the production of test scores. Because of all of this, any relationship of the score to the quasi-theoretical entity it purports to measure is simply not specifiable.

This argument is not offered as a corrective to testers, such that better tests could be produced. Considering the large numbers of interfering factors operating between the concept and the measure of tests, this author doubts that such a correction is possible. It seems better to consider the factors to be integral aspects of score production than to consider them independent interferers. Be that as it may, to date, statements of group differences in a general intellectual quality have been made on the basis of a very weak set of data. While implications of this have been given more fully in the previous chapter, it bears repeating that the weaker the relationship of the measure to the concept, the less valid will be statements of group or individual differences regarding the quality in question.

It is not argued that clinical psychologists are unaware of this fact. On the contrary, since the beginning of testing, it has been common to state that the test score itself is a limited datum, and that one must investigate an individual very closely before making imputations of competence (see Terman 1916, pp. 109-10). However, when group comparisons in intellect are made, the same scores are used without the same cautions. In fact, since scores are considered to consist of a true measure plus a small number of uncorrelated errors, reliability theory holds that the errors will cancel one another out, given a large number of observations. If the argument presented here has merit, then scores can in no way be considered to consist of true plus error measures. Rather, they must consist of the totality of effects covered herein, in a complex interaction. That being the case, use of a large number of observations does not solve the psychologists' problem.

While this chapter has concentrated on the general problem of measurement, the specific problem of group differences deserves brief mention, since it is with group differences that most interest lies. At least much of the explanation of black-white and middle-class/lower-class differences in scores can probably be traced to test-construction procedures. It is well known that the reason boys and girls get the same IQ scores is that Terman and Merrill (1937) deliberately standardized their Stanford-Binet revisions to eliminate sex differences. Prior to that, such differences had been apparent, and Terman's and Merrill's actions reflected their sexual equalitarianism. Standard intelligence tests have not been standardized to eliminate ethnic differences, though when test-standardization procedures have been experimentally manipulated, it has been possible to reverse the direction of group differences in test scores (for a review, see Loehlin, Lindzey, and Spuhler 1975, pp. 66-69).

Standardization of items is only the second step in the production of tests. Prior to that step, the items themselves must be constructed. At this point, Harrington's findings are a step removed in importance. Recall that he generated items in a manner that, on the face of it, did not appear to discriminate against different strains of rats. In the construction of human intelligence tests, the items used have often been discriminatory on the surface. Summarizing a study of the early intelligence tests, including the Stanford tests, the Army tests, and the National Intelligence Test, Karier (1975) concludes that "certain characteristics emerge. They all reflect the euphemisms, the homilies, and the morals which were indeed the stock and trade of Poor Richard's Almanac, Noah Webster's blue-back speller, and McGuffy's readers" (p. 350). The Army even relied on tests which were given to immigrants in pantomime, which it was felt would eliminate problems of cultural bias. As late as 1960, the new revision of the Stanford-Binet included items in which the child was to discriminate the pretty person from the not-pretty person. The pretty individual was a very neatly dressed, Anglo-American, while the ugly figure had a broad nose, thick lips, and was poorly dressed. Culture-loaded items remain embedded within present tests. As an example, Wechsler (1958, pp. 65-67), the developer of what have become the most popular intelligence tests on the market, explicitly includes culturally loaded items in his tests, because such an inclusion increases the correlation between test scores and other criteria. When one includes, with the above, the fact that poor people tend to be relational in cognitive orientation, while middle-class people (including test constructors) tend to be analytic, and the fact that tests aim at basically analytic problems, it becomes clear that gross artifacts operate.

More than a mere artifact operates here, though. Recall that the introduction of motivating factors in the experiments cited operated to raise the test scores of black and lower-class children but not the scores of middle-class white children. Every study cited in that context has indicated that middle-class children tend, as a group, to react quite differently to test situations as compared with other children. With blacks, we have a historical precedent for the types of reactions cited by Labov for example. What can be termed <u>withdrawal actions</u> on the part of blacks are a normal feature of the traditional black reaction to white authority (Dollard 1949, p. 303), which some writers have traced to the days of slavery (Elkins 1963; Osofsky 1969; Wellman 1968). As a traditional response to authority ("Don't stand out, play dumb"), this way of behavior is passed down across generations. But it would be a mistake to consider it an irrational response to a situation that no longer exists. Recall that in the Rist study, kindergarten children learned to withdraw from the classroom situation as a response to a deplorable situation. The behavior was situation specific, but it came to have castelike qualities in a very short time. As much as any other factor, the tradition of behavior marking the interactions of blacks with those in authority, along with the tacitly patronizing attitudes of people in the middle class, will have an effect on the scores that ultimately emerge.

3

THE STRUCTURE
OF INTELLIGENCE

For the hereditarian position in the IQ controversy to remain valid, it is logically necessary that one be able to stratify people hierarchically, in terms of some global mental ability. It is easy to stratify people by any of a number of criteria, but the crucial issue in the controversy focuses on how reasonable such a practice is regarding general intelligence. Does a mental scale mirror nature, or is it imposed on a more multiform entity?

Since intelligence has yet to be satisfactorily defined, there is no strictly theoretical reason to suspect that a general entity exists. Yet IQ scores are commonly considered satisfactory measures of intelligence, so it appears that, at least tacitly, the general or monolithic view is accepted. Indeed, one commentator on the controversy, who professes to take no side, has stated that both hereditarians and environmentalists accept the "theory of general intelligence" (Urbach 1974, p. 112; for a reply, see Deakin 1976).

For hereditarians, the postulation of a general intelligence is necessary. Thus, Jensen (1969a, p. 9) has made the strong claim that general intelligence is a " rock of Gibraltar" in psychometrics. Likewise, Herrnstein (1971, 1973) speaks of intelligence in terms of a gradient. Strong statements aside, however, two questions need to be addressed regarding the alleged natural stratification of humans. First, what is the nature of the evidence supporting the idea? Second, is there evidence that tends to disconfirm the idea, and, if so, what is it?

In this chapter, first the psychometric evidence for a central mental process will be discussed. Problems of data and interpretation will be mentioned. Then, psychometric evidence for the existence of a diversity of intelligences will be presented. Following this, the evidence from animal studies on the generality of behavior will be presented briefly. Since it is possible to hold that a large set of intelligences exists, but that only a small subset of these are important in modern affairs, a study of the characteristics of research scientists will be provided. This study will foreshadow a much more extensive documentation of the specificity of human action, which will appear in the following chapter. Finally, a simple model of human intelligence will be presented. All of these sections of the chapter will support the idea that the specificity of performance in a given context is related not just to social and interactional phenomena (as discussed in Chapter 2), but also to the very nature of human intelligence.

THE EVIDENCE FOR GENERAL INTELLIGENCE

The idea of a general intelligence is most often represented by the letter g, which was first used by Charles Spearman (1904a, 1927) to stand for the general factor that appeared in factor analyses of test-item scores. In his most comprehensive treatment of intelligence, Spearman divided the entity into a general-ability factor and an unlimited number of other factors (or s factors), each specific to a given task or type of task. The two-factor view of intelligence does not necessarily enable one to talk in terms of gradients of ability, since s factors might be very important in the performance of socially important tasks; however, this is the only position that can logically support such a tendency and that has a degree of empirical support. The monolithic view simply has no theoretical base at all, and other views of intelligence do not effectively support the idea of a gradient.

Historically, the evidence for a g factor has taken two forms. First, factor analyses of intelligence test scores usually reveal the presence of a major general factor (the problems with this line of evidence will be shown below). Second, Spearman showed that were a particular score dependent on two intellectual factors (g + s), then tables of intercorrelations would take peculiar forms. Specifically, the tables would take a hierarchical form, with score magnitudes generally falling from left to right and from top to bottom. Expressed mathematically, this meant that given the correlations r_{ap}, r_{bq}, r_{aq}, r_{bp}, where a, b, p, and q are four different tests, the equation $r_{ap}r_{bq} - r_{aq}r_{bp}$ would yield 0 (see McGuire and Hirsch 1977, p. 5). Spearman and his colleagues showed such an equation to hold.

Two problems with this procedure soon appeared. First, it was shown that, mathematically, any of a number of different arrangements could yield tetrad differences of zero. In fact, it was shown that a table of correlations based on chance would yield such differences (for a review, see Tuddenham 1962). Since this was merely a different interpretation given to a well-known phenomenon, this attack did not seriously shake faith in the concept of a general intelligence.

However, a second form of attack proved more potent. This was focused on the fact that tetrad differences of zero simply did not always appear. Spearman (1927, p. 157) himself reported instances of this but explained them in terms of heterogeneity of samples and other disturbing factors. Others (for example, Tryon 1932a, 1932b) took the absence of zero tetrad differences as prima facie evidence of the multiple-factor nature of intelligence. Reviews of the development of psychometrics (Tuddenham 1962; Thomson 1951) have mentioned the slowness with which Spearman's supporters took cognizance of this important problem. Commonly, various disturbing factors were postulated to account for the failures that were encountered. For example, Tryon (1932b, pp. 403-5), in reviewing the literature on tetrad differences, found no less than 41 disturbers postulated, and he chided the Spearman group for presenting what "threatens to become a multiple factor theory in its own right."

With these basic problems, the idea of a general factor (g) entered a period of decline, and multiple-factor theories of intelligence gained in importance. In the mid-1930s, Tryon (1935) himself introduced a theory of "psychological components" that he contrasted with "mathematical factors." Tryon complained that the use of mathematical factors represented a retreat from psychological explanation, because no attempt was made to describe the "psychobiological properties" of the factors that emerged, and because any factor-analytic manner of research required some fundamental assumptions about the entity in question that were unlikely to have psychological or biological meaning (1935, pp. 426-32). Tryon's own theoretical position, based as it was on studies of behavioral responses to different situations, called for an unlimited number of components of intelligence.

The most popular view of intelligence to develop during the 1930s, however, was a factor-analytic view. Presented by Thurstone (1933, 1934, 1938), this position used techniques of factor analysis that were different from those used by Spearman and showed anywhere from five to nine major factors to exist when factor rotation was performed. Thurstone claimed to have shown that the major factors were independent of one another, such that the old g factor did not exist. However, when others followed up Thurstone's studies, it was found that some variance remained after the extraction of factors and that the factors obtained were slightly positively related to one another. Raymond Cattell (1941) then claimed that Spearmen's g factor should be retained as a second-order factor. In this manner, the g factor was retained even as it lost explanatory importance and even though other writers added more factors to the list of primary mental abilities.

THE EVIDENCE FOR DIVERSITY

One fact that is seldom commented upon is that factor analysis of test scores occurs after such scores are obtained. Recall that in the preceding chapter it was noted that items are chosen for inclusion in tests to the extent that they correlate well with the final score on the test—that is, to the extent that they share variance.

As mentioned, Terman and Merrill pragmatically dropped from consideration tests that did not correlate well with full test results, "even though they were satisfactory in other respects" (1937, p. 33), thus showing their commitment to a unitary intelligence. More explicit is Wechsler (1958), who has admitted that the "combining of a variety of tests into a single measure of intelligence, ipso facto, presupposed a certain final unity or equivalence between them" (pp. 9-11).

Thus, it would be surprising if no general factor were to emerge during analysis. In fact, Thurstone's factors were extracted from a series of tests, many of which he chose because they showed a "high g loading." It appears that at least much of the variance explained by the general factor is in truth present as an artifact of test-construction procedures. Indeed, those who have not been content to stop with a few primary factors have had no difficulty in radically increasing the number that they find. Thus, French (1951) found 20 factors of intelligence, while Guilford (1967, 1968) has developed a three-dimensional "structure-of-intellect" model that predicts at least 120 factors of intelligence, many of which he has found.

Psychologists (including Guilford) have found, upon close inspection of various specific factors, that those factors themselves differentiate into still more factors (Guilford 1968, p. 11; Vernon 1970, pp. 102-3). It appears that the greater the effort employed to delineate test factors, the more multidimensional the object under study appears. Thus, the total number of factors may actually range in the millions, as proposed by Tryon (1935; see also Garcia 1977, p. 11). There certainly does not appear to exist a simple scale by which people can be fitted into their proper place on a gradient.

While there is little use in challenging Jensen on his claim that about half the variance in a standard IQ test seems to load onto a single factor, neither is there much use in assigning importance to that fact. According to the psychological-components position (the position that the author will hold throughout this work), items should be correlated to the extent that they are psychologically similar. However, in investigations of individual test items, it has been found that even when many items are chosen in the common manner, some of them tend not to correlate well with one another. For example, Guilford (1964) has shown that if one takes, as the criterion of "zero intercorrelation," a correlation coefficient of less than 0.10, then 18 percent of the items do not correlate. If one takes, as the criterion of correlation, the common $p < 0.05$ confidence level, then fully 24 percent of the items do not correlate.

Other examples of the lack of importance of a g factor have emerged. Bloom (1963a), for one, has shown that if "gifted" means that a child falls in the top 10 percent on one of Thurstone's Primary Mental Abilities tests, then fully 60 percent of all children fall into the talented tenth for at least one ability. Guilford (1967, p. 28) adds (not tongue in cheek, it appears) that were the number of tests to increase without limit, the number of gifted children might approach 100 percent as an asymptote. This is what one should expect to find, given that since the early 1920s it has been known that the degree of interrelationships among different kinds of learning rates is low (this will be discussed later). Since only tasks that are similar should correlate well, one would expect that scores on different types of tasks would be shown to be independent of one another. As a test of this, Vandenberg (1965, 1967) analyzed scores on six Primary Mental Abilities tests (numerical, verbal, spatial, word fluency, reasoning, and memory) and found four independent hereditary components of the various tasks. Elsewhere, Vandenberg (1968a) found a wide divergence in the presence of hereditary components, depending on the populations sampled, the types of tests used, and so forth.

A further argument against the presence of a real psychological universal comes from examinations of tests of different sorts. Recall that IQ test items tend to be of the multiple-choice variety. This is absolutely essential for test takers to be able to answer a large number of items and thereby generate reliable scores. However, what the use of such items does is exclude from consideration performance on more time-consuming tasks. For example, as mentioned in the preceding chapter, IQ test scores do not correlate highly with scores on tests in which the subjects are expected to work out involved problems (for a review, see Evans 1969). If intelligence is what an intelligence test measures, then intelligence is not very much implicated in the completion of more complex tasks. This point will be returned to later, when the relationship between IQ scores and academic achievement is considered.

One other source of evidence against the idea of a simple gradient of ability for humans comes from the study of creativity. Briefly, since the surge of interest in creativity, following the launching of the first space satellites, it has been repeatedly shown that very little relationship exists between creativity (as either measured on a scale or inferred on the basis of professional work) and scores on standard intelligence tests (for example, Getzels and Jackson 1962; Wallach 1976). According to Guilford (1968, p. 128), such findings were met with "surprise, alarm, and disbelief" when rediscovered in the 1960s (see McNemar 1964), though they had been known half a century earlier. In fact, Terman (1906) first excluded tests of inventive and creative imagination from the investigation of intelligence precisely because such tests did not distinguish between children whom he commonsensically considered bright and stupid. It was the presupposition of a general "monolithic ability, all-relevant and unanalyzable" that led Terman and others to exclude such items from tests (Guilford 1968, p. 138). In any event, the intellectual giftedness of humans seems generally separate from their creativity.

EVIDENCE FROM ANIMAL STUDIES

The evidence for humans clearly suggests that the search for a general intelligence has been fruitless and that the artificial stratification of people by means of IQ tests does not represent a natural stratification. However, problems with the use of people as subjects in the study of individual differences (treated in the previous chapter) suggest that studies employing animal subjects may be useful. While one must, to some extent, reason by analogy from the results obtained in these studies, social interferences are eliminated. What is more, genetic and environmental variables can be strictly controlled.

Interesting information has come from the study of the behavior of infrahuman animals. One long line of investigation has come by means of breeding experiments with white rats. Beginning in the 1920s, Tryon (1929, 1940) and others selectively bred white rats for quickness in learning mazes. By the eighteenth breeding generation, two quite different groups had been bred: those who made few errors in running mazes and those who made many errors. Moreover, there was very little overlap in the number of errors made by those in the maze-bright and maze-dull groups.

Jensen (1969a, pp. 30-31, 40-41; 1969b, pp. 455-56) has taken such studies as showing that rat intelligence has been bred, though he has hedged somewhat in affirming that only "molar behavior" has been observed and that it "makes little difference whether one refers to this ability as rat 'intelligence,' or 'learning ability' or [by] some other term." The important point is that Jensen feels that some sort of general ability has been readily bred and measured. Further, this ability yields itself to unilinear analysis.

A quite different picture emerges if one examines the conclusions drawn by others from such studies. A general review by Anastasi (1958) indicated that the differences found were "not to be found in 'intelligence' or even general learning capacity" (p. 91). Instead, the so-called maze-dull rats equaled or excelled the maze-brights in other types of learning tasks. Other studies (for example, Searle 1949) found that the maze-bright rats were food driven, economical in the distance they cover, low in motivation to escape from water, and timid in open spaces. The maze-dull rats were fairly disinterested

in food, had good water motivation, and were timid around mechanical apparatuses. The differences between the two strains were apparently emotional and motivational rather than intellectual.

Jensen cannot be faulted for suggesting that a specific behavioral
trait can be selectively bred in rats, or that such could be the case for
humans. However, he presented the rat studies in the middle of an
extended discussion of the inheritance of a general ability in humans.
When this discrepancy was pointed out (by Cronbach 1969b), Jensen's
response was that he had found no literature suggesting a general
learning factor that operated across different types of learning for
animals, but that "this fact is actually irrelevant to the question of a
general factor in human intelligence" (Jensen 1969b, p. 456). If the
literature cited previously in this chapter has any validity, then Jensen is incorrect, and the existence of a specificity of differences is
of major importance.

If one wishes to be generous, to grant that motivational and
emotional factors should be included in definitions of intelligence,
something which several writers will not do (see Block and Dworkin
1976, pp. 431-32, 454-56), then at most the rat studies demonstrate
that a small number of properties, out of an n-numbered behavioral
repertoire (that we can term intelligence) can interact to affect additively the accomplishment of a limited task. These same properties
do not affect the accomplishment of other tasks, and they affect the
accomplishment of a third series of tasks in an inverse manner.
This is the reason that maze-dull rats were able to outperform the
maze-bright rats in a number of tasks. Note that this hypothesis of
the specificity of task accomplishment is directly supported by the
Harrington study reported in the previous chapter.

The specificity of behavioral differences has been made explicit
in a number of other studies. For example, in one study (McGaugh,
Jennings, and Thompson 1962), the mere change in the amount of
time between learning trials for the two strains of rats completely
obliterated strain differences in scores. In another study (Cooper
and Zubek 1958), when both strains of rats were raised in restricted
environments, strain differences were eliminated. Further, when
both strains were raised in stimulating environments, average differences were almost, but not quite, eliminated. A major review of
rat studies found that "all of the analyses have been consistent in
denying the existence of a universal factor" (Royce 1950, p. 256).
Among one series of studies, correlations between performances on
different sorts of tasks ranged from -0.64 to 0.77, and 9 of 13 correlations fell in the range of plus or minus 0.20. Further, the correlations of learning rates in rats were found to be direct functions
of the degree to which the behaviors being measured resembled one
another (Tomilin and Stone 1934). As noted earlier, this is hardly

surprising. What is surprising, again, is that the presence of inter-correlations among test items that are indeed designed to correlate is so often taken to be evidence of a unifactorial intelligence in humans.

It should be noted that the finding of numerous quasi-independent factors in the outcome of any behavioral task is not a product of research on rats alone, though much of the relevant work has been performed here. Other work has been performed on, among other species, fruitflies and blowflies (for example, McGuire and Hirsch 1977), and the lack of general behavioral categories has been well documented (Hirsch 1963).

DIVERSITY AND CRUCIAL ATTRIBUTES

As mentioned, it may be argued that there is no really general intelligence, but that there does exist a limited set of attributes whose presence is crucial, at least for academic endeavors. This appears to be the argument that Jensen makes, though in several places he gives this set a more global significance: that is, with his call for eugenic action. Here, we find several problems.

For one thing, the granting of such a global significance shows a bias toward this group of abilities that may not be warranted on the basis of the types of activities that are really necessary in order to competently manage one's life in the modern world. As put by Eisenberg (1966), the general issue is this:

> By what eternal scale of values can it be said that a competent physicist is better able to act purposefully, to think rationally, and to deal effectively with his environment than a competent cabinet maker, politician, farmer, housewife, or, for that matter, con artist? [P. 504]

There are an unlimited number of physical and behavioral traits located within a population (Williams 1969; McKusick 1966, p. ix; Haldane 1946; Hogben 1939). With such a diversity to choose from, using any discrete number in order to make social judgments of worth inevitably involves a set of elitist assumptions.

Related to this is the assumption that, say, physicists have a greater amount of these basic abilities than do people in general. But, as will be shown in depth in the next chapter, we do not now know what leads to eminence in physics or other academic domains. The standard intelligence and achievement tests simply do not effectively discriminate those who achieve eminence from those who do not. Where positive correlations between test scores and such accomplishments as the obtaining of a Ph.D. degree are found, there is evidence of a self-fulfilling prophecy, operating through the use of test scores to screen potential academicians. Where the personal characteristics of eminent scientists have been investigated, it has been found that there are "a number of subjects for whom none of the test material would give the slightest clue that the subject was a scientist of renown" (Roe 1953a, p. 52). This does not mean that just anyone can be a physicist. The study of individual differences leads us to expect that people will be differentially suited for any given task or small set of tasks. Yet this differentiation should be specific to the task set, and as of now we do not know how to perform such differentiations.

This leads to a further problem with the position just described. It would have us believe that those who engage in intellectual-type tasks are better able to arrange their lives than are other people. Yet the evidence does not support such a position. For example, in an in-depth study of research scientists, Anne Roe (1953a, 1953b) found them to be subject to a number of personality quirks, which seemed functional to the accomplishment of their research but which could well interfere with their everyday lives. For example, physical scientists could almost be described as cold. They tended to withdraw from intense emotional situations. On the other hand, social scientists showed a great deal of concern for such situations. Biologists and physicists showed considerable emotional independence from their parents, but social scientists demonstrated considerable rebelliousness and guilt with respect to their parents. With respect to expressions of aggression, social scientists were the most free, and biologists were the most restricted. In general, achievement motivation was surprisingly low (Roe 1953b, pp. 191-93). In discussing the pattern of her subjects' interests, Roe (1953) concluded that "the biologists showed up as very concerned with form . . .; the physical scientists as being more concerned with 3-dimensional space and inanimate motion than the others and the social scientists as extremely concerned with (in fact, practically haunted by) people" (p. 228).

Roe considered these emotional differences as component parts of the matrixes of attributes that would lead to success in the various fields. One important point here is that strong differences in emotionality were indeed important for that success. Another point is that the people she studied appeared not to be superior in rationality to normal people in the population. They had specific kinds of emotional problems that might be functional to their work, but they certainly did not result from any ability to think rationally (see also Roe 1963). Instead, these were arational (or even irrational) tendencies.

Another point to emerge from the Roe studies was that scientists in different disciplines also differed in intellectual qualities; there was no single differentiator acting (Roe 1953b, pp. 160-70). For example, on a verbal test for which the items were supplied by the Educational Testing Service (ETS), experimental physicists had by far the lowest scores, while theoretical physicists and anthropologists had the highest scores. On this 80-item test, actual scores ranged from 8 to 75. On a 24-item test of spatial abilities that was supplied by ETS, biologists and anthropologists scored lowest, while theoretical physicists again scored the highest. The range of scores was from 3 to 22. On a 30-item mathematical test, physicists had no trouble on any of the items. Of the other groups, biologists and psychologists performed much better than did anthropologists (respective averages were 16.8, 15.6, and 9.2). Correlations among various tests were low, despite the broad range in scores. While the tests were not fully standardized, it should be noted that they consisted of stock ETS items.

These data support the idea that success in academic spheres does not depend merely on a single constellation of attributes. Roe herself came away convinced that the most important determinant of success in science was to be found in a home atmosphere in which a high value was placed on learning "for its own sake" (1953b, p. 231). Be that as it may, if no single set of attributes is sufficient to account for even scientific eminence, then how, in general, shall people be placed on a scale? The argument made here is that the search for such a scale will in principle be in vain.

A MODEL OF INTELLECTUAL-TASK PERFORMANCE

The various lines of evidence discussed previously indicate that performance on intellectual, as well as other, tasks depends on a shifting constellation of variables. Given this, as put by P. B. Medawar (1977): "No single figure can embody itself in a constellation of values of all these variables in any single real instance" (p. 13). Why this is so deserves discussion. It will be done here by presenting a model of task performance. It is not argued that mental functioning directly mirrors the model, which utilizes simple additive assumptions; but it is argued that the more complex workings of the brain are well-enough represented here to make the important points of this chapter.

Take the situation in which a given task (T) exists among an array of tasks. Assume, also, that there exists an array of human attributes (A). Following the literature cited above, for task T_{ijk}, A_i represents those attributes that additively affect the performance of the task in a positive direction. Further, A_j represents those attributes that do not affect the performance of the task, and A_k represents those attributes that affect the performance of the task in a negative manner. Attributes are continuous and at least partially independent.

Given such an arrangement, it logically follows that no averaging of the differential levels of representation of the various attributes A_{ijk} will tell, in general, how well one will do on tasks.

For each given task, a different constellation of attributes will act differently to affect task completion in a unique manner. To the extent that tasks are similar, performance will be similar, though by no means identical. For fairly complex task sets, any average representation of a set of attributes will not be very predictive of the level of task-set accomplishment, because of the large number of attributes called into play in different combinations. This aspect of the model calls into question even the weak general-overview type of general intelligence. Not only the presence or absence but also the weighting of each attribute will shift as the tasks in the set shift. Any simple summary score will simply fail to represent the complexity of task performance and will, hence, lack strong predictive ability.

According to this sketchy model of task performance, a simple placement on a hierarchy will be possible only in the limiting instance where one approaches a single task. To the extent that the task is very limited, a hierarchy will at least approximate differentials of performance. The more complex the task, the less sense a hierarchy will make and the less predictive of actual performance will any ranking scheme be. It is the contention of the author that the research into the relationships between standardized test scores (where a test is a form of task) and performance on real-world tasks supports this model. That is, intelligence, as represented by intelligence tests, is simply not a very important variable in the socioeconomic world. The following chapter will investigate this contention.

SUMMARY

In sum, the evidence presented in this chapter leads one to seriously question the degree to which the idea of a general intelligence can have usefulness in real-world pursuits. Instead, all the various lines of evidence indicate that behavior is too multiform to be encapsulated under the label of intelligence, unless what we intend by intelligence is something quite a bit different from that which is usually intended. But if this difference is taken seriously, then what happens to calls for eugenic action? Indeed, what happens to any statements about group differences that do not have strictly defined contexts? The conclusion of this author is that such statements must be ruled out of order; that a serious consideration of behavioral diversity is incompatible with statements of inferiority-superiority in any general sense. Thus, success in a specified sphere should not be used to generalize about other spheres.

4

THE SOCIAL IMPORTANCE
OF INTELLIGENCE

For the hereditarian position in the IQ controversy to stand, it is essential that measured intelligence play a crucial role in the social world. This is because the hereditarian position relies on a simple meritocratic model of achievement in which social stratification mirrors intellectual stratification (for example, Herrnstein 1973; cf. Chomsky 1976). If this model is correct, then it follows that, at the minimum, strong correlations will be found between meritocratic indicators and various indicators of achievement. While IQ test scores are the most frequently employed meritocratic indicators, such things as school grades and achievement-test scores are also assumed to reflect one's intellectual ability.

If the alternative model of intellectual functioning presented earlier is valid, then none of the relationships that one finds between the various indicators and various forms of achievement should be very strong. Where correlations are positive and at least moderate in magnitude, the statistical effects of the indicators should not be direct. Rather, it should be possible, at least in principle, to show that they are mediated by other variables, and/or that they are largely spurious relationships. That is, the indicators should lack functional importance. Once one leaves the arena of education (where test scores are designed to correlate with grades), the relationships discovered should be negligible.

By way of foreshadowing, it should be noted that a weak relationship between meritocratic indicators (including IQ scores) and achievement is one of the most solidly documented facts to emerge from the IQ controversy. But while the most widely discussed attacks on the social importance of measured intelligence have stressed recent studies (especially Jencks 1972), data indicating this weakness have been available for over half a century (for example, Hoyt 1965).

Evidence on this issue comes from several sources. First, there are studies that trace the achievement patterns of people with low IQs. Such studies are important because it is commonly supposed that people low in measured intelligence are unable to cope satisfactorily with modern-life situations (for example, Harlow and Harlow 1962). This is an idea that can be traced at least to Herbert Spencer, in the mid-nineteenth century, and its history will be sketched later. For now, it should be noted that if it can be shown that people who, in the face of low scores on various standard measures of intellectual ability, still lead productive lives, then the status of intelligence as being fully necessary for social achievement must be at least open to question.

The second source of evidence on the social importance of intelligence is the category of studies investigating the relationship between meritocratic critcria (especially standardized test scores and school grades) and nonacademic achievement. Two subsets of studies are included here. First, we have studies documenting the relationship between intelligence and future income or occupational status. This is the set of studies most frequently encountered in the literature. Second, we have the set of studies investigating the relationship between intelligence and academic success not related to grades in school and between intelligence and the nonacademic success not directly related to economic achievement.

The third source of evidence is the group of studies investigating the general relationship between intelligence and educational achievement. The 0.50 correlation between IQ scores and school grades is the single most important source of validation of the simple meritocratic idea of achievement. If it can be argued that the correlation is, to a considerable extent, attributable to external causes—that is, that it is largely spurious—then the use of intelligence as a criterion of merit becomes questionable.

The fourth source of evidence for the relationship between intelligence and success is the set of studies investigating the relationship between intelligence and success in highly intellectual occupations. We will examine each of these four lines of evidence in turn.

DULLNESS AND ACCOMPLISHMENTS

As mentioned, a fear expressed by many psychometricians is that a population of people with low IQ scores will be unable to cope with the exigencies of a complex modern world. Jensen (1969a, p. 88) presented such an argument in a discussion of the general topic "why raise intelligence?" However, the little evidence available on the topic indicates that even people with very low IQ scores on intelligence tests prove often to be very capable, when given the opportunity.

Much evidence on this topic has been anecdotal. An early example of this was Trabue's (1922) example of a 40-year-old woman with an IQ of about 75, who was a successful businesswoman, a housekeeper at a fashionable Fifth Avenue hotel, and the owner of a small factory. It can, of course, be argued that any given exception to the general rule does not count against the rule—that other factors operated in the specific case, or that the score was not representative of the person's true ability. This contention will be examined shortly. Trabue's own position was that testers had too great a confidence in the accuracy of test scores, that the division of people into homogeneous groups on the basis of scale scores was uncalled for, and that the making of social pronouncements on the basis of test scores was not valid.

The problem of the differentiation of feeblemindedness from low test scores had actually arisen some time prior to Trabue's complaint. The earliest U.S. version of the Binet intelligence tests had been developed by H. H. Goddard. Goddard, an ardent antiimmigrationist, had used his tests at Ellis Island to measure the intellect of immigrants and had shown that over 80 percent of Eastern and southern European immigrants were feebleminded (1913, 1917). Wallin (1916) used the Goddard revisions of the Binet scales to measure the intelligence of prosperous businessmen, farmers, and housewives in Iowa, and found that as a group they also were shown to be feebleminded. Of course, Wallin's findings were quickly taken to indicate that the Goddard tests were invalid measures of intelligence, because so many very solid citizens failed them.

By the time of the Trabue article (1922) the well-standardized Stanford-Binet revisions were available, and his complaints were directed at these more refined tests. The studies that have followed have, in the main, supported his position. For instance, Sarason and Gladwin (1958), in a rather long monograph, investigated the abilities of "subnormals." They found that those with extremely low scores on tests, including people who had been institutionalized, were "capable of a completely adequate degree of sustained problem-solving activity" (Sarason and Gladwin 1958, p. 41). Included in the study were examples of retarded citizens who had been awarded medals for coolness and bravery under fire, who had commonly carried out complex laboratory tests as medical assistants, and so forth. The most striking finding of the study was that subnormality in general intelligence was not as a rule associated with a lack of competence. In fact, many similarities between the retarded and the nonretarded appeared. One striking difference between the two groups was that those who fell in the retarded category generally had a very negative attitude toward school. Guilford (1967, p. 27) has cited the study as evidence that intellect is a multidimensional entity that will not correspond to summary scale scores, an idea which dovetails with the model of intellect presented in the previous chapter.

A study that did not deal specifically with those labeled retarded but that did compare the achievements of high test scorers with those who scored in the middle or low part of the relevant scale, was performed by Elton and Shevel (1969). These authors sampled 22,000 takers of the American College Test (ACT) and divided subjects into three groups: those who had an average score, those who had a score of one or more standard deviations above the mean, and those who had a score of one or more deviations below the mean. The subjects were compared on 48 different items, across six general categories of nongrade-related achievement (leadership, music, drama/speech, art, writing, and science). There was very little relationship found between test scores and achievement. In some areas, high scorers showed greater achievement, whereas in other areas middle-range or low scorers showed greater achievement. Since this study will be treated at greater length later, only one comparison will be presented here, that contrasting male high and low scorers on the 48 items. Briefly, on 29 items, no significant differences appeared between the two groups. On 12 items, high scorers showed a greater tendency to achieve, and on 7 items low scorers showed greater achievement. This compares favorably with a study by Wallach and Wing (1969), which found significant differences between high- and low-ability groups on only 3 of 34 achievement items.

The most comprehensive study of the relationship between low test scores and general social competence has been performed by Mercer (1973) and her associates. Like those authors already mentioned, Mercer is critical of the view that low test scores indicate a lack of competence. Specifically, she criticizes the "clinical" perspective on mental retardation, in which "a low IQ is interpreted as a pathological sign and treated as if it had been identified as a symptom by functional analysis" (Mercer 1973, p. 8). She argues that this occurs because statistical abnormality is confused with functional pathology. Since extremely low scores are rare, they are treated as evidence of pathology, and those who score low are treated as though they shared a syndrome (see Mercer 1973, chap. 1).

In order to investigate the clinical perspective on intelligence, Mercer studied black, white, and Chicano subjects with IQ scores in the bottom 3 percent of the population by grading them on behavioral indicators of intelligence: being able to travel alone, do one's own shopping, read books and magazines, hold a job, stay in school, and so forth. She found that while no whites with IQ scores below 70 (the criterion) were able to perform these tasks efficiently, 60 percent of Chicanos and 90 percent of blacks who fell below the criterion were able to do so.

When Mercer revised her definition of retardation to include behavioral indicators of intelligence, and then took into account pluralistic norms for IQ and adaptive behavior, the rates of retardation for blacks and Chicanos plummeted. The rate for whites remained at 4.4 per thousand people, no matter how the criteria were changed; but the rate for Chicanos fell from 149 per thousand to 15.3 per thousand, and the rate for blacks fell from 44.9 per thousand all the way to 4.1 per thousand, a figure slightly lower than that for whites (Mercer 1973, p. 253). Lest these results appear overly surprising, it should be noted that others have obtained similar results (see, for example, Cooper et al. 1967).

As noted by Block and Dworkin (1976, p. 529, n. 81), a writer like Jensen might explain Mercer's findings in terms of differential distributions of "Level I" and "Level II" intelligence, where intellectually dull blacks and Chicanos could have high levels of the ability to operate in noncognitive spheres. However, to postulate this would be to abandon the idea that these groups are inferior in their ability to competently manage their real-life situations. It might not affect arguments concerning the ability to succeed in specialized occupations like the sciences.

A second objection to the Mercer analysis might be that it really only documented the continuing presence of test bias, rather than the abilities of low-IQ people. The argument might be made that were test bias removed, the IQ scores of minority groups would accurately represent their ability to perform everyday activities. This argument has cogency. However, the previously mentioned study by Sarason and Gladwin (1958) documented competence among low scorers without regard to ethnicity—even among those who had been institutionalized for retardation. Also, the other studies mentioned all indicated that low scorers, as a group, were well represented in various achievement categories. For example, it has been found that about 10 percent of those who are employed as accountants have IQ scores of less than 88 (Thorndike and Hagen 1959).

It must also be mentioned that standardized tests are often justified on the grounds that they tap abilities that are necessary in this specific society. If this is so, and if the measurement of those abilities is biased, then it follows that the tests should remain valid predictors of performance. Common activities that are important for success in this culture should show a bias against minorities, but for cultural rather than genetic reasons. This, essentially, is the cultural-deficit position. But the studies presented indicate that any deficit may be specific to the cultural group and the task studied. Again, the issue of the meaning of test scores must be raised.

Recall Labov's (1972) study of black children in IQ-test situations. In a related study, Labov and Robins (1969) investigated the relationship between gang membership and a standard meritocratic indicator: reading level. Labov and Robins found that all those who were full or marginal members of teenage gangs read below grade level, none read above the fifth-grade level, and no increase in reading skills followed advancement in number of years of schooling. That is, the older youths read as badly as did the younger youths. Meanwhile, those who were nonmembers of gangs, while they averaged two years below grade in reading, followed the usual trend of increases in reading skills with increases in grade. Further, some of these people read at or above grade level.

While the above findings would appear to substantiate the idea that gang members were those who simply did not have the intellectual ability to succeed in the school system, Labov's and Robins's analysis indicates something quite different (1969; see also, Labov 1972, pp. 255-92). Specifically, the authors showed that gang membership was highly prestigious for the black teenagers included in the study. Success in school simply did not connote prestige to gang members. Instead, focal concerns of members included toughness, smartness (ability to manipulate others), trouble, excitement, autonomy, and a variable called fate. Such activities as reading were seldom engaged in outside of school.

Further, the authors indicated that gang members, as a group, were superior to nonmembers in a number of socially important attributes. So striking indeed were the differences found that nonmembers came to be termed lames, a term that indicated that it was "the normal, intelligent, well-coordinated youth" who would be a gang member (Labov 1972, p. 286). Gang members, much more than lames, were skilled in games requiring complex verbal manipulations, in fighting, and in those skills that served the function of social integration. Implicit in this analysis is the idea that those who ranked high on common meritocratic criteria did so as a result of isolation from their peers. Within the specific cultural context of the gang subculture, these people were failures, and those who scored low could be successes. *

This set of studies is important as regards the issue of achievements of dull people, because gang members, by standard measures, would have to be considered dull. And these people, within the frame of reference of their subcultural group, were clearly successful as a group.

In combination with the other studies cited here, these studies lend support to the idea, previously developed, that behavioral attri-

---

*It would be interesting to compare the cultural milieus operating in the case of Labov and in the previously mentioned Rist studies.

butes are specific rather than general, and that performance in any one sphere should not be used to generalize about other spheres. What studies like Mercer's and Labov's do is add the dimension of situational and cultural context to the model of performance given in the previous chapter. It is not just the combined effects of individual characteristics and situational requirements that determine performance, but also the cultural context within which performance takes place. Put differently, it is not merely that intellectually dull people manage to do well in certain spheres, but that the measures of dullness simply cannot take into account what is required for success in any given area of endeavor.

INTELLIGENCE AND NONACADEMIC ACHIEVEMENT

The evidence in the previous section indicates that those who score even very low on intelligence tests can be competent members of society. However, the fact that measured intelligence does not appear to be strongly related to competence in everyday life situations does not prove that intelligence is not implicated in the performance of exemplary tasks. It might yet be the case that true success, as opposed to mere "making do," will require a greater amount of some set of intellectual abilities, such as might be measured on an intelligence test. Two forms of achievement can be studied in this regard: economic and noneconomic. The latter will be discussed first.

Noneconomic Achievement

Earlier, it was mentioned that scores on intelligence tests and on some other kinds of tests (for example, those measuring creativity) did not correlate highly. As an example, Getzels and Jackson (1959) and Torrance (1963) have estimated that if one selects the top 20 percent of scorers on IQ tests, one will exclude 70 percent of the top 20 percent of scorers on tests of creativity. This is only 10 percent fewer than would be excluded if IQ and creativity were totally independent of one another. Does the same relationship hold for activities outside test situations? In a word, yes. The study by Elton and Shevel (1969), briefly mentioned in the preceding section, investigated the relationship between scores on the ACT and forms of nonacademic achievement, and in fact found very little relationship at all. A summary of the authors' findings appears in Table 3. The most striking fact to emerge from the study is the degree of independence of test scores from nonacademic achievement. For combined categories of analysis, fully 68 percent of the comparisons yielded no significant

TABLE 3

Comparisons of High, Average, and Low ACT Scorers on Various Achievement Categories

Category	Comparisons of High and Low[a]			Comparisons of High and Average			Comparisons of Average and Low		
	Favor Highs	Favor Lows	No Difference	Favor Highs	Favor Averages	No Difference	Favor Averages	Favor Lows	No Difference
Males									
Leadership[b]	3[c]	2	3	2	0	6	0	3	5
Music	3	0	5	4	0	4	1	0	7
Drama	1	1	6	2	1	5	0	0	8
Art	0	4	4	0	6	2	0	0	8
Writing	2	0	6	5	0	3	2	1	5
Science	3	0	5	8	0	0	0	2	6
Totals	12	7	29	21	7	20	3	6	39
Females									
Leadership	2	2	4	2	0	6	2	1	5
Music	2	1	5	1	1	6	1	0	7
Drama	0	2	6	0	1	7	0	0	8
Art	0	1	7	0	0	8	0	0	8
Writing	3	1	4	6	0	2	2	1	5
Science	1	0	7	4	0	4	0	0	8
Totals	8	7	33	13	2	33	5	2	41

[a]High means that the American College Test (ACT) score was one standard deviation or more above the mean. Low means that the ACT score was one or more standard deviations below the mean.

[b]There are eight comparison categories for each of the six major categories listed (for example, there are eight forms of leadership in which scores are compared.

[c]A difference in comparisons is found when the differences in percents of subjects is significant at p < 0.01.

Note: Sample size was 22,000.

Source: C. F. Elton and L. R. Shevel, Who is Talented? An Analysis of Achievement, ACT Research Report no. 31 (Iowa City: American College Testing Program, September 1969), p. 10. Reprinted by permission.

differences between groups, despite the rather large sample size
(n = 22,000). Where there were significant differences, the higher-
scoring group tended to rate higher more often than not, but there were
numerous exceptions. For example, as a whole, the average scorers
rated more poorly than either the high or the low scorers, showing
superiority only 17 times and proving inferior in 42 instances. Low-
scoring males attained greater levels of achievement than high-scoring males in 7 of 19 comparisons in which a significant difference was
found. Low-scoring females outperformed high-scoring females in
7 or 15 categories.

Those differences that emerged were interesting. Among males,
contrasting high and low scorers, high scorers tended to outperform
low scorers in the areas of music, writing, and the sciences. Low
scorers were superior in art, and there were few differences in leadership or in drama-speech. High scorers were more likely to have participated in a student, change-oriented movement, but low scorers
were more likely to have initiated such movements. Low scorers
were also more likely to have exhibited works of art in local or re-
gional-state shows and to have won prizes in those shows. High
scorers were more likely to have entered a school speech or debate
contest, but low scorers were more likely to have had minor roles in
plays (not high-school or church sponsored).

Mention should be made of the meaning of superiority in this
study. Comparisons were based on the percentage of those in each
group who had shown achievements in a given area. For example, 12
percent of low-scoring males had edited a school yearbook or paper,
while 7 percent of middle-scoring males and 11 percent of high-scoring males had done the same. In this case, both the high- and low-
scoring males significantly (p< 0.01) outperformed middle-scoring
males, as a group. However, the actual percentage differences were
slight. Put differently, 93 percent of middle-scoring males, 89 percent of high-scoring males, and 88 percent of low-scoring males had
not edited a school paper or yearbook. Even at the 0.01 level of significance, the size of the sample caused differences of as little as 2
percent to reach statistical significance. Thus, the authors correctly
noted that the degrees of difference might have "little practical importance" (Elton and Shevel 1969, p. 11). The differences in achievement among the groups were thus overstated because of the method
employed, and the real differences in achievement patterns among the
groups were slight, despite the fact that over two standard deviations
in ACT scores separated the high and low groups.

A study by Holland and Richards (1965) shows just how slight
the relationship between ACT scores and nonacademic achievement
is. These authors measured the same categories as those in the
previous study, and added a list of 143 things from which students

were asked to check those that "you can do well or competently" (Holland and Richards 1965, p. 7) as well as three scales that will not be discussed here. Their sample, rather than being drawn from among all those who took the ACT, was made up of college freshmen (N = 7,262) from 24 different colleges and universities.

Intercorrelations among ACT subtests, high-school GPA, and the various indicators of achievement were obtained. While the subtests and high-school grades correlated moderately well ($0.34 \leq r \leq 0.64$), the correlations with the other items were quite small. The highest correlation was 0.23; 27 percent of all correlations were negative; and the median correlation was only 0.04. The authors checked for restriction of range and for curvilinear relations and found evidence of neither.

Economic Achievement

Research on the relationship between intelligence and nonacademic achievement began in the late 1950s and early 1960s, but research on the relationship between intelligence and economic achievement has a much longer history. As early as the early 1920s, Gambrill (1922) presented data that indicated that the correlation between college GPA (a surrogate for intelligence) and salary was only 0.10, and research since then has tended to support the finding. In his review of the major studies aimed at this issue, Hoyt (1965) concluded that "we can safely conclude that college grades have no more than a modest correlation with adult success no matter how defined" (p. 45).

The first major longitudinal attempt to demonstrate the relationship between IQ and achievement was performed by Terman and his associates at Stanford University (for a summary, see Terman 1954). In these studies, the progress of schoolchildren with high IQ scores was followed for a number of years and their accomplishments were recorded. The group as a whole showed a great deal of achievement by any standards. Yet Terman never answered the question of why these children became high-achieving adults. For example, he apparently never bothered to look upon high IQ scores in terms of accreditation processes (Blum 1978, pp. 75-76).

Further, the Terman studies were marred by problems that could well serve to introduce biases into the findings presented. For example, in addition to IQ scores, children were chosen on the basis of teachers' recommendations; school grades; information on their home life, their health, racial, ethnic, home, occupational, economic backgrounds, their interests, and so on. Clearly, more than just IQs were used. Further, the children were overwhelmingly from semiprofessional, professional, and business-oriented families. Only

6.8 percent were the children of semiskilled or unskilled parents (for a review, see Sorokin 1956, pp. 70-82).

Even with these biases in sample selection, the group was not totally outstanding in its accomplishments. For example, about a third of the subjects would have to be considered economic failures by the standards of the social classes from which they were drawn. Most of the rest proved merely adequate by these criteria. In fact, of the group accomplishments so often proclaimed regarding these subjects, almost all were performed by a group of about 14 percent of the total sample. It is evident that the problems with the study were great, since no other major study that has controlled the independent effects of such variables as social class has been able to repeat Terman's findings. (This will be shown later in this chapter.) Likewise, no other study, to this author's knowledge, has shown IQ scores to be terribly important. The Terman studies stand as isolated instances among a large collection of studies that simply does not support his contentions.

Another early, large-sample investigation of the relationship between various meritocratic indicators and economic achievement was performed by E. L. Thorndike et al. (1934). The study required eight years to complete and was longitudinal in nature. Briefly, tests of intelligence, GPA, and the grade achieved before the subjects left school (along with other measures that will not be covered here), were recorded when the subjects (N = 2,225) were 14 years old; and the subjects' economic achievement was recorded at ages 20 and 22. A summary of results appears in Table 4.

Again, the most striking fact to appear is the dearth of strong correlations. For the various indicators, the range in correlations was from -0.36 to 0.65, but the range of weighted means for the indicators was only from -0.02 to 0.26. Fully two-thirds of all weighted means were in the range of plus or minus 0.10, and the median correlation was only 0.08. The four strongest relationships found were between the two intelligence measures and the two indicators of occupational achievement for clerical workers (range = 0.17 to 0.26), which follows from the fact that clerical skills figure prominently in the completion of such tests (for example, McClelland 1974, p. 165). But even here, less than 7 percent of the variance is accounted for.

As will be documented in Part II of this study, Thorndike was a eugenicist who believed that various intellectual and ethical traits would strongly overlap, and that there would, therefore, be a strong relationship between meritocratic criteria and human achievement. After giving the findings just mentioned, he rather lamely concluded that one could predict performance, "but only in probabilities of rather small magnitudes" (Thorndike et al. 1934, p. 68). Elsewhere, perhaps in a more truculent mood, he stated that test scores would be at

TABLE 4

The Relationship between Various Meritocratic Indicators and
Economic Success

Meritocratic Indicator	Earnings at Ages 20 and 22	Job Level at Ages 20 and 22
Clerical intelligence		
Mechanical work	-0.05 to 0.09 (0.01)	-0.12 to 0.06 (-0.02)
Mixed work	-0.22 to 0.42 (0.10)	-0.21 to 0.28 (0.07)
Clerical work	0.21 to 0.31 (0.26)	0.18 to 0.35 (0.21)
Abstract intelligence		
Mechanical work	-0.08 to 0.21 (0.08)	-0.12 to 0.07 (-0.01)
Mixed work	-0.16 to 0.43 (0.12)	-0.18 to 0.28 (0.10)
Clerical work	-0.02 to 0.40 (0.17)	0.16 to 0.19 (0.18)
School grades		
Mechanical work	-0.04 to 0.17 (0.04)	-0.05 to 0.20 (0.07)
Mixed work	-0.28 to 0.33 (0.04)	-0.25 to 0.30 (0.08)
Clerical work	0.00 to 0.23 (0.11)	-0.05 to 0.23 (0.13)
Grade reached at leaving school		
Mechanical work	-0.03 to 0.22 (0.07)	-0.06 to 0.29 (0.09)
Mixed work	-0.36 to 0.65 (0.04)	-0.29 to 0.47 (0.06)
Clerical work	-0.05 to 0.26 (-0.01)	0.03 to 0.32 (0.16)

Note: Data are ranges of correlations between the indicators and economic success. The weighted averages furnished by the authors appear in parenthesis.

Source: E. L. Thorndike et al., The Prediction of Vocational Success (New York: Commonwealth Fund, 1934), pp. 224-27. Copyright © 1934 by the Commonwealth Fund. Reprinted by permission.

least better predictors of performance than "prejudices and superstitions" (Thorndike et al. 1934, p. 118).

In the late 1950s and 1960s a number of works critical of the use of standard criteria for inferential purposes appeared. One major work (McClelland et al. 1958), commissioned by the Social Science Research Council (SSRC), obtained the same pattern of results as did the studies previously mentioned. David McClelland, the chairman of the Committee on Early Identification of Talent of the SSRC, in his words, "found this hard to believe" until he independently checked the achievement of eight straight-A students and of eight truly poor students (C- or below), all from college classes in the 1940s. He found no distinguishable differences in their achievement patterns by the early 1960s, except that those with better grades had been able to parlay them into admission to better postgraduate institutions. However, even with attendance at superior institutions, the straight-A students had not been able to achieve more, on the average, than had the poorer students.

This general independence of academic from nonacademic achievement has been verified not only for the United States (see Berg 1970, for a summary) but also for Great Britain (for example, Hudson 1960). The independence of test scores from achievement has been similarly well documented. Perhaps the first national-sample attempt to discover a relationship here was performed by Thorndike and Hagen (1959), who followed the careers of some 10,000 men with military records, in the process of which they calculated some 12,000 correlations. Most germane to the discussion here is their finding concerning the relationship between intelligence-test scores and occupational achievement in general. Briefly, of all the correlations obtained that related to this issue, only 6.2 percent were significant at the common 0.05 level. More bluntly, the number of significant correlations was about what one would expect to find by chance alone. In this manner, the authors properly interpreted their findings.

This does not mean that one never finds significant relationships between test scores and achievement, nor that such must never occur. The argument made here is merely that test scores are not (except for purposes of certification) very important in social success. For example, it has been shown that father-son differences in IQ test scores show a correlation of 0.29 with father-son differences in occupational status (Waller 1971). This correlation, however, accounts for less than 9 percent of the variance in such differences. Further, almost all of this variance is accounted for among the three middle classes of a five-class index. Poor and rich people seem little affected by test scores. Moreover, the study assumes that the relationship is causal, and reasons for it are not investigated. This is an important omission, since it has been shown that somewhat less than

20 percent of the correlation between education and occupational success is attributable to test-score differences, when other variables are brought to bear (for a review, see Bowles and Gintis 1976, pp. 294-97). One should ask, in an analogous fashion, how much of the relationship between test scores and success is actually itself attributable to an underlying ability matrix tapped by tests. Since the 9 percent mark is found when only the effect of social class is controlled, the true effect is likely to be much smaller.

One review, which has attempted to document the importance of intelligence for performance in various occupations (Ghiselli 1966), estimated that test scores correlate 0.42 with trainability, and 0.23 with proficiency, across all types of jobs. The second correlation is so weak as to be virtually negligible, while the first seems moderate in magnitude. Yet Ghiselli did not state how either concept was measured in the different studies he reviewed (McClelland 1974, pp. 168-69). We are not privy to information on the meaning of the two terms, though McClelland conjectures that proficiency is the same thing as supervisors' ratings, along with other indirect indicators of how well one does a job (for example, turnover, salary, and promotions). Further, Ghiselli's data were strictly correlational, and as such did not account for any possible causes of the correlations, but rather took them at face value.

The search for sources of spurious relationships has yielded interesting results. For example, Brenner (1968) found a significant correlation between GPA and supervisors' evaluations of on-the-job performance. But Bowles, Gintis, and Meyer (1975) reanalyzed Brenner's data and found the following: When personality traits (as measured by school absences and by teachers' evaluations of work habits and cooperation) were controlled by linear regression, GPA no longer had predictive power. The issue of the importance of personality patterns in the determination of occupational performance, while it strays somewhat from the subject at hand, has some value. It has been shown, for example, that factors such as strength of character constitute important nonintellective correlates of success (Smith 1967, p. 982). Further, whereas a factor named rule following has been shown to predict performance in low-level jobs, a factor named internalization of norms is more predictive at higher levels (Edwards 1977). For some summaries of studies of the role of personality patterns in the marketplace, see Bowles and Gintis (1976, chap. 5).

Major sociological and economic investigations of the role of intelligence in the determination of success can be traced very clearly to the national-sample studies that were undertaken in the mid- to late-1960s along with the federal antipoverty programs. One of the first studies to gain general recognition was performed by Duncan

(1968), who investigated the combined influences of IQ scores and education on occupational achievement (see also, Blau and Duncan 1967). Duncan found that the overall correlation between IQ and occupational achievement was a modest 0.31. That is, slightly less than 10 percent of the variance in achievement was accounted for by intelligence-test score variations. This was a large contribution, by common sociological standards, but was still almost minute when compared with the full range of human achievement.

When Duncan controlled for the effects of education, the influence of IQ scores fell to almost zero ($R^2 = 0.017$), leading him to conclude that while there was "some role for general ability," it operated almost completely through the process of education and certification (Duncan 1968, p. 9). Other studies have supported these findings in the main, but there has been a great deal of discussion concerning the role of intelligence in the relationship between schooling and achievement. Some studies have found positive interactions between IQ and schooling, but others have found no interactions; and several studies have found negative interactions (for a summary of studies, see Bowles and Gintis 1976, pp. 314-16, especially n. 8 and 14).

A focal point of discussion has been the relationship between meritocratic predictors and achievement among minorities, as contrasted with the same relationship among male Anglo-Americans. In this regard, Weiss (1970) documented a strong "discrimination effect" on black income, relative to white income, for given amounts of education. The presence of a "cost" of belonging to a minority group has also been documented for Chicanos (Poston and Alvirez 1973; Poston, Alvirez, and Tienda 1976) and for women. Weiss (1970, p. 159) also found no significant relationship between education and income for blacks, though he did find one for whites.

If substantial amounts of the income differentials between dominant and subordinate groups cannot be accounted for by meritocratic criteria, then a prima facie case is made for considering social processes that are independent of a simple ability dimension as having major importance. Discrimination is merely one form of such social processes. The massive study by Jencks (1972, p. 218) estimated that at least half the income disadvantage of blacks must be related to discrimination or unmeasured cultural differences. In the more general case, if the population were homogeneous with respect to measured intelligence, then income inequality would be reduced by only about 3 percent (Jencks 1972, p. 221).

The relationship between Armed Forces Qualification Test (AFQT) scores and occupational achievement has consistently proved small or negative. Jencks (1973), using National Opinion Research Center (NORC) data, indeed found a clear negative relationship between AFQT scores and the rate of economic return for education.

Similarly, Griliches and Mason (1972), again using the AFQT, found
that "the direct contribution of heredity to current income is minute.
Its indirect effect is also not very large" (p. S99). A study by Butler
(1976), using army data, found that even when AFQT scores, level of
education, and type of job were controlled, whites consistently rose
faster in military rank than did blacks. More germane to this analysis was his finding that AFQT scores were negatively related to the
rate of promotion in many categories.

As mentioned, among the attempts to estimate the importance
of IQ-score differentials in the relationship between schooling and occupational success, little relationship between score differentials and
success has been found. One longitudinal study (Rogers 1969, p. 122),
using a benefit-cost analysis, found that no net differences in economic
return per year of education could be shown for any level of IQ. In
fact, depending on the discount rate applied, graduate education was
shown not to be cost effective for the individual unless it was sub-
sidized about 50 percent. A reanalysis of Rogers' data (Hause 1972)
showed that a difference in gross income was slightly dependent on a
positive IQ/years-of-education interaction. With a college degree,
people with IQs of 121 could expect to earn about 12.7 percent more
than could individuals with the same education and IQs of 86. Note
that this moderate difference in income was associated with IQ differences amounting to 2.3 standard deviations. Further, this positive
interaction worked only at high levels of education. For low levels,
ability differentials had a negligible impact. Over the full range of
IQ levels and educational levels sampled, the impacts of the two were
modest.

What, then, is the source of Duncan's findings, mentioned
above? According to the writers who most strongly attack the meritocratic position (Bowles and Gintis 1974, 1976), the answer lies in
a compendium of characteristics—specifically, a pattern of noncognitive personality variables (as previously mentioned): sex, age, race,
and educational credentials (Bowles and Gintis 1974, p. 11). Since
these variables (with the exception of sex) are differentially distributed
by social class, the relationships among intelligence-test scores,
education, and occupational achievement are considered to be primarily results of the selection and legitimation functions of education.
That is, education is designed to stratify, and those who share certain
favored characteristics will be advanced. This Marxist conclusion,
as well as Bowles's and Gintis's specific mathematical-modeling procedures, have been controversial; but even critics (for example,
Heyns 1978) have not disagreed with the general empirical points.
Whether one accepts the conclusions of those who state that some
variance in achievement may be accounted for in terms of strictly
meritocratic criteria (for example, Blau and Duncan 1967) or agrees

with this more radical argument, the fact remains that ability, as portrayed by common meritocratic criteria, does not have overwhelming importance in the attainment of occupational achievement. The general conclusion of Jencks, that occupational achievement is largely independent of these other criteria, still holds.

INTELLIGENCE AND EDUCATION

Intelligence scales were first developed in a context of educational reform, and the use of tests has been linked to educational practices ever since. Thus, it should not be surprising if the relationship between test scores and educational achievement is greater than that between the scores and noneducational achievement. Yet if the argument developed here has validity, then even that relationship should not be substantial.

A challenge to the importance of test scores for educational purposes is not attempted lightly. It is probably true that the single most-often-employed validation of such scores has been the correlation, of about 0.50, between IQ scores and school grades (somewhat higher for years of schooling), which has held now for several decades. One writer even went so far as to count 4,096 validity coefficients in order to prove the case of the importance of IQ, and almost all of the coefficients dealt with grades (for a critique, see McClelland 1974). Yet the relationship is surely less than it appears, if only because it is purely correlational, and other effects are seldom controlled. For example, in the Labov studies previously mentioned, it was implied that a positive correlation between IQ scores and school marks would be caused by a matrix of social relationships having to do with the tradition of hostility marking ethnic relations. A similar set of relationships was shown to operate in the study of black kindergarteners by Rist; and both the Labov and Rist studies support the conclusion by Jencks (1972, p. 146), that the factors affecting educational attainment (here considered to be years of schooling, rather than grades) were "overwhelmingly social, not biological."*

---

*It should be mentioned that the majority of studies dealing with the relationship between meritocratic indicators do not deal with GPA, but with years of schooling obtained. This is unfortunate, because on its face it seems that the relationship between intellectual characteristics and number of years of schooling should be more tenuous than the relationship between those characteristics and actual performance in school tasks—except as the indicators are used for promotion and selection. Yet this is the type of evidence available.

Actually, this conclusion should not be very surprising, for even the common 0.5 correlation accounts for merely 25 percent of the variance in school grades, and controlling for other variables in correlation and regression studies should quite naturally lessen the explained variance. As far as this author knows, the lowest estimated direct effect of intelligence-test scores on educational attainment is the slightly under 3 percent of variance found by Wilson and Portes (1975, p. 355). These authors consider this a "major" predictor of educational attainment (years of schooling), and interpret it in terms of "active institutional recruitment and selection" (Wilson and Portes 1975, p. 360). The argument presented here holds that a direct effect of such magnitude, while it is important for the interpretation of path-analysis models, for the most part has almost insignificant real social meaning. But be that as it may, the results definitely demonstrate that the supposed relationship is much smaller than often thought, and a host of educational-attainment studies in the sociological literature bear out the general conclusion. Moreover, the idea that institutions seek out and recruit people on the basis of meritocratic criteria presents quite a different underlying reason for the existing relationships than is usually proffered.

With respect to this point, it should be pointed out that even prior to 1920, Terman (1916, pp. 16-17) held that promotions should be based chiefly on IQ-test scores, and that "information standards" would have to give way to test-score standards. As will be shown in Part II of this study, Terman was the dominant force in the first half century of testing in the United States, and his prescriptions have become sources of traditional wisdom. Thus, standardized test scores (especially IQ-test scores) are part of the congeries of elements that teachers and administrators depend upon in the assignment of students to college and noncollege tracks (Cicourel and Kitsuse 1963, pp. 16-17).

Placement in a given track has effects on a student's eventual GPA and, not surprisingly, on the total number of years of schooling he or she will receive. One study (Jencks 1972, p. 145) has estimated that between a sixth and a third of the relationship between test scores and years of schooling may be accounted for on the basis of curriculum placement alone. The advantage of being in a high, as opposed to a low, track is the same for students with low test scores as it is for those with high scores (Jencks 1972, pp. 157-78). *

---

*As a personal example, in the author's high school it was common for students in enriched (that is, high-track) courses to gain a double-grade advantage over other students. First, they found it easier to obtain good grades in such classes, perhaps because teachers

When we turn to studies of students who have achieved excellence in some academically related area that is not directly related to grades, considerable independence of test scores from this form of academic achievement appears. For example, in assessing the novelty and effectiveness of projects submitted to an annual science talent search, it was found that no commonly employed criterion discriminated the creative from the less creative (Parloff et al. 1968). These criteria were age, Science Aptitude Test scores, Scholastic Aptitude Test (SAT) verbal scores, high-school GPAs, socioeconomic status, and birth order. Yet the sample covered was not totally homogeneous, for geographic, urban-rural, and ethnic differences were found, as were a series of personality differences. Among the personality factors showing differences were self-control, the making of a good impression, well-being, achievement via conformance, tolerance, socialization, and, to a lesser extent, responsibility and intellectual efficiency. The last factor is interesting, in that it is considered a nonintellectual-intelligence test. It is made up of a number of questions that tap aspects of neuroticism, none of which are intellectual (Gough 1953). Yet it predicts school grades for girls slightly better than do standard IQ tests (0.59 versus 0.56), though it is substantially less able to predict grades for boys (0.31 versus 0.51).

The weakness of standard tests for predicting creative production within an academic setting is further documented by Mednick (1963), who took measures of graduate psychology students' GPAs, and added scores from the commonly used Miller Analogies Test (MAT), the Remote-Associates Test (RAT)— designed to measure creativity—and a creativity-rating scale (CRS). The latter scale was a Thurstone-type device designed to measure the creativity of student-research projects. Results are found in Table 5. Briefly, neither students' GPAs nor their MAT scores were positively related to their degree of creativity. What is more, the MAT and the GPA did not

----

felt that they were superior and should not be given poor grades. Be that as it may, a great deal of cutting up occurred in these classes, and those students took their studies no more seriously than did others; yet grades were higher. Second, the school administration added bonus points to a student's grades in enriched courses, because of the supposed difficulty of making good grades when one competed against other superior students. Thus, a grade of B was given the number of points that an A in a standard course would bring. A grade of A was similarly increased. Conversely, in low-track classes grades were decreased.

TABLE 5

Relationships among School Grades, the Miller Analogies Test, a
Measure of Creativity, and Creativity of Student-Research Projects

Measure	RAT	GPA	MAT
CRS	0.55^a (N = 43)	0.06 (N = 16)	-0.08 (N = 24)
RAT		-0.11 (N = 26)	0.41^b (N = 25)
GPA			-0.03 (N = 25)

CRS = creativity-rating scale
RAT = Remote-Associates Test
GPA = grade point average
MAT = Miller Analogies Test

$^a p < 0.005$
$^b p < 0.025$

Source: Martha Mednick, "Research Creativity in Psychology
Graduate Students," Journal of Consulting Psychology 27 (1963):
265-66. Copyright 1963 by the American Psychological Association.
Reprinted by permission.

correlate. However, scores on the RAT correlated moderately with
the creativity criterion. *

There seems to be little relationship between standardized test
scores and creative production, though often a relationship between
test scores and GPA appears (it did not do so in the above study). The
role of test scores in creative production will be further investigated
later, while the relationship between test scores and progress in
graduate school will be discussed here.

---

*This is not to imply that creativity tests are the keys to future
accomplishment. Generally, their relationship to achievement is
lower even than is that of the IQ tests, and it appears that creativity
may be itself a complex of different attributes. For a critical review
of the work on creativity scales, see Blum (1978, pp. 132-44).

Commonly, a small positive correlation has been found between relevant scores and grades in graduate school. For example, Lannholm (1968) found correlations of 0.24 and 0.32 between quantitative- and verbal-test scores on the Graduate Record Examination (GRE) and student GPAs, and in some cases higher correlations were found. However, Lannholm, Marco, and Schrader (1968) found that a composite index made up of GRE quantitative and verbal scores, and undergraduate GPA correlated with success-failure in graduate school in a range from -0.39 to 0.55, depending on the department surveyed. The median finding was 0.22. Using GRE scores alone, verbal-score correlations with the criterion ranged from -0.27 to 0.35, and quantitative-score correlations ranged from -0.24 to 0.45.

Using the MAT, Gough (1965) found the correlation with faculty ratings of students to be 0.21, but the correlation with actual survival in the program was only 0.02. The lesser relationship with actual progress in an institution has also been documented for undergraduate students. In comparisons of regular students with those who had been admitted under a special admissions system, Astin and Rossman (1973) found that regular students did get better grades than did the special admittees, but that progress through the grades was similar for the two groups. Slightly over 60 percent of regular students had completed 24 hours of work after the first year, while 50 percent of special admittees had done so. (This was despite the fact that these people qualified for university admission on none of the standard criteria employed.)

One may question why students with high test scores tend to get better grades than students with low scores. If the reason were that these students are superior, and therefore learn more, then one would expect them to have learned more by the end of their educational careers. Yet this is not the case. Despite the fact that they tend to go to better colleges and universities, smart students appear not to learn much more than do regular students (Astin 1968). In fact, institutional excellence has as little effect on learning at the college and university level as it does at the public-school level.

This author rejects the argument that the average difference found in grades received between high- and low-scoring students is tied, in any more than a tenuous manner, to a general difference in interests and abilities. There are two reasons for this. The first is the general independence of creative production from either test scores or school grades. The second is the (perhaps counterintuitive) fact that those who score very high and who enter challenging and creative fields tend to have a narrower breadth of interests than do other students (Campbell 1971, pp. 642-46). It has been noted by Campbell that such interests tend to center on reading, and that "creative achievement requires a concentrated focus of interests, almost a fanatical disregard for the rest of the world. " If this is true, it indicates that specialized competencies require, in principle, certain incompetencies, and that those who do well in one area (for example, making good grades), will do only so-so, or even poorly, in other areas. This position corresponds to the model of task achievement presented in the previous chapter.

Given this position, a possible explanation of the test/classroom-grade correlation is that classroom situations are much like test situations. The same general list of characteristics, or behavioral repertoire, is required for excellence in these two areas. Once the situation is changed, the correlation magnitude drops. Thus survival in graduate or undergraduate programs is clearly not related to test scores, to grades, or to creative production outside the classroom. Survival likely requires a set of attributes substantially different from those required merely to make a good grade in a given class. Neither of these need have much to do with learning or cognitive complexity, or any such construct. In fact, one can make a case for students employing different repertoires of behavior, depending on whether they want to obtain an A in a course, or whether they are merely interested in getting through it. Similarly, instructors can be depicted as giving grades according to different criteria, depending upon the situation. There is at least anecdotal evidence for each of these phenomena (for example, Axelrod 1968).

Along this line, one finds low correlations between test scores and achievement in any but classroom-type situations. For example, Gough, Hall, and Harris (1963) found that the correlation between scores on the Medical College Admissions Test (MCAT) and first-year medical-school grades was 0.18. The correlation with fourth-year grades, however, was only 0.07. The reason seems to be that the fourth year in medical school (and to a lesser extent, the third year) is devoted to clinical rather than classroom learning.

This finding has been corroborated by others. Richards, Taylor, and Price (1962) found that none of the MCAT scores, or the undergraduate GPA, predicted either performance in medical internship or the quality of the intern's hospital. This is presented in Table 6.

Of the 12 MCAT subtest correlations with the three criteria of intern performance (rating of performance, quality of hospital, and a composite indicator), only one, a -0.20 correlation with the knowledge-of-science subtest, was significant. The only positive relationship was a 0.01 correlation between the quantitative test and the quality of the intern's hospital. To a small extent, first- and second-year medical-school grades predicted performance, but the only moderate predictor was performance in the clinical year of training.

This line of evidence suggests that even if standardized test scores can tell us something of the likelihood of a person's making a

TABLE 6

The Relationships between Performance as an Intern and a Variety of Predictors

Criterion	Predictor							
	MCAT–V	MCAT–Q	MCAT–So	MCAT–Sc	U–GPA	MED–1	MED–2	MED–3
Rating of performance	−0.09	−0.07	−0.06	−0.20[a]	0.06	0.15	0.16	0.33[b]
Quality of hospital	−0.07	0.01	0.00	0.00	0.01	0.17[a]	0.21[a]	0.36[b]
Composite	−0.11	−0.04	−0.04	−0.13	−0.03	0.21[a]	0.24[b]	0.45[b]

MCAT = Medical College Admissions Test
V = verbal subtest
Q = quantitative subtest
So = knowledge-of-society subtest
Sc = knowledge-of-science subtest
U–GPA = undergraduate grade point average
MED–1 = first-year medical-school grades
MED–2 = second-year medical-school grades
MED–3 = third-year (clinical) medical-school grades

[a]$p < 0.05.$
[b]$p < 0.01.$

Source: James M. Richards, Calvin W. Taylor, and Phillip B. Price, "The Prediction of Medical Intern Performance," Journal of Applied Psychology 46 (1962): 142–46. Copyright 1962 by the American Psychological Association. Reprinted by permission.

good grade in a course, they can tell us little else about the person. And, as put by Ronald Flaugher (1974) of ETS, no one will seriously defend freshman GPA as "an important gauge of anything very important in life's list of desired values" (p. 15).

INTELLIGENCE AND THE PROFESSIONS

If the simple meritocratic position is to be fruitful anywhere, it should be so in the world of science and the professions. Indeed, the early ideas regarding the nature and nurture of intelligence were developed in a context in which only the specific accomplishments of those in elite occupations were seen as representative of intelligence (for example, Galton 1869). Even if those who are high in this intelligence are not generally more competent than others, it could easily be the case that they are more competent at science. All that is required, in order to expect to find a strong relationship between intelligence tests (or other indicators of ability) and accomplishment in the intellectual professions, is the belief that the tests tap attributes that are specific to success in these areas. In this fashion, the argument for success in this limited set of spheres would be independent of general arguments concerning differential competence.

However, even this limited argument faces problems, in that the relationship between indicators of ability and professional success is not strong. The weakness is not newly discovered, but has been known for over a century. As early as 1874, Francis Galton, in his classic study of English men of science, expressed surprise "at the mediocre degrees which the leading scientific men who were at the universities have usually taken" (Galton 1871, p. 257). This finding was rediscovered by Hudson (1960).

A common source of justification for the idea that scientists have very specialized attributes has come from the fact that, in general, such people do very well on standard intelligence tests. Recall the studies by Roe (1953a, 1953b) mentioned earlier. Similarly, Berelson and Steiner (1964, pp. 223-24) found the IQ scores of lawyers, engineers, and chemists to range from roughly 100 up to the mid-150s. Yet the question remains as to how much of the restriction in scores is a function of the selection and accreditation practices of institutions. For example, in the Berelson and Steiner study, the fact that the bottom end of the scale for the professionals studied fell almost exactly at the mid-range mark, for the country as a whole, suggests that persons who seem average might accasionally be admitted to professional training, while those who are below average would be screened out automatically. Otherwise, it seems unlikely that the population average would be the ultimate screening level. The reason for this is that there can be no a priori reason for supposing that any given level of score will be that below which an acceptable level of accomplishment is not possible. Such a fact would have to be empirically determined; it could be 140, or 115, or 75, for example. But there is a strong tendency in our society to believe that being below average is unacceptable. With this line of thought, 100 could well be a cutoff point, whether it was empirically justified or not. *

Some evidence for this comes from the Berelson and Steiner study. In areas of study in which IQ scores were not used as primary screening devices—for example, art and music—the scores of professionals ranged as low as 89 and 56, respectively. This line of evidence is merely suggestive. More important is the evidence that low scorers are screened out of academic competition at a very early period (for example, Taylor and Holland 1962).

It has been extensively documented that standard ability tests and GPAs are heavily weighted in the admissions process for both undergraduate and graduate programs. For example, Wing and Wallach (1971, p. 53) found that the selection of over 75 percent of those who would be admitted to high-selectivity colleges could be predicted on the basis of either the Scholastic Aptitude Verbal Test (SAT-V), the Scholastic Aptitude Mathematics Test (SAT-M), or high-school rank. When the three were combined, over 84 percent of eventual selections could be predicted. This occurred despite statements by various college admissions programs that they searched for a wide range of competencies in coming to selection decisions, and despite the fact that it had previously been demonstrated that academic and life accomplishment were essentially independent of each other (Wallach and Wing 1969). Further, this independence was known by the examiner's offices of at least some universities as far back as the early 1960s (Bloom 1963b).

When Taylor and Holland (1962, p. 93) stated that admissions to the world of science are based on screening "through a long, formal, academic program" in which only a handful of characteristics are employed in making decisions, they indicated that it is not only admissions to graduate programs that are based on scores. Rather, admissions to both undergraduate and graduate programs are so based, as is the excellence of the school one attends (Astin 1968). Further, the regard in which students are held by faculty is partially dependent on their relative scores (Gough 1965), and so are their chances of

---

*This is demonstrated by the perhaps apocryphal story of the member of Parliament who complained that studies had shown half the British population to be below average and who questioned what was going to be done about it.

financial aid and academic recognition. At the university where this author received his doctorate, by far the single most important determinant of whether a student will be granted a universitywide fellowship is his or her GRE score. *

Given the above, the fact that scientists and other professionals tend to have high test scores is not evidence that they are more able at performing the sets of activities required by their professions. What is needed is evidence that high-scoring professionals will outstrip low-scoring professionals. The evidence now available suggests that they do not do so.

There is a long history of research that attempts to provide a prediction of professional accomplishment, and such attempts have ended largely in failure. A previously mentioned example, from Harmon (1963), consisted of an attempt to develop a criterion of scientific competence. When such a criterion was constructed (consisting of the judgments of experts, the number of publications of writers, income from technical and scientific work, the number of levels of people supervised, the type of job performed, the type of employer, and the number of years since the obtaining of the Ph. D. , if any), it was found that correlations with standard ability indicators were not strikingly different from zero. The findings regarding the obtaining of Ph. D. 's are presented in Table 7. In Harmon's study, over 38 percent of the correlations were negative. Over 58 percent fell in the range of plus or minus 0.10. Of those that actually had a magnitude of plus or minus 0.20 or greater, two were positive and two were negative, though two other positive correlations came close to this cutoff point.

As mentioned earlier, Harmon attributed the lack of predictive ability to the criterion itself, a position for which he was criticized by Wallach (1971; see also, Wing and Wallach 1971). Wallach's (1971) position was that "excellence in real-world pursuits has a different structure to it and concerns a much more diversified range of products and performances" (p. 334) than does academic excellence. Further, Wallach (1971, p. 335) contended that those who did well on standard tests, and in education, were most apt to memorize "formulas to be regurgitated," activities that are basically independent of the use of strategies of problem solving (for example, Evans 1969). Some confirmation of this comes from a study by Guilford (1963), in which active scientists were asked to rank 28 characteristics of individuals that they thought were important in scientific research. Of the top 20 characteristics cited, 19—while intellectual—were not clearly related to intelligence.

---

*Louis Zurcher, Jr. 1978: personal communication.

TABLE 7

Correlations between a Criterion of Scientific Competence and
Standard Ability Indicators

Predictor	Physical Scientists, Year When Ph. D. Was Obtained			Biological Scientists, Year When Ph. D. Was Obtained		
	Early	Middle	Late	Early	Middle	Late
Verbal test	0.09	0.04	-0.01	0.06	0.08	0.35
Quantitative test	0.04	-0.03	-0.02	-0.03	0.19	0.19
Advanced achievement test	-0.05	0.13	-0.32	0.06	-0.04	0.30
Undergraduate GPA	-0.03	0.12	-0.20	0.14	0.10	0.13
N =	216	91	39	65	54	38

Source: Lindsay R. Harmon, "The Development of a Criterion of Scientific Competence," in Scientific Creativity: Its Recognition and Development, ed. Calvin W. Taylor and Frank Barron (New York: John Wiley and Sons, 1963), pp. 44-52. Originally presented at the second University of Utah Conference on "The Identification of Creative Scientific Talent," August 1957. Reprinted by permission of John Wiley and Sons and the University of Utah Press.

This is a reason often given for the low correlations between grades or standard tests and future production. Bloom (1963b) has estimated that only about 10 percent of all Ph. D.'s actually produce much at all, if we take the number of publications as the criterion of accomplishment (see also, Price 1963). In fact, about two-thirds of all articles are produced by that talented tenth. Despite the relative rareness of this achievement, it is predictable on the basis of earlier achievement, though not on the basis of standard criteria (for example, from a slightly different context, Richards, Holland, and Lutz 1967).

Considering such accomplishments as professional publishing, Kelley and Goldberg (1959) found a correlation of 0.16 between number of publications and the MAT. However, Marston (1971), using a sample of 111 psychology Ph. D.'s from the University of Southern California, obtained a correlation of -0.05 between GRE and the number of publications for clinical psychologists and a nonsignificant 0.18 correlation for nonclinical psychologists. Since the distribution of numbers of publications was so skewed, Marston computed a point-biserial correlation (with scores dichotomized as no versus some publications), and found relationships of 0.02 and 0.24 for clinical and nonclinical psychologists, respectively. Neither of these was significant.

Notably, the GRE scores of these scientists were not greatly restricted. Instead, they ranged from 740 to 1490, and were generally symmetrically distributed. The average GRE score of nonclinical psychologists with publications was 1157, while for those with no publications at all, it was 1094 (not significant). For clinical psychologists, the average respective scores were almost identical, and in the direction opposite to that expected (1071 versus 1073).

Using GPA to predict performance as measured by a creativity criterion produced by factor analysis, Taylor, Smith, and Ghiselin (1963) found that the mean GPA of the top third of the scientists was 2.73 (out of 4.0), while the mean GPA of the bottom sixth of the scientists was 2.69. For the full sample, the triserial correlation was a nonsignificant 0.06.

In other studies using GPA as a predictor, MacKinnon (1968) found a -0.19 correlation between the predictor and rated creativity of research scientists, while Price et al. (1964) found no relationship between grades and the performance of physicians.

Using scores on the Terman Concept Mastery Test, various researchers have found low-to-nonexistent correlations with various forms of competence. Gough (1961) found a correlation of -0.07 with a measure of on-the-job creativity. In the same study, the Minnesota Engineering Analogies Test and the General Information Survey correlated 0.13 and 0.07, respectively, with the criterion. None of the correlations was significant. MacKinnon (1962) found a correlation of -0.08 between the Terman test and rated creativity among architects. This occurred despite the fact that no restriction of range occurred. Rather, scores on the test ranged from 39 to 179. Meanwhile, masculinity, as measured on the Strong Vocational Interest Blank, correlated -0.49 with the criterion. This supports the common finding that personality factors seem to have more to do with achievement than do ability factors. Finally, Taylor (1963) found no significant correlations between the Terman test and creativity or productivity, as indicated either by a rating of the immediate supervisor or by the average ratings of two supervisors. This lack of a significant correlation held whether the originality of work, quality of work, quantity of work, degree of initiative, attitude toward work, or skill with people was being measured. Meanwhile, a test of productive thinking, and upper-division GPA, both gave small positive relationships with creativity.

This same general finding has emerged when the Wechsler intelligence tests are employed. For example, Helson and Crutchfield

(1970) found no significant differences between creative mathematicians and average Ph. D. 's on the Wechsler Adult Intelligence Scale (WAIS), in either the verbal test, the performance test, or the total score, though a significant difference did appear for the comprehension test. Personality factors did differentiate the two groups. Also, Meer and Stein (1955), using the Wechsler-Bellevue tests, found no significant correlations between intelligence and 24 different categories of creativity, for chemists with Ph. D. 's. Using 11 Wechsler-Bellevue subtests and ratings of professional creativity, correlations for Ph. D. 's ranged from -0.52 to 0.70, and only 2 of 33 correlations were significant. For non-Ph. D. 's, correlations ranged from -0.22 to 0.61, and 5 of 33 were significant. Further, when the non-Ph. D. 's were given a chance to perform, they proved as productive as those with doctorates.

SUMMARY

The general conclusions from the foregoing lines of evidence are clear. In none of the several areas discussed were standard measures of ability strongly predictive of achievement. Where a moderate positive correlation was discovered (for example, between IQ scores and GPA), several variables besides test scores could reasonably account for large portions of the observed correlations, either in conjunction with, or independent of, an intelligence dimension. In fact, the seldom-investigated phenomenon of the self-fulfilling prophesy may account for the preponderance of the relationships, though there is as yet little evidence on this point.

It is not necessary to posit that there is nothing about intelligence-test taking that could be used to generalize about future achievement. Rather, the argument made here is only that the relationship between the two is very small. Also, it is not necessary to posit that the very creative are not different from other people. In fact, they tend to differ in a number of ways, most commonly in personality traits.

This fact supports the model of achievement presented in the previous chapter. If a number of largely independent attributes, rather than a single scalar attribute, are implicated in various forms of achievement, then comparisons of individuals or groups, on the basis of differences in any one attribute or a handful of attributes, will be socially trivial. If ability is important, then it is a multiform entity; if it is unitary, then it is relatively unimportant. An alternative hypothesis could be that intelligence is both unitary and important, but that tests do not accurately measure it. However, even here, judgments of neither individual nor group ability are warranted on the basis of test-score differences. This conclusion cannot be stated too forcefully: <u>There is no empirical justification for making broad predictions of an individual's or a group's place in a social hierarchy on the basis of common meritocratic criteria, including test scores.</u> This conclusion holds also when policy statements are being considered: <u>There is no empirical justification for calling for differential treatment of individuals or groups on the basis of standard meritocratic criteria, including test scores.</u> This holds whether or not the standard criteria measure anything about the individual or group that has a substantial genetic component. This last point will be considered in the next chapter.

5

THE NATURE AND NURTURE
OF INTELLIGENCE

To some extent, the question of the genetic inheritance of intelligence should now be considered superfluous. The lines of evidence presented in the previous three chapters strongly suggest that even were IQ 80 percent inherited, it would not have a strong bearing on the outcomes of social competition within generations. It might still be argued that intelligence would have a screening effect over a number of years, but even here the effect would be quite gradual. This is because the transmission of a trait occurs not steadily, but over generations (roughly 20-25 years). Recall that we are only 100 generations removed from the Roman republic (Feldman and Lewontin 1975, p. 1165), and that the attributes required for success have probably changed a great deal in that time.

Still, the question of the inheritance of traits has been central to the IQ controversy. Major hereditarian writers (for example, Jensen 1969a, 1969b; Shuey 1966), with few exceptions, have limited their arguments to discussions of the supposedly large genetic component of intelligence and/or to discussions of the relative immunity of IQ scores from environmental manipulation. Environmentalists, likewise, have generally taken the nature and nurture of IQ scores to be the important question in the controversy.

If for no other reason that this subjective centrality of the question, genetic inheritance requires some discussion. However, there are two subsidiary reasons for such a discussion. The first of these has to do with the abovementioned intergenerational transmission of attributes. According to Herrnstein (1971, 1973), if IQ is even moderately related to success, and if it is substantially genetically inherited, then eventually societies would naturally stratify on the basis of the set of abilities it measures, should the meritocratically ideal society ever develop. According to this argument, social classes (though not races), in principle, must eventually become ever more stratified on the basis of these abilities. *

The second reason for a discussion of the inheritance of intelligence has to do with the ever-present interest in the sources of test-score differences between blacks and whites. Here, we may ask if blacks are naturally inferior in the limited attributes tapped by tests. Further, we may ask if natural inferiority indicates immutability.

The question of genetic inheritance of intelligence is multifaceted, and requires a discussion of two complex topics. The first of these topics is that of the heritability of intelligence, where the term heritability refers to the technical apportionment of the sources of variance for a trait. Four interrelated questions bear strongly on heritability as a topic. First, what is the meaning of heritability? Second, what is the relationship between heritability and the environmental control of traits? Third, what are some problems with the estimation of heritability for human populations? Finally, what is the magnitude of the heritability of intelligence?

The second major topic has to do with changes in measured intelligence over time. This is closely related to the question of the relationship between heritability and environmental control of traits, but is empirical rather than theoretical. Put differently, whatever the genetic component of intelligence, can it be pragmatically raised (or lowered)? What determines changes in intelligence? And are cultural elements successful in affecting intelligence?

HERITABILITY

While the central question of the IQ controversy has been the inheritance of traits, the central part of the debate over inheritance has been the question of the magnitude of heritability of human intelligence. This is unfortunate, for several problems with heritability

---

*Concerning Herrnstein's argument, if H^2 is 0.80, and if the relationship between IQ and success is as low as we have previously seen it to be, then even accepting a simple linear view of inheritance will lead to the inescapable conclusion that "genotypic IQ" is negligibly related to the intergenerational reproduction of economic inequality (see Bowles and Nelson 1974). If we accept the viability of linear models, the lower the H^2, the less are genetic factors implicated in ultimate social outcomes, even over a number of generations. Of course, the evidence given above suggests that linearity does not hold. In any event, the Herrnstein argument is dealt a serious blow.

estimation make it a very weak sort of evidence upon which to make any inferences at all about the inheritance of traits. So weak a line of evidence is magnitude of heritability that two critics of the Jensen position in the controversy call it "nearly the equivalent of no information at all for any serious problem of human genetics" (Feldman and Lewontin 1975, p. 1168). There are four interrelated sets of reasons for this weakness, corresponding to the four questions mentioned previously. To the extent possible, they will be dealt with separately.

The Meaning of Heritability

Heritability takes two forms. The most important form—the one found in animal husbandry—is termed narrow heritability (h^2). In the analysis of variance of traits, this is the proportion of the variance of a trait that is accountable in terms of additive genetic differences among individuals in the population measured. That is, it is the source of the fact that relatives tend to resemble one another. In an experimentally controlled environment, where none but small random differences in environment will affect individuals, h^2 gives an estimate of the amenability of the trait in question to selective breeding, for the specific environment in the study. Parameters used in determining h^2 are the correlations among relatives for the given phenotype (trait), the correlations predicted by Mendelian theory, and the correlations between mates (Feldman and Lewontin 1975, p. 1164).

It should be understood that narrow heritability does not state how much of a trait is genetically and environmentally determined. It merely gives an index of the relative impact of minor genetic and environmental perturbations on the average representation of a phenotype in the population, given a standard environment. Indeed, mathematically, the set of procedures employed is termed local perturbation analysis (Feldman and Lewontin 1975, p. 1163). Thus, narrow heritability is a manner of estimating the effects of gene substitutions over a very narrow range of analysis, where genes are assumed to have incremental effects on the phenotype in question (McGuire and Hirsch 1977, p. 17).

The second form of heritability is termed broad heritability (H^2). With H^2, it is recognized that gene effects are not always additive. In fact, various types of gene action lead to the fact that relatives do not always resemble one another. For this reason, agricultural experimenters do not employ heritability in the broad sense. To arrive at a coefficient of broad heritability, the additive genetic variance is added to the variance attributed to gene dominance, to epistatic interaction (interaction between alleles at different loci), to genotype-environment interaction, and (often) to genotype-environment covariance. The effect of this is to boost the coefficient of heritability considerably, except in the limiting instance where all variance is additive.

The reason that heritability in the broad sense is not used by agriculturalists is that, in seemingly paradoxical fashion, the inclusion of other sources of genetic variance lessens the usefulness of the heritability coefficient. The addition of the extra information makes the coefficient nonpredictive, since the other sources of variance do not operate in anything approaching an incremental fashion.

It might be thought that broad heritability, since it includes all sources of genetically related variance, might stand as an inverse index of the amenability of a trait to environmental manipulation. That is, it might indicate the degree of freedom from environmental control. Jensen (1969a, p. 59), for example, has indicated this. This is apparently related to the fact that heritability coefficients are commonly considered, at least by psychologists, to be nature-nurture ratios, or indexes to the causes of variation of traits. However, this view is mistaken. A high heritability does not indicate that environmental manipulation of a trait is illusory. In fact, as shown by Lewontin (1970a), a heritability of 100 percent can be associated with strong environmental control over a trait. Conversely, a low heritability does not indicate that a trait does not have an important genetic component.

Consider the problem of skin color. It is well known that some people tend to be lighter-skinned than others. This would seem to be a hereditary trait. Yet if half of a genetically homogeneous population were to winter in Miami, while the other half wintered in Fairbanks, the skin-color differences between the two groups would be entirely environmentally caused. Likewise with corn; special hybrid corns, developed in the U.S. Midwest, contribute a great harvest. Yet these same strains, when planted in other countries, do not do well. In different situations, often the local stocks of a given product prove much superior to the hybrid strains (Feldman and Lewontin 1975; Garcia 1977, pp. 9-10). Moreover, heritability coefficients themselves change widely with changed environments.

This being the case, broad heritability has no practical usefulness. It can give one no information on the applicability of either eugenic or euphenic measures. Thus, heritability is not used in the determination or treatment of genetically related diseases, for the cure is always environmental manipulation. Narrow heritability at least is useful in the construction of breeding programs, where one can control environments.

It may be asked why psychologists continue to employ broad heritability in discussions of intelligence differences among humans.

An answer often given is that H^2 gives an estimate of "the extent to which differences [in a trait] in some population are associated with genetic differences among individuals in that population" (Loehlin, Lindzey, and Spuhler 1975, p. 81). It will be noted that this answer comes perilously close to the nature-nurture ratio approach to characteristics. An investigation of why such an approach is popular with psychologists will appear in Chapter 9. Here it is important to recognize that the answer given above has no practical genetic usefulness. If one is interested in the nature and nurture of intelligence for any pragmatic reason—and the policy implications of the IQ controversy are stressed by virtually every commentator on the subject—then broad heritability cannot help one. The coefficient in question can tell us neither the causes of individual or group differences in a trait, nor the ways in which those differences can be ameliorated.

Heritability and the Environment

The independence of heritability from the causes (or control) of differences in a trait deserves a more thorough discussion. The general reason for this independence has to do with the interactional nature of the genotype-environment connection (Loevinger 1943; Anastasi 1958).

For any given genotype, phenotypic development is a complex function of a number of elements. For the genotype, the sources of variation include dominance, epistatic interaction, recombination (or crossing over), and mutation. The genetic material is massively complex, and its reactions to the innumerable environmental elements with which it comes into contact are likewise unnumbered (Dobzhansky 1962, p. 126). For the individual genotype, development is specific to the environmental variables that it contacts, the time periods in which they are contacted, and the order in which they are contacted. The result is a unique norm of individual reaction that cannot be predicted in advance.

The term norm of reaction indicates that phenotypic development is contingent on both the specific genotype and the specific environmental milieu contacted. It was the reality of norms of reaction that led to the varieties of behavior emitted by the so-called maze-bright and maze-dull rats, discussed in Chapter 3. As put by Lewontin (1976a, p. 184), the relations between phenotype and genotype, and between phenotype and environment, can be characterized as "many-many" relations; that is, "no single genotype corresponds to a single phenotype, or vice versa."

Lewontin provides the following hypothetical norms of reactions shown in Figure 1; in each norm, two phenotypes are plotted as func-

FIGURE 1

Hypothetical Norms of Reaction for Genotype (G_1, G_2) and
Environments (E)

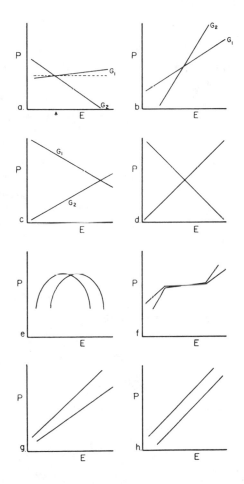

tions of·an environment (E) and of two genotypes (G_1, G_2). What the eight norms in Figure 1 demonstrate is a subset of the wide array of norms of reaction that one will encounter in experimental research. Some are linear, and some are curvilinear. In the first six norms shown, a determination of which genotype is superior in whatever trait is being measured will depend on where in the environmental continuum measurements are made. For several of the norms, no environmental effect will be noticeable, in the aggregate, if the populations are balanced about the line intersects. Note that in several instances the slope of the reaction line is not generally positive. In fact, the curved lines in norm e of the figure are the general type most commonly found.

It is no accident that Jensen (1969a, p. 64) has employed a model of norms of reaction similar to norms g and h in the figure, for it is only when such lines emerge that one can make clear statements about superiority and inferiority. It is also no accident that his environmental index has been a general favorableness of environment. However, what is favorable for one genotype may not be favorable for another, and vice versa. Further, environment is not a general phenomenon, but consists of a massive set of specific elements, many of which will affect the ultimate development of the phenotype. Consider the following empirical work with fruitflies.

FIGURE 2

Norms of Reaction to Temperature Variations Affecting the Viability of Fourth-Chromosome Homozygotes of <u>Drosophila Pseudoobscura</u>

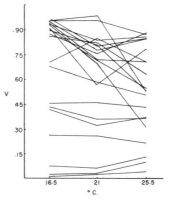

Source: Richard Lewontin, "The Analysis of Variance and the Analysis of Causes," <u>American Journal of Human Genetics</u> 26 (1974): 400-11. Copyright © 1974 by the University of Chicago Press. Reprinted by permission.

Figure 2 shows the relative viability for the larvae of 21 different lines of fruitflies. Note how widely survival rates vary as temperature (the only environmental variable) is manipulated. While there appears to be some general trend for viability to decrease with increasing temperature, there are exceptions to this trend. Further, the viability of the different strains, relative to one another, changes with changes in temperature. It should be recalled that numerous other environmental variables will also affect viability. No matter what the heritability of larval viability, one cannot make meaningful statements about the relative inherited viability of the different strains, unless the environmental parameters of those comparisons are made explicit, except in the limiting cases where the same relative differences occur across all experimental conditions.

This fact is not newly discovered. In fact, as early as 1933, Lancelot Hogben had chided the statistical biologist R. A. Fisher on just such grounds. In response to Fisher's belief that correlations among relatives could provide simple nature-nurture "balance sheets," Hogben (1939) responded that "no statement about a genetic difference is clear, <u>unless it includes or implies a specification of the environment in which it manifests itself in a particular manner</u>" (p. 14). Hogben's examples made it clear that by "specification of the environment," he meant strict experimental control of variables. This will be discussed more thoroughly below.

Heritability and Human Populations

From the above, it is seen that a heritability coefficient is a very limited datum. All admit that narrow heritability has usefulness in situations where both genotype and environment can be strictly controlled; but what is the case when one can no longer control relevant variables?

It must be remembered that the construction of heritability estimates requires both a standard environment and somewhat standard genotypes. A standard environment is required in order that only small random fluctuations in environmental variables may affect genotypes differentially. A standard genotype is required in order that population averages in phenotype expression may have meaning for individuals in the population. With human populations, neither of these conditions is met.

On environmental standardization, Hogben (1939) concluded his critique of Fisher as follows:

Are we to understand that the "standard environment"
[the homogeneous environment postulated by the biome-

trician] which must be defined to give any meaning to a
balance sheet of nature and nurture is a statistical average? True, such an average would have a definite significance in [an experimental study where one element
of the environment would be manipulated]. It would not
have an equally definite significance for the study of human populations exposed to an indefinitely large number
of as yet unmeasurable and unidentifiable environmental
differences. Nor would any balance sheet drawn up on
such an assumption entitle us to set limits to changes
which could be produced by controlling the environment. * [P. 116]

If genetic standardization is lacking, then the norms of reaction for
the varied members of a given population will make it impossible to
know what elements in the environment affect which members in what
ways (Williams 1969).

These problems appear not only in studies of wild-type populations, but also within the laboratory. For example, genotype-environment interaction is a problem that often affects agricultural applications of research (Feldman and Lewontin 1975, p. 1164). Further,
even within the laboratory, it is difficult to develop homogeneous lines
of the species with which one works, so that the genetic usefulness of
research is sometimes questioned on this basis alone (for example,
Hirsch and Vetta 1977). With freely-mating populations, in which
few controls on genotype exist at all—and for which only such crude
devices as the statistical average of assortative mating are available
—the usefulness of heritability estimates is so eroded that a number
of writers have insisted that such estimation is of no value whatsoever,
or even that it cannot be properly accomplished at all (for example,
Layzer 1974; Moran 1973; McGuire and Hirsch 1977; Feldman and
Lewontin 1975; Goldberger 1976).

The strongest attack on the viability of heritability estimation
comes from those who posit a high degree of genotype-environment
interaction and/or covariance (for example, Moran 1973; Layzer
1974). Interaction does not always show up in estimates of heritability,
where limited populations and environments are employed, but is
readily seen when different studies are compared. For example, I.

---

*Such arguments may have proved telling for Fisher (1951), for
two decades later, he condemned "the so-called coefficient of heritability, which I regard as one of those unfortunate short-cuts which
have emerged in biometry for lack of a more thorough analysis of the
data" (p. 217).

TABLE 8

Variations in Estimated Heritability of IQ, for Various Types of Data

Data Source	Range of H^2 Estimates
Parent-child data	0.29 to 0.76
Identical-fraternal twin data	0.45 to 0.60
Identical twins raised apart	0.29 to 0.50
Siblings and unrelated children raised together	0.00 to 0.25

Source: David Layzer, "Science or Superstition? A Physical Scientist Looks at the IQ Controversy," Cognition 1, no. 2/3 (1972): 265-99. Reprinted by permission of Elsevier Sequoia S. A., publisher of Cognition.

M. Lerner (1972) has shown how heritability estimates derived from half-sib correlations in the open field are considerably and systematically lower than are estimates constructed from half-sib correlations made in test labs (p. 399). These were correlations for metric traits in milk cows, but the same holds for humans.

For example, Layzer (1976, p. 223) has tabulated the variations in estimated heritability of IQ scores for four different kinds of data. These findings (originally reported in Jencks 1972) appear in Table 8. These are the sorts of findings that one would expect, were one operating on the assumption that the heritability of the trait in question was inextricably tied to the contingencies of measurement. The source of data, the age groups for which measurement is intended, and other factors seem to operate strongly when an overview of heritability estimation is provided. The importance of age groupings is underscored by two sets of studies (Wright 1931; Rao, Morton, and Yee 1974) relying on data from a famous study of adopted children by Burks (1928). In both studies, the variance in IQ attributed to genotypic differences was high for children, but low for adults. Such a conclusion was required before path diagrams could be employed in the analysis of heritability. Wright (1931) interpreted this phenomenon as evidence that mid-parent IQs were "a much better index of home environment than of child's heredity" (p. 161); Rao, Morton, and Yee (1974, p. 355) concurred.

Other studies have also noted wide discrepancies in the data used for the construction of heritability estimates. For example, the

FIGURE 3

Range of Familial Correlations across
Different Types of Relationships

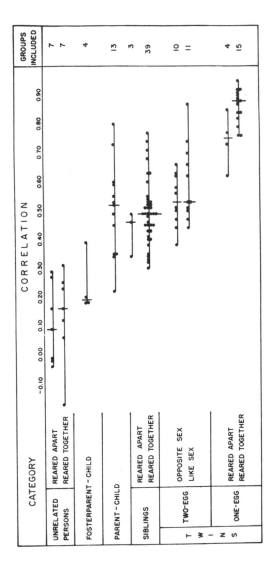

Note: Data are correlations in intellectual abilities, from 56 publications, for 1911–62. More than one study per category was reported for several populations. The medians are indicated by vertical lines.

Source: Lissy Jarvik and L. Erlenmeyer-Kimling, "Survey of Familial Correlations in Measured Intellectual Functions," in Psychopathology of Mental Development, p. 451 (New York: Grune & Stratton, 1966). Reprinted by permission of Grune & Stratton, Lissy Jarvik and L. Erlenmeyer-Kimling.

comprehensive review of the literature on familial correlations by Jar-vik and Erlenmeyer-Kimling (1966) revealed a wide latitude of corre-lations for most categories of data. This is shown in Figure 3.

Jensen (1969a) has used the median findings for each category of relationship in order to support his herditarian stance. The use of medians does indeed indicate that hereditary factors affect score differences. However, the range of findings also indicates a decided degree of genotype-environment interaction. For example, parent-child correlations, for 13 studies, range all the way from about 0.2 to about 0.8, or most of the distance from zero to one. Even identical twins raised together had scores correlated at as low as about 0.7, and fraternal twins ranged in correlation from 0.4 to 0.9. Also, note the great deal of overlap in the ranges for different sorts of data.

The variability in heritability is not unique to IQ studies. In ad-dition to the findings of the study of milk cows, mentioned above, ex-perimental studies with open-field behavior in mice have shown fa-milial correlations to increase, decrease, of fluctuate randomly, on successive days. This fluctuation seems to be a function of repeated testing (Hegmann and DeFries 1968). While it is possible to consider this fluctuation a function of measurement error, it may also be a function of interaction effects. The latter hypothesis is actually more likely than the former in discussion of test scores, for the graph in Jarvik and Erlenmeyer-Kimling represents, not individual scores, but correlation coefficients from various studies. If the differences found were merely those of error, then the degree of error must have been immense to give the variation in correlations discovered. Par-enthetically, the use of median scores as true representations of fa-milial correlations, while a simple method, is likely to give a biased estimate of any central tendencies. More proper would have been the use of weighted means, were such data available.

The other major problem with heritability estimation has to do specifically with the source of data. Here, even excluding a general environmental-genotype interaction, a great deal of bias in reported results appears. For example, the data sources most often used when the issue of the heritability of intelligence is discussed are of two types. First, there is the classic twin study. Here, the correlations of monozygotic (MZ) and dizygotic (DZ) twins, raised together and apart, are compared with correlations based on a Mendelian model, in order to arrive at appropriate estimates of heritability. Second, there is the classic adoption study, in which adopted children are com-pared with either their adopted parents or their adopted siblings, in order to determine heritability.

Here, various problems emerge. With twin studies, it is nec-essary to assume that the environments of MZ and DZ twins raised together are identical. If MZ twins are treated more alike than are

DZ twins, then twin IQ correlations will be biased upwardly for the MZ twins (for example, Hogarth 1974; Linn 1974). Yet it is well known that MZ twins raised together are treated much more alike than are DZ twins (for example, Smith 1965; Bronfenbrenner 1975b, pp. 127-33).

For studies of MZ twins raised apart, a necessary assumption for heritability estimation is that twins are randomly placed. Here, two issues arise. First, there must be no correlation between important elements in the original and the adoptive homes; second, there must be no correlation between the environments of the adoptive homes of twin pairs (Hogarth 1974; Linn 1974; Miller and Levine 1973). Again, these requirements are not met. Regarding MZ twins raised apart, it has been found that strong biases in placement are indeed prevalent. Newman, Freeman, and Holzinger (1937), in their study of the adoption of twin pairs, found an intraclass correlation of 0.55 between twins, for the number of years of education received. Further, ratings of the educational, social, and physical environments for twin pairs revealed very low differences. In the same study, the average difference in IQ scores for separated twins was correlated with the environmental differences of the pairs.

In the study by Shields (1962, p. 47) on 44 identical twins raised apart, 30 of the 44 were raised "in different branches of the same family"; further, it was noted that "large differences in social class do not often occur in the present material." In the Burt (1966) study of separated twins, over two-thirds of all cases fell in the bottom two of five social classes. Kamin (1974) uses such confounding cases, and a number of others that he documents, to indicate that there are no grounds for positing a genetic component of test-score differences. That position goes much too far. Yet he is correct in noting that heritability estimates will be biased upwardly, to an unknown degree, by the use of such data. (For a major review, see Bronfenbrenner 1975b, pp. 115-22.)

Some of these same types of problems affect studies of adopted children, as compared with their adoptive families. For example, selective placement has been shown to operate in these studies, as well as in twin studies. Thus, a final correlation between adoptive children and their true parents should be boosted. Further, adopted children in better homes should do better than do other children. In the major study by Skodak and Skeels (1949), very low correlations obtained between children's ultimate IQs, and the occupational and educational background of their foster homes, a point that hereditarians have frequently noted. However, in the same study, it was found that the home environments of superior homes were striking. Here, environment means "the type of atmosphere and social interaction that took place within the family" (Bronfenbrenner 1975b, p. 125), and not occupation or education. When compared with the children's homes of birth, atmosphere differences were even more striking. Adoptive homes as a group were superior. This fact is consistent with a strong average gain shown in the IQs of children in the adoptive homes. *

What are the effects of violations of the requisite assumptions? A few studies have estimated the effects that would be obtained, given specific violations. For example, Linn (1974), using data reported by Burt, assumed a magnitude of 0.20 for both the genotype-environment correlation of adopted twins, and the correlation of adoptive environments with original environments. While these correlations were slight, they were still sufficient to drop the heritability of IQ from 0.80 to 0.60.

Likewise, Goldberger (1976) found that heritability estimates derived by Jensen required the estimation of six unknowns, while only two pieces of data on twins were available. Accepting Jensen's data, Goldberger then estimated the effect on H^2 if the correlation between a DZ twin's genotype and his twin's environment were not the same as the correlation between an MZ twin's genotype and his twin's environment. Crucial in Jensen's formula was the assumption that genotype-environment covariance was identical for MZ and DZ twins. Changing the ratio of DZ to MZ covariance from 1.0 (as with Jensen) to 0.4, Goldberger (1976, p. 5) lowered H^2 from 0.72 to 0.15. Ratios higher than 0.4 (arbitrarily chosen) gave H^2 figures falling between Goldberger's and Jensen's original figures. For example, a ratio of 0.5 yielded an H^2 of 0.24.

The above armchair manipulations were undertaken in order to demonstrate the sensitivity of heritability estimates to arbitrary specifications (for example, Hogarth 1974; Goldberger and Lewontin 1976). However, in addition to parameter estimation, measurement variation affects outcomes. In a related paper, Goldberger lowered H^2 from 0.81 to 0.68 by merely replacing a simple measure of home environment with a more elaborate measure. Goldberger's argument is that heritability is boosted to the extent that the environment is treated as being homogeneous. This is important, because only measured environment is used in the construction of heritability coefficients, and virtually all studies have used, as their measure of environment, one or another index of socioeconomic status (SES). Use of such a measure, while it facilitates the estimator's task, has the effect of boosting estimates. This occurs because indexes force the multiplicity of elements constituting environment into a simple scale

---

*Still, the generally low correlation of the IQ scores of adopted children with characteristics of their adoptive parents deserves further study.

arrangement. Here, three effects operate. First, any compound index includes elements whose relationships to the trait in question may
be positive, negative, complex, or nil. Various elements affect a
trait in question in various manners. Thus, multiple inclusion guar-
antees that the total effects of environment will be muted, washed out,
as it were (for a different position, see Rao, Morton, and Yee 1974).

Second, the effect of any specific element is masked in the
course of index formation. Use of indexes, then, weds one to a
methodological approach that excludes, at the start, consideration of
reaction norms for specified variables. Third, indexes will only show
environmental effects on traits to the extent that important environmental elements are used in scale construction. Indexers commonly
rely upon readily counted cultural processes. They commonly include,
in their scales of environment, such variables as income, SES (for
example, the Duncan scale), years of education, and types of living
accommodations. But as mentioned earlier, the IQ debate concerns
the relationship between sociocultural milieu and test scores. In the
debate, much discussion has surrounded the effects of cultural differences on test scores. The culture concept, since the work of Boas,
has largely had to do with the day-to-day interactions of members of
collectivities, language usage, and so forth. The variables employed
in index formation are noncultural once they are removed from meaningful interaction. Investigators hope that indexes and important cultural processes correspond in simple, linear ways, but this has not
been demonstrated. Those few investigators who have studied the effects of cultural differences in interaction patterns have found, for
example, substantial differences in scholastic achievement between
groups that were not tied to any measured mental ability (for example, Cohen 1971). It appears also that the researchers who have
studied ways to raise IQ scores have succeeded largely by changing
the usual puzzle-solving techniques used by their subjects. It thus
appears that important interactional processes are being bypassed
in the construction of heritability estimates, and that environmental
effects are being understated.

It should be noted that changes in the specifications of heritability estimates can lower, as well as raise, the magnitudes of such estimates. For example, Loehlin, Lindzey, and Spuhler (1975, pp.
300-2), by changing a specification in the path models provided by
Jencks (1972), have increased the H^2 from 0.45 to 0.60. In light of
these wide variations made possible by relatively tiny changes in
specifications, Garcia (1977) notes that you can "make your own assumptions to fit your own prejudicial values of human diversity and
arrive at your own heritability estimate" (p. 10). More generally,
Morton (1974) holds that estimates of heritability, "both within and
between groups, depend on the credulity of the investigator" (p. 327).

The Magnitude and Importance of Heritability

What, then, is the best estimate of the heritability of IQ? The foregoing indicates that the answer to that question is neither important nor possible to determine. There will be no single estimate of heritability. Since it is a population statistic that is dependent on a variety of parameters, it will vary from study to study. For general interest, it may be noted that while hereditarians continue to claim that IQ is, for the most part, genetically determined (the figure $H^2 = 0.80$ is commonly employed), the greater number of studies actually show H^2 to fall in the range of 0.40 to 0.80, with roughly 0.60 as a median. However, many newer studies indicate that H^2 falls in the range of 0.00 to 0.45 (for example, Jencks 1972; Rao, Morton, and Yee 1974; Schwartz and Schwartz 1974; Adams, Ghodesian, and Richardson 1976).

Still, the fact is that whatever the heritability of IQ scores is, it is not a datum that can help us in answering the question of the role of genetics in group differences in a trait. Thus, even with a low estimate of heritability we cannot know for certain the reasons for racial differences in IQ scores. The position so often stated, that one must remain agnostic on the basis of this type of evidence, still stands. The only thing we know for certain, that whatever underlies IQ scores is not perfectly transmitted to offspring, is hardly a new fact. Thus, in order to determine genetic and environmental effects, different sorts of data are required.

IQ AND EXPERIMENTATION

If heritability studies cannot help us, perhaps studies in which environmental or genetic factors are varied can. Considering the environment, is there evidence that one can permanently change IQ scores by environmental intervention? Since it is commonly admitted that nutrition plays a role in development, and since the IQ controversy has centered around the problem of cultural versus genetic causation (for example, Jensen 1969a, p. 65), this question can be changed so as to ask if intervention in social and cultural environments can affect IQ scores. Here, four types of studies are of interest. First, there are studies of IQ changes in populations over time. Any changes, except in special instances, would have to be culturally induced. Second, there are studies of adopted children (already mentioned briefly). Third, there are studies of the much-maligned Head Start-type programs. Finally, genetic (that is, breeding) studies, while limited in scope because of the lack of genetic controls in the population, can provide clues to the differences between blacks and whites in test scores. This last type of study will be considered first.

Black-White Mixture and IQ

Racial intermarriage presents us with a natural experiment concerning black-white differences in IQ scores. While there can be problems of interpretation concerning mixed-breeding results, breeding studies are the only ones that can give physical proof of the determination of score differences. A review of the few extant breeding studies appears in Loehlin, Lindzey, and Spuhler (1975, pp. 120-33). It should be noted that breeding studies are not the same things as studies employing anthropometric characteristics in the determination of racial admixture, for surface characteristics are not reliable guides to degrees of admixture.

These authors discuss five actual studies of black-white mixture and scores on common intelligence tests. None of the studies supports the specific hypothesis that blacks are inferior to whites, on any genetic substrate, related to IQ scores. An old study of such a mixture, based on genealogical data (Tanser 1939, 1941), revealed that while a Negro group scored lower than a mixed group, a more refined breakdown of data showed that those judged one-half Negro were outperformed by those rated as three-fourth Negro on two of three tests. A study of the relationship between blood groups common in the white population and standardized scores (Loehlin, Vandenberg, and Osborne 1973) yielded correlations of 0.01 and -0.38. The larger correlation was in the direction opposite to that expected on the hypothesis of black inferiority, but it was not statistically significant. A study of interracial matings (Willerman, Naylor, and Myrianthopoulos 1970, 1974) found that mixed-race children of white mothers averaged nine IQ points higher than those of black mothers, a finding suggesting a social-interactional cause of score differences. Studies of the illegitimate children of servicemen and German nationals, following the U.S. occupation of West Germany, found no overall differences in IQ scores between those whose fathers were white and those whose fathers were black (Eyferth 1959, 1961; Eyferth, Brandt, and Hawel 1960). Finally, a study of the degree of white admixture in black children with IQs above 140, as contrasted with the proportion in the general black population, revealed no significant differences (Witty and Jenkins 1936). In fact, there was a slight difference in favor of the more-black-than-white ancestry group, though this was not statistically significant. These results are presented in Table 9. More extensive data reported by the same authors, on black children with IQ scores above 125, revealed the same trend.

It should be stressed that there are problems with each of these studies (extensively discussed by Loehlin, Lindzey, and Spuhler 1975), as there are with any empirical undertakings. However, since a black-inferiority hypothesis is not supported by any of these diverse

TABLE 9

The Degree of White Admixture in the Black Population as a Whole,
as Compared with the Proportion among Black Children Who Are
Gifted (IQs above 140)

| Ancestry | Gifted Black Children[a] | | The Black Population[b] |
	N	Percent	Percent
All black	6	21.4	28.3
More black than white	12	42.8	31.7
About equal	6	21.4	25.2
More white than black	4	14.3	14.8

[a]Ancestry reported by parents.
[b]Based on data by Herskovits (1930).

Source: John C. Loehlin, Gardner Lindzey, and J. N. Spuhler,
Race Differences in Intelligence (San Francisco: W. H. Freeman and
Company, 1975), table 5.7, p. 131. Copyright © 1975. Reprinted
by permission.

sorts of evidence, the null hypothesis of racial equality cannot be rejected. It is the only hypothesis to find any support at all. If we are
to make statements based upon empirical evidence, the black-inferiority position must be, at least for the present, rejected.

However, the authors do not take this position. Instead, they
report that "such studies can probably be assessed as offering fewer
explanatory difficulties to environmentalists than to hereditarians,
although they admit interpretations from a range of viewpoints"
(Loehlin, Lindzey, and Spuhler 1975, p. 133). Later, in the conclusion to their monograph, these authors strongly imply that genetic
factors are at least partially responsible for the range of average
white-black score differences (pp. 238-39). In fact, it seems almost
as if the authors construct strongly implausible arguments in order
to keep the racial-differences hypothesis from being discarded (the
reader is directed to the relevant pages, cited above). This fact has
led at least one commentator (Lewontin 1976b) to charge that the authors have willfully held to the inferiority position despite a knowledge

of its weakness (see also Blum 1978, chap. 9). Such a charge is, almost undoubtedly, overly strong. However, the apparent resistance of the authors to the equality hypothesis may serve as an index of the degree to which a belief in racial differences—in the context of a long tradition of racial thought in which blacks were considered naturally inferior to whites—has become somewhat immune to empirical disconfirmation. This position will be discussed at greater length in Part II of this work.

IQ Differences across Time and Space

Since intelligence is considered by hereditarians to be a preset quantity, it follows that changes in IQ across the general population should not generally be predicted from their perspective. Such changes might be predicted for isolated groups, on the grounds that these groups were isolated from the cultural milieu of the general society, and that therefore they could not be expected to measure up to the standards of the major groups. However, such a position introduces the bugbear of cultural differences into discussions of group differences. Conversely, differences between different isolated groups could be expected on genetic grounds, but in that case such groups should maintain their distinctiveness even when culturally integrated with the greater society. However, any changes over an entire society raise real problems for genetic determinists, for while it is certainly possible to conceive of cultural changes leading to differences in test performance, widespread changes would bring into question the grounds for making inferences of genetically induced group differences. What we find in the literature is evidence for both temporal and geographic differences in test performance that can be readily fitted to environmentalist models of score differences.

The study most frequently cited as evidence of the malleability of test scores was Otto Klineberg's study (1935a) of differences in test scores, for blacks and whites in northern and southern states. The data used by Klineberg came from the army studies of intelligence performed during World War I, with what was the first large, national sample to undergo psychometric analysis. The data clearly showed blacks (as well as other ethnic and immigrant groups) to score lower than Anglo-Americans. Yet, when Klineberg and others cross-tabulated the data, interesting regional variations in test scores appeared. The ones most germane to this discussion appear in Table 10.

In all within-state comparisons, whites outscored blacks. However, the range of median scores, by states, was much greater than would have been expected on the basis of theories of genetic drift regarding selective migration in a small group. For whites, the median scores ranged from 62.2 down to 35.6 (in the states discussed), while

TABLE 10

Median Alpha Scores of White and Black Army Recruits from Five
Northern and Eight Southern States

State	White	Black
Northern		
Ohio	62.2	45.5
Pennsylvania	62.0	34.7
Illinois	61.6	42.2
New York	58.3	38.6
Indiana	55.9	41.5
Southern		
Tennessee	44.0	29.7
Texas	43.4	12.1
Oklahoma	42.9	31.4
Kentucky	41.5	23.9
Alabama	41.3	19.9
Mississippi	37.6	10.2
Louisiana	36.1	13.4
Arkansas	35.6	16.1

Source: Ashley Montagu, Race, Science and Humanity (Princeton, N.J.: Van Nostrand Reinhold Co., 1963). Copyright © 1963 by Litton Educational Publishing, Inc. Reprinted by permission.

for blacks, scores ranged from 45.5 down to 10.2. When first reported, such data were used to support beliefs of white supremacy; however, when Klineberg reinterpreted the data, a different position became viable.

First, Klineberg showed that there was a general tendency for northerners to outscore southerners. Second, blacks in several northern states were shown to outscore whites in several southern states; more specifically, blacks in four northern states outscored whites in three southern states. Blacks in the three highest-scoring states equaled or outscored whites in five states. Finally, blacks in Ohio outscored whites in eight different southern states. *

---

*Some writers (notably, Garrett 1960) objected to the findings by Klineberg and his associates, but these objections were based on

Earlier in the century, attempts had been made to demonstrate that southern citizens were, on the average, genetically inferior to northerners, though such attempts did not prove very fruitful (for example, see the account on the thought of J. McK. Cattell, in Pastore 1949). Klineberg's data, likewise, were treated as being of genetic significance. Specifically, it was assumed that northern blacks were a highly select group—that selective migration had led superior blacks to flee the south, leaving their less-talented relatives behind. However, this raised three problems. First, why was it that the average test scores of both blacks and whites were tied to their state of residence? It strained a genetic argument to posit that inferior whites and blacks both just happened to settle in the same areas, yet no other genetic argument was immediately apparent to explain the relationship. Likewise, why was it that bright blacks and whites happened to appear so commonly in the same states? An explanation that most readily fits the data centers on the idea that conditions specific to the states in question (specifically, the state of education in the states in question) were responsible for the relationships found.

Second, if one posited an environmental explanation for differences within one group, was it reasonable then to posit genetic explanations for the differences in the other group, or for differences between the two groups (for example, Feagin 1978, p. 244)? Third, Klineberg (1935a, 1935b) was able to show that the level of scores achieved by blacks was predictable on the basis of the amount of time they had spent in the north. Those who had most recently migrated scored essentially the same as did blacks in their home states, while those who had lived a long time in the north approached northern norms. This finding was later replicated by Lee (1951), and strongly supported the environmental-conditions position, though it was not evidence of no racial differences.

In point of fact, there have been a number of studies of test-score changes in populations over time. Commonly, these have shown such changes to be upward in direction (for a review, see Loehlin,

---

the strength of the findings, not on the general trends discovered. For example, Garrett felt that the data on northern states in which blacks obtained the highest scores were restricted to too-few cases to be fully representative. Further, he faulted the environmentalists for not pointing out that blacks were inferior in army scores in all within-state comparisons, and that education did not fully do away with the racial differences in scores that were found. Yet even he mentioned the positive impact of education on test scores (Garrett 1945a, 1945b); he merely felt that education was not potent enough to bring about intellectual equality.

Lindzey, and Spuhler 1975, chap. 6), though the actual direction of change is not important. For the population as a whole, test-score norms indicate a rise of the equivalent of 12-14 IQ points between the two world wars (Tuddenham 1948), and this trend apparently continued through the early 1960s (Tupes and Shaycoft 1964). The same occurred in more specific populations. For instance, in Hawaii, the various ethnic groups, en masse, increased test scores an equivalent of about 13 points between 1924 and 1938 (Smith 1942). Likewise, among East Tennessee mountain people, the regional IQ average jumped over ten points between 1930 and 1940 (Wheeler 1942). *

As in the case of blacks and whites, the Hawaiian study showed almost no change in the rank order of groups, in average IQ, a point that can be used to support an argument that the groups differed in relative ability. However, it is not the case that great changes in rank order do not occur. For example, as late as World War II, Chinese-Americans failed army entrance exams at a rate 25 times that of white failures in the exams, and over twice that of black failures (Vetta 1974; Hyde and Chisholm 1944). This was consistent with data dating to the World War I army studies, which showed all ethnic

---

*The Wheeler study is interesting because Jensen (1969a, pp. 62-63) used it to demonstrate that "great improvements" in general socioeconomic and cultural conditions could not keep the IQ scores of children from showing a consistent drop from ages 6 to 16. This drop was considered as great in 1940 as it had been in 1930, when, presumably, the children were more deprived. Jensen interpreted this consistency as demonstrating a native intelligence that, as it were, seeks its own level with age, and is resistant to environmental impact.

It is apparent that the 16-year-olds did considerably worse in each year than did the 6-year-olds. In 1930, their scores were 74 and 95, respectively. In 1940 they were 80 and 103 (according to data presented by Jensen). However, the two studies are cross-sectional; they show differences by age group, rather than declines with increasing age.

We can treat the study as though it were longitudinal by comparing the 1940 teenagers with the 1930 six-year-olds. Doing so, we find a mean IQ decline of 15 points over the span. This is considerably less than the 21-to-23-point decline that we would have expected from the evidence given for either of the two years alone. The 1940 teenagers had an average IQ score some six points higher than would have been expected in 1930, despite the fact that they were tested in the final days of the worst depression in U.S. history. Further, the regional average rose by two-thirds of a standard deviation in the same period, a fact that Jensen admitted and then ignored.

groups to fall far below Anglo-Americans in test scores. Among other groups, native Americans, Mexican-Americans, and Italian-Americans scored very poorly when compared with Anglo-Americans (Klineberg 1935b). However, by the mid-1960s, Oriental-Americans (including Chinese-Americans) were second only to northern urban Anglo-Americans in cognitive-test scores, and some writers (for example, Jensen 1969b) suggested that the Oriental-American group, as a whole, might be superior to even Anglo-Americans in native endowment. This rise, in at least the case of Chinese-American test scores, coincides with the growth of a U.S.-born Chinese-American population, a segment of the Chinese-American population that was almost nonexistent prior to the 1940s, because of a poor sex ratio among immigrants (Lyman 1974, pp. 112-15).

Summing up the above studies, there is unambiguous evidence that social factors (or something to do with social climate) can have major effects on test scores in the time period of a generation. While it is not understood just what occurs to change test performance, the fact that such changes occur is not contested.

Efforts at Boosting IQ Scores

If populations change in average test scores over time, then it seems reasonable to assume that individuals within the populations would also change, relative to the population average. In fact, the average spontaneous change in IQ scores between the ages of 2.5 (when such scores first become predictive of later test scores) and 17, for middle-class children, is 28.5 points (McCall, Appelbaum, and Hogarty 1973). About one-seventh of all children show changes of 40 or more points, and isolated changes of up to 74 points have been reported.

At least in early childhood, the congeries of elements leading to test behavior is obviously malleable, or at least is developmentally plastic. However, this fact is not very important here. What is important is the problem of the direct manipulation of the environment in order to pragmatically change IQ scores. Recall that the IQ controversy began in an atmosphere of frustration over the seeming inability of liberal social scientists to affect either the test scores or the achievement patterns of poor people. Jensen's (1969a) article, "How Much Can We Boost IQ and Scholastic Achievement?" was a direct challenge to the liberal position. For, while we know that scores change over time, attempts at intervention in the developmental process have historically given mixed returns for the effort put into them.

The first efforts at changing test scores through changes in schooling were undertaken in the late 1930s, and almost universally failed to produce significant changes in relevant variables (National Society for the Study of Education [NSSE], 1940). However, adoption studies consistently did show changes (NSSE 1928, 1940). Following the institution of Head Start and other intervention programs, the major review of such attempts (Coleman et al. 1966, p. 523) reported relatively little effect on test scores. The same holds for grade school and high school, where the most comprehensive review of evidence (Jencks 1972, p. 89) reported modest effects of schooling on test scores.

However, "modest" does not mean "nonexistent." The Coleman and Jencks studies both showed some impact on test scores, based on time spent in school, and at least Coleman indicated that this gain was larger for blacks than for whites. That being the case, some gain in scores can be expected from such an everyday activity as going to school. But if schooling itself can offer such returns, what can intensive intervention accomplish?

Jensen's (1969a) conclusion on the effects of "intensive educational intervention" was that "massive compensatory programs have produced no appreciable gains [while] the majority of small-scale experiments have produced significant gains" (p. 97). In the next sentence, without documentation, he asserted:

> It is interesting that the magnitude of claimed gains generally decreases as one proceeds from reports in the popular press, to informal verbal reports heard on visits at research sites and in private correspondence, to papers read at meetings, to published papers without presentation of supporting data, and to published papers with supporting data.

The clear implication of this was that intervention schemes had simply failed to boost scores much. Yet there is evidence (not all of it was available in 1969) that intensive programs can lead to gains of ten or more points on tests (for example, Frost and Rowland 1971; Averch et al. 1972).

The largest, and most long-lasting, gains have been produced in those studies in which the families of the target children have been made an integral part of the intervention process, especially when this has been done during the children's first three years of life. In a major review of research, Bronfenbrenner (1975a, p. 304) reports several studies in which gains of 7 to 21 points (over scores of control groups) were obtained. One study that emphasized the involvement of mothers in the process of intervention (Karnes et al. 1969) found gains of 16 points over the scores of controls, and gains of 28 points over the scores of older siblings at an earlier age. One study indicated that the younger siblings of target children in a family intervention program benefited more than did the target children (Gilmer, Miller, and Gray 1970). There is also evidence that such gains tend to be somewhat long-lasting (for example, Bronfenbrenner 1975a, pp. 306-8).

Overall, some evidence indicates that significant gains in test scores can be achieved with the use of appropriate intervention strategies. Further, such gains, on the basis of the little evidence available, can be expected to last for at least several years after termination of the programs. The two main drawbacks with such strategies, according to Bronfenbrenner, are ethical and economic, rather than empirical. Specifically, if capital-efficient large-scale programs do not work, can we afford the small programs that do work? This leads to the second problem: Is our society willing to make conditions suitable for all its families?

SUMMARY

The argument in this chapter has been as follows: First, heritability coefficients do not give important information about the genetic/environmental causes of traits. With unstandardized human populations, a number of arbitrary assumptions are required in order to estimate heritability and these assumptions (which can have strong effects on ultimate estimates) are almost certain to be incorrect. The end result of this is that true heritability is, almost certainly, considerably lower than the estimates making the rounds. Modern-day estimates of the heritability of intelligence tend to show it to be somewhat lower than had been estimated in the past.

Second, it is known that societal changes can have very profound effects on the test scores of citizens. Such factors as geographic location also affect test scores. Changes in scores over time can (but do not always) change the rank orders of various groups on standard tests. With respect to differences in scores between blacks and whites, the results of studies that correlated degree of black-white mixture with test performance have, without exception, shown no significant differences by amount of mixture. Finally, appropriately designed intervention strategies have successfully raised the test scores of children.

The inference to be drawn from this set of diverse sorts of evidence is not that there are no genetic inputs to group differences in the narrow range of attributes leading to test performance. However, the evidence does not support a position claiming genetic inputs and suggests that even if genetic differences are implicated in test-score differences, they can be overcome by appropriate strategies, if we are willing to make the required sacrifices.

Viewing Chapters 2-5 as a unit, we have seen that each of the required assertions supporting the hereditarian position in the IQ controversy is open to considerable empirical and theoretical criticism. Yet, in the main, those who may be called environmentalists have been slow to point out these weaknesses. Indeed, most environmentalists appear to be as unaware of them as are their opponents. In the opening rounds of the controversy, incisive documentation of these major weaknesses was conspicuous by its almost-complete absence (a few writers have since commented upon them).

This fact raises the interesting question of why so many debatable assertions have been allowed to lie unchallenged for so long. It is the contention of this writer that this has occurred because both groups of scientists in the controversy operate within a tradition of research in which those issues are seen as having been resolved long ago. That is, neophyte psychologists are taught very early that (for example) mental testing is "psychology's most telling achievement to date" (Herrnstein 1971, p. 45). Likewise, neophytes are taught that IQ is the correct index to intelligence, that IQ is very important in social affairs, and that IQ differences are largely hereditary in nature. Since we have seen that none of these is necessarily true, it becomes important to trace aspects of the development of psychometric psychology, in order to determine the ways in which these issues came to be seen as settled. The existence of these assumptions as deeply embedded beliefs cannot be denied without difficulty. While such a comprehensive treatment of the hereditarian argument as that given in Part I of this study has not been done before (to this author's knowledge), the facts and ideas presented are hardly new. Indeed, the evidence for the assumptions was never strong, and evidence against each of them had been presented long ago. Indeed, many writers who took strongly hereditarian positions in the early debates over race and intelligence severely questioned various of these assumptions in their own works. Yet, when social pronouncements were made, the writers ignored their own theoretical positions and even their own evidence. Strong evidence of this will be presented in the following chapters. Such a disjuncture between private and public pronouncements is logically inconsistent, but it makes sense in terms of the embedded nature of the assumptions. Briefly, there was more to the early debates over nature and nurture (or race and intelligence) than merely the development of scientific positions. Tacit commitments were equally important, and these proved more decisive than individual positions when public policy came to be at issue. It is proposed that the same thing occurs in the modern IQ controversy.

What follows is an investigation of the historical development of each of the four assertions, in order. Part II, therefore, will parallel the structure of Part I. Whereas Chapter 2 detailed problems with the idea that paper-and-pencil tests clearly measure human intelligence, Chapter 6 will demonstrate the manner in which a commitment to the use of such tests grew in psychology, such that contemporary writers could be taught this commitment in the normal course of undergraduate and graduate education (for example, Kuhn 1962). In like manner, where Chapters 3 through 5 discussed problems with the conception of intelligence as being unitary in structure, socially important, or necessarily genetically inherited, Chapters 7 through 9 will detail the growth of each of these ideas as a major commitment of psychometric psychology. In this way, each of the following chapters will help us understand how we came to where we are, in the absence of strong empirical support.

Chapter 6 will be a keystone for the second half of this study: It will delineate the general idea of meritocracy upon which the testing movement was based. For there to be a desire for a unitary measure of intelligence, there must first be the assumption that such an intelligence exists, and it is this feeling that there exists such an intelligence that will be shown first in the chapter. Then, the work of the early testers, especially Binet, will be traced in order to show how this unitary intelligence came to be operationalized in mental scales.

Chapters 7 and 8 will show in more detail the ways in which the pioneers of testing worked with the assumptions of both the unitary nature and the importance of this measured intelligence. These are the two complementary aspects of the idea of meritocracy, and they deserve special attention, apart from the general discussion that will be provided in Chapter 6.

Finally, Chapter 9 will provide both a historical overview of the manner of conceptualizing heredity, which is still largely followed in psychology, and a discussion of the manner in which psychologists kept this conception even when alternative approaches to studies of heredity developed in biology. Of course, it is this subject that divides hereditarians and environmentalists, who for the most part do not disagree on any of the aspects of the idea of meritocracy. The dispute concerns whether or not the meritocracy is hereditary.

In each of the following chapters, it will be shown that the pioneers of testing worked hard in order to fit each of the given assertions in question into the fabric of psychological research; it will be shown that these scientists had difficulty accomplishing this. Indeed, nature proved at times intractable. Yet, their prior commitments were so strong that ultimately they were able to treat the assertions as though they had received the empirical support that we now know was lacking.

Although a considerable shifting of gears is necessary as we move from the analytic chapters of Part I to the historical discussion of Part II, the two parts constitute separate aspects of a single thesis.

Neither portion of the work is, by itself, sufficient to allow an understanding of the controversy, but together, the two parts tell us how we
we got to where we are, and they give clues as to where we may go
in the future. Some aspects of this latter point will be touched on in
Chapter 10.

PART II

THE HISTORICAL DEVELOPMENT OF HEREDITARIAN PSYCHOLOGY

6

THE HISTORICAL DEVELOPMENT
OF INTELLIGENCE TESTING

We saw in Chapter 2 that there exists no clear definition of intelligence, even though those involved in the controversy, for the most part, appear to believe that a real entity exists. Further, we saw that real problems exist regarding the measurement of this poorly defined entity. In this chapter, two related phenomena will be investigated: first, the historical development of the idea that a simple entity exists that serves to differentiate people; and second, the way in which mental tests were derived in order to mirror this supposed entity.

The first portion of the chapter is essential if we are to understand the commitment to hierarchical thought that ultimately developed in the United States and Britain. To this end, first a general history of the idea of inequality will be presented. This presentation will stress those elements from traditional European social thought that called for a hierarchical conceptualization of nature. Stressed also will be the impact of those social institutions (especially slavery) that gave impetus to attempts at ranking peoples in a hierarchy. The work of Herbert Spencer and Francis Galton will then be sketched, in order to show how these unformed ideas of ranking were given scientific validation.

The second portion of the chapter will investigate the way in which ideas of a hierarchy (or mental stratification) came to be incorporated into mental tests. The growing commitment to simple indicators of rank will be explored first, in order to make explicit the intellectual forces driving the pioneers of mental testing. Then the pragmatic motivations of those testers will be discussed. It will be shown that the enthusiasm for testing that had marked the 1890s waned to a considerable extent by the early 1900s, as a result of the inability of testers to give operational meaning to their ideas about inequality. Finally, the work of Alfred Binet will be discussed, and it will be shown how Binet's commitment to the idea of a simple scale of inequality led to the construction and popularization of his mental scales.

THE DEVELOPMENT OF THE IDEA OF INEQUALITY

Conceptions of hierarchical inequality among humans existed long before the age of science (Ossowski 1963; Banton 1967, pp. 12-13). Speculation over the sources of human differences, however, increased following European exploration of the new worlds; some of this speculation undoubtedly stemmed from St. Augustine's statement that it would "be excessively absurd" to suppose that any of Adam's descendants had sailed to faraway lands (Banton 1967, p. 14). Thus, European speculative thought centered on the nature of the Africans and Indians. Were they, perhaps, not human? Or had there been multiple creations? Such questions were inchoate, however. Capacities of sorts were discussed, and the relative capacities of white and colored peoples were questioned, but capacity here referred almost exclusively to capacity for religious experience, rather than any secular ability (Jordan 1968, pp. 187-90).

When African enslavement began early in the seventeenth century, justifications for it were not couched in the well-developed inequalitarian ideology that later marked discussions of slavery following the U.S. revolution. In fact, Jordan (1968, pp. 44-100) has referred to black enslavement as an "unthinking decision." The almost total degeneracy of the Africans, in English eyes, set them off from Europeans in a quantum sense that required little elaboration. * A human hierarchy was at least tacitly felt to be present, but the development of such an idea was hindered by the fact that people were still considered spiritual rather than secular beings.

Secular thought regarding humans is tied closely to the work of the biologist Linnaeus, who gave eighteenth-century biology an empirical basis with his delineation of species and family boundaries on the basis of degrees of physiological resemblance. So successful was

---

*The differences between the English treatment of blacks and the Spanish treatment of Indians deserves mention. The Indians were seen as primarily lacking religious instruction, and a Spanish royal commission ultimately decided that religious conversion afforded the savages a degree of protection by the church (Barzun 1937; Banton 1967, pp. 14-15). Among the English, whose church was not as powerful as a political force, conversion did not confer privilege. When discussion began over this, laws were passed making the point both explicit and official (Jordan 1968, pp. 180-81).

this attempt to bring order to the diverse biological realm that, until the development of population genetics in the 1920s, Linnaean classification was a central aspect of biology. Linnaeus's contribution to racial thought came through his treatment of humans as part of the natural world. He included humans in his great classificatory "webs" of life (Handlin 1957, chap. 4); divided the species (most commonly) into four categories, corresponding to the common "red and yellow, black and white" scheme of the children's song (see Barzun 1937, p. 66); and ascribed behavioral characteristics to each group.

This was not racism in the sense of the nineteenth-century racial ideologies, for Linnaeus was convinced of the unity of the species. This monogenesist conviction caused him to resist imputations of black biological inferiority. For example, commenting on a report in 1755 that a rabbit and a hen had crossbred, Linnaeus stated that one should not draw any "general conclusions" from such research, and that to do so would lead to "frightful conclusions" about mankind. Specifically, they would lead to questions about the origins of the Moors. Here, Linnaeus was adamant about not wishing to entertain theories of "strange" origins (see Jordan 1968, p. 236).

Linnaeus was conscious of the diversity of criteria required for his typological classifications, and therefore could not rashly place beings in a hierarchy. But his work extended a general secularization of theory, and in conjunction with the idea of the Great Chain of Being (Lovejoy 1942), this had unfortunate results.

The chain idea, dating from Plato, but especially strong in the eighteenth century, treated the realm of creation as extending from the lowest to the highest of organisms. As a metaphor for treatment of social place, the chain worked quite well, though one immediately faced problems when attempting practical applications. Nevertheless, the new fact that humans were animals suggested to scholars that they, too, should be ranked. There is no inherent reason to conceive of life as constituting a chain, rather than a Linnaean web. The two were, in fact, incompatible, for implicit in the concept of diversity is the idea that no simple ranking of beings is possible. The metaphor of the chain, however, proved irresistible. Instead of pursuing the one devastating defect of the chain idea—that the qualities by which ranking should occur were ultimately arbitrary—eighteenth-century thinkers incorporated hierarchical conceptions into their biological schemes, and to an ever-greater extent considered the Africans to lie at a lower link than the Europeans.

Mental Inequality

Arguments concerning black inferiority first emerged in the mid-eighteenth century in the same period—but not coincidentally—

that the natural and moral philosophers began being read and discussed (see Jordan 1968, p. 294). The driving belief of the natural philosophers was the equality of humanity. In fueling an assault upon traditional Christian theology, however, these writers opened the way for the invidious comparisons of human beings that had been muted by doctrines of human oneness.

While it has been claimed by some that inferiority was used as a justification for slavery, this was not the case, except on a tacit level. Indeed, the issue of mental ability was never clearly addressed until after the publication of Locke's mechanistic "Essay Concerning Human Understanding" in the last decade of the seventeenth century (Jordan 1968, pp. 440-45; Barzun 1937, pp. 58-60). Locke's view of the mind as a blank page, on which were imprinted sensations, led to the conclusion that understanding consisted of the manipulation of those sensations. Capacity came to be the ability to manipulate sensations, and a hierarchy of intellectual ability received a philosophical base.

For Locke, people were equal insofar as they all had understanding. This idea of understanding itself had roots in the chain idea, in that at least since Elizabethan times, understanding had constituted half of the highest mental faculty: reason. The lowest aspects of the mind were the five senses. Above this were common sense, fancy, and memory. Finally, there came reason, consisting of understanding and will. Remaining within the metaphor of the chain, reason separated humans from the animals (Tillyard 1944, p. 71). Locke's essay dealt with the understanding aspect of reason. With Galton, and then through Spearman to modern psychometrics, understanding came to be the general intellectual quality upon which all people would be ranked. This point will bear more emphasis later. For now, it should be noted that Locke's view of creation led him to abandon the idea of rigid species boundaries in favor of the idea that such boundaries were more apparent than real (Lovejoy 1942, pp. 228-29). In view of the early reports from Africa that the people there copulated with apes, this vision of continuity reinforced claims of black inferiority.

The twining of beliefs about the mind and the ranking of nature led to attempts to measure mental inequality. Linnaeus may have been unwilling to ascribe bestiality to the Africans, but others were not. More important, however, the way now seemed open to determine the degree to which such people fell below the plane of the Europeans. Thus, among the several measures designed to determine the qualities of racial types, there were a number of indexes aimed specifically at determining the relative magnitudes of the brain. It is instructive that the indexes of racial difference that became most popular in the latter part of the nineteenth century were these same cranial measures.

The most widely used indicator of racial and intellectual differences was the facial angle, suggested by Petras Camper in the late eighteenth century (Barzun 1937, p. 52; Haller 1971, pp. 9-11). This measure, which consisted of the angle formed by the face and a horizontal plane, ranked all animals on a one-dimensional scale. A large angle indicated superior station. A small angle indicated stupidity (according to Camper), and an angle of less than 70 degrees was considered less than human. In 1842, the facial angle was joined by the cephalic index (a ratio between the length and breadth of the head), which its inventor, Anders Retzius, felt could classify individuals by their appropriate races (Handlin 1957, pp. 60-61). So potent was the cephalic index as a classificatory device that such scholars as Karl Pearson, Franz Boas, and Binet used it into the twentieth century. It was the malleability of the supposedly stable (by race) cephalic index that ultimately led Boas to his critique of racial formalism (Stocking 1968, p. 173; 1960, pp. 222-26).

A third measure of racial differences popular in the United States, and tied to inchoate conceptions of the role of the brain in human action, was cranial capacity, a measure developed by Samuel Morton and his associates in the 1830s (Stanton 1960, chap. 3). Like the measures discussed above, cranial capacity assumed a direct relationship between the brain and behavior. The popular and general idea of a unidimensionality to this relationship marked Morton's work, so that he conceived that a proper measure of station would be the average volume of the skull enclosure, as measured by white-pepper seed, lead shot, or other handy materials (Stanton 1960, pp. 30-33). Again the diverse differences among peoples were forced onto a scale of being. And again, people of color ranked lower than did white people. *

The important question is: Why was it at this particular period that massive efforts were made to demonstrate the smaller brain

------

*Recently, Stephen J. Gould (1978) has reanalyzed Morton's original data, and has found that Morton's conclusions about racial differences in cranial capacity are not supported by the data when they are treated in a consistent manner. Gould has found that all the groups investigated had average cranial capacities in the narrow range of 83-86 cubic inches. Further, the differences found were largely related to differences in stature. According to Gould, Morton found great differences in cranial capacity, favoring Caucasian groups, by unconsciously manipulating his data. He gives evidence of a consistent shaping of data in the "desired" direction and suggests that "unconscious or dimly perceived finagling is probably endemic in science, since scientists are human beings rooted in cultural contexts" (Gould 1978, p. 503).

sizes of nonwhite people? The answer is surely that it was at this time that attacks on slavery were based on the natural-equality philosophy. Slavery advocates who espoused the rights of man needed to respond in the same terms. If nothing else, the constant discussion of the issue of inferiority would lead to the following question: Were there scalar differences? If the men who answered the question were not all apologists for slavery—and several, especially Morton, were not (Stanton 1960, pp. 37-39)—the continuing claims of black inferiority certainly affected the direction of research.

It should be noted that hierarchical thought was not unchallenged at this time. Locke had held that all men were at least potentially equal in understanding, barring differential early experiences. Given his one-dimensional view of understanding, equality was equivalent to identity (Manuel 1963, p. 296). Identity, like hierarchy, was difficult to maintain when one got down to cases: physiologists always found human differences. During the French Revolution, Talleyrand had broken from the Lockean tradition to assert that men were born with diverse faculties that fitted individuals best for specified positions in the social sphere. This workshop idea was clearly related to Adam Smith's emerging ideas about economies (Manuel 1963, pp. 296-97). Later, Cabanis and others developed typologies of humans and human conduct that related to Talleyrand's assertions, and the phrenological movement was born with the work of Gall and Spurzheim.

Though phrenology, like other sciences, saw "an exact correspondence between body and mind" (Barzun 1937, p. 59), it stressed the diversity of human mental attributes. Different complexes of behavior were tied to independent, localized areas of the brain; the degree of a specified faculty corresponded to the size of that area of the brain; and measurement of the outside of the head could tap internal structures (Barzun 1937, p. 56; Stanton 1960, pp. 35-37). Different cultural patterns were assumed to parallel different skull profiles. Since traits were localized and independent, questions of inferiority were difficult to formulate. Phrenologists could speak of superiority and inferiority, but they did not do so often, and their statements were muted.

In the United States, phrenology is aligned with the romantic-racialist movement, which held that races as well as individuals, had special attributes (see Gossett 1963, pp. 71-73). Romantic racialists tended to stress the natural qualities of the slaves, and clearly rejected the idea of a racial hierarchy (see, for example, the discussion of the romantic-racialist roots of the writings of Harriet Beecher Stowe, in Frederickson 1971, pp. 110-17). However, phrenologists were never able to tie traits to combinations of bumps and hollows, and they faced hostility from Lockean theorists. Long before the end of the nineteenth century, the discipline was in disrepute.

This, along with a decline in the romantic aspects of romantic racialism, brought about a shift in thought from the thesis of localized function to its antithesis, general action.

THE SCIENTIFIC SUPPORT
OF UNITARY INTELLIGENCE

Herbert Spencer

It was at this time that sophisticated views of intelligence began being developed. The most important of these was that of Herbert Spencer, who tied the idea of a general intelligence to early laws of evolution. For Spencer, life was a very fragile property, which could easily be disrupted. The maintenance of life required a struggle for existence in which only those organisms that met certain criteria could survive and prosper. These criteria Spencer subsumed under the term fitness, and they could conceivably include almost any properties functional to the organism in a specified environment. However, for Spencer the one paramount criterion of fitness was self-mobility (Spencer 1899, vol. 1, p. 4), which indicated that events within the organism had to correspond to events outside the organism in order for the organism to survive. Organisms needed to make correct choices of action, given external contingencies. Given this, evolution was the way that organisms came to develop ever-greater repertoires of responses to a hostile environment. This ability to generate responses of varied types was what Spencer meant by intelligence, and its development was an evolutionary universal—it differentiated the fit from the unfit.

Spencer's ideas fitted well not only with the emerging evolutionary perspective but also with the Chain of Being idea as well. Thus, at the low end of the scale were those creatures capable of only reflex action, while at the high end there developed, successively, instinct, then memory, reason, the feelings, and will (see Spencer 1899, vol. 1, p. 4). All of these were manifestations of increasing amounts of nerve tissue; there was a tie between "the quantity of nerve and the quantity of motion" (Spencer 1899, vol. 1, pp. 8-11).

Notice that Spencer placed reason and will squarely toward the top of the hierarchy of intelligences; in this manner, he recapitulated the traditional Elizabethan view of the faculties. In both cases, this was what differentiated humans from the animals, though in Spencer's case the division was not that of a dichotomy, but rather of a continuum.

Spencer's work had multiple effects on nineteenth- and twentieth-century ideas concerning intelligence. First, there was the establishment of a theory of unilinear mental functioning, with a basis in the emerging evolutionary world view. Second, there was Spencer's personal view of primitive peoples, women, and members of the lower social classes, whom he considered inferior in intellect to upper-class males. Third, there was his view of society as a superorganic entity that became ever more complex, thus requiring ever more intelligent societal members. This effect has much to do with the social importance of intelligence, and will be discussed in the following chapter.

Spencer's lay and scientific popularity reached its peak in the last third of the nineteenth century (Hofstadter 1959), coincident with the origins of the testing movement. That being the case, it would have been surprising were there not efforts to develop metric intelligence scales, because hierarchical intelligence did not simply exist for Spencer, but existed in an evolutionary perspective in which the primary analogy was the scale of being. All living things had places on the scale, and while gradations between links were, in Spencer's view, "insensible," they nonetheless existed. The reasons for intelligence differences were evolutionary. This had far-reaching effects when Spencer considered the differences among peoples, for the principles were the same as with other species. Differences in this prime evolutionary quality were necessarily the result of hereditary differences between those engaged in the struggle for existence, and if some were less intelligent than others, this was merely a function of their less-well-developed nervous systems.

Francis Galton

Following Spencer, the most important figure in the development of the idea that a scientific method could be established for properly stratifying people was Francis Galton. The scion of a wealthy banking family, Galton (1892) was an outspoken hereditarian elitist: "I object to pretensions of natural equality" (p. 56). In that he wrote during the century after the French Revolution, his attitude is understandable. In fact, he disapproved of revolutions. Of France, he wrote that "the Revolution and the guillotine made sad havoc among the progeny of her abler races" (Galton 1892, p. 47). He also contended that the lack of exceptional works emerging from the United States, as opposed to Great Britain, demonstrated that the openness of a society had little effect upon such works—that is, ability would show, whatever the circumstances, and would not be nurtured were it not already present (Galton 1892, pp. 77-80).

Galton's sources of influence were many, and not all of them can be discussed here. However, among them was the fact that he based his elitism upon evolutionary principles, though it was a Darwinian rather than a Lamarckian evolution (as had been the case with Spencer). He introduced the use of population statistics—first developed by the Belgian statistician Quetelet—in studies of intelligence. * Further, he was instrumental in developing a methodology for determining the roles of nature and nurture in the development of traits, a fact that will get more scrutiny in Chapter 9. It was he who set up the first testing laboratory, and several early testers (for example, J. McK. Cattell) worked with him or his students. Finally, he was central to the development of the eugenics movement in the late nineteenth and early twentieth centuries. For all these reasons, he has central importance, and his work must be seen in some detail.

The primary thrust of Galton's work was the demonstration of the unchangeable hereditary aspects of human behavior. In places, Galton indicated certain environmental influences that could keep a man from achieving eminence in a field, but this was of almost inconsequential importance for him. For example, the fact of specialization was seen as keeping one from achieving eminence in more than a handful of fields (Galton 1892, pp. 63-64); but genius would eventually show in some area. Thus, "the men who achieve eminence, and those who are naturally capable, are, to a large extent, identical" (Galton 1892, p. 78).

Following Quetelet, who had spoken of the normal distribution of numerous attributes, Galton focused on the distribution of "ability," the word that, along with "intelligence," most often replaced Locke's "understanding." While he could discuss the distributions of such diverse qualities as mental imagery and number forming, he constantly returned to discussions of ability. The Lockean tradition was, in fact, extremely influential with Galton. For example, the bifurcation of reason into understanding and will is found almost unchanged in Galton's discussions of ability and eagerness. Thus he stated that he did not know how a gifted and eager man "should be repressed" (Galton 1892, p. 79). Eminence needed, besides intellect, "zeal and power of work" (Galton 1892, pp. 85-87). But intellect, or ability, constantly intruded as a sine qua non.

Galton was not completely consistent in his approach to ability: In places, he spoke in terms of specialized abilities that functionally

---

*Quetelet had spoken of the normal distribution of intelligence some time before Galton, but he had been concerned primarily with group or racial differences in this quality. Moreover, he had never quite fully broken with the phrenological tradition, though in the main he was Lockean (Quetelet 1842, p. 98). In contrast, Galton was interested in variation within populations, and he operated much more clearly in the tradition of Spencer.

suited people for specific positions in society, thus mirroring the workshop metaphor used by Talleyrand. * But while people might have diverse attributes, they would also be ranked, from those with worth to those with less worth. Racial and class stratification would be given a justification in scientific terms. Thus, the workshop would have a boss who presided over laborers. And if natural ability were too low in supply, one would breed for it. It was in terms of his feeling that a hierarchy existed that he called for breeding, for if a multitude of important qualities existed, and these were independent of one another, then how could the improvement be accomplished? In this manner, Galton introduced an ambiguity in thought regarding intelligence that exists to this day: intelligence is at the same time complex and simple. When he spoke of the attributes required for success in a given occupation, he stressed the large number of attributes that might exist. Yet, when he compared individuals or groups outside a specific context, he spoke in hierarchical terms.

Thus Galton was never clear as to what led to success, even within a specified sphere of activity. For example, regarding the criteria for judgeship, he wrote (1892):

> The majority of judges belong to a strongly-marked type. They are not men who are carried away by sentiment, who love seclusion and dreams, but they are prominent members of a very different class, one that Englishmen are especially prone to honor for at least the six lawful days of the week. I mean that they are vigorous, shrewd, practical, helpful men; glorying in the rough-and-tumble of public life, tough in constitution and strong in digestion, valuing what money brings, aiming at position and influence, and desiring to found families. The vigour of a judge is testified by the fact that the average age of their appointment in the last three reigns has been fifty-seven. The labor and responsibility of the office seem enormous to lookers-on, yet these elderly men continue working with ease for many more years; their average age at death is seventy-five, and they commonly die in harness. [P. 108].

---

*Several direct references to emerging capitalist conceptions of social structure appear in Galton's work, often metaphorically. The metaphorical references demonstrate how deeply the view had penetrated his thought (see Galton 1883, pp. 29, 236, 300; 1889, p. 36).

These diverse attributes were depicted by Galton first as "remarkable gifts and peculiarities," but later as the "peculiar type of ability" required for judgeship (1889, p. 111). It is apparent that Galton was aware, on at least a tacit level, of the complexity of the behavioral repertoire constituting a judgeship, yet in his theoretical statements he drew these disparate elements together into a unified whole. At times this was explicitly done, such that he would claim that "natural ability" indicated "those qualities" that ultimately led to one's reputation (1892, p. 77).

Ability, then, had a dual nature for Galton: It was at once unitary and diverse. Diversity was exposed in his descriptions of the display of ability; singularity surfaced through his methodological precepts. While he could recognize the diverse nature of abilities, he could not arrange them into his hierarchical social philosophy.

Part of this dualism may have stemmed from the semimystical quality that Galton attached to genius. * Time and again, he wrote of the irrespressibility of genius, calling it, for example (1892):

A nature which, left to itself, will, urged by an inherent stimulus, climb the path that leads to eminence, and has strength to reach the summit—one which, if hindered or thwarted, will fret and strive until the hindrance is overcome, and it is again free to follow its labour-loving instinct. [P. 77]

The mystical, upward-striving (and very Victorian) quality of genius stands in stark contrast to Galton's coldly mechanistic descriptions of the normal-curve distribution of traits in populations.

Galton's inconsistency operated at two distinct levels of application. At one level, it dealt with the determinants of success in a given field of endeavor (as with judgeships). At a second level, Galton was inconsistent regarding a general, across-occupations ability. In this regard, he vacillated between pronouncements of specialization and of inferiority. He could, in one place, state that the "instincts and faculties of different men and races differ in a variety of ways almost as profoundly as those of animals in different cages" (Galton 1883, p. 2). Later, in the same work (Galton 1883, pp. 305-8), he

---

*Some of this mysticism may have served to replace the free will that had been denigrated since at least the time of Quetelet, and that Galton considered thoroughly unscientific (1892, p. 25). That he himself spoke of "eagerness" and "zeal" indicates that he had not completely gotten rid of the teleology he so despised, and his description of upwardly-mobile genius is definitely teleological.

could talk of the qualities of "higher and lower" races. In the second edition of his classic Hereditary Genius (1892), he wrote, on consecutive pages, of a "man endowed with superior faculties," and of "the natural ability, of which this book mainly treats" (pp. 26-27). In one place, faculties are considered "blends of ancestral qualities . . . mosaics, patches of resemblance" (Galton 1883, p. 43), but classes and races were clearly to be ranked from the "best" to the "worst" (Galton 1892, p. 37). What is more, evolution was conceived not as a differentiating process, but, in Spencerian fashion, a movement "upward" (Galton 1883, p. 303).

It becomes clear that Galton was moving toward the idea that there were diverse human differences, but that one congeries of qualities was paramount. This was a purely typological form of thinking, in that good and poor qualities were largely separated from one another. In a mystical, morality-play fashion, the world was ultimately divided into two classes. Thus, those qualities that marked judges amounted to the quality that separated whites from blacks and the Scots from the Irish. In an age marked by the serious search for pure racial types, such an approach was not only not seen as ludicrous but also was widely respected.

Galton had to be inconsistent in order to maintain a meritocratic position. In order to think in hierarchical terms, he had to postulate an all-encompassing ability that could be manipulated by linear statistical means. He had to lump all the diverse elements he discussed into a mass, or else he had to relax his simple mechanistic conception of human achievement. He could not think of what ability constituted and still treat it hierarchically. Hierarchical treatment required that those things that were considered ability be glossed over, or Galton would have been left with the unhappy idea that British elites did not have more worth than the "inferior races" (cf. Galton 1883, pp. 305-8; 1892, pp. 392-404.)

In his comparisons of groups, Galton consistently spoke of averages and distributions. This is important, for it shows that he was thinking in terms of quantitative, overlapping differences. Thus, he was modern in his thinking. For example, while even exceptional blacks might be inferior to most whites, some Africans were superior to most whites. His influence at the time probably rested on four facts. First, he used what were considered rigorous statistical techniques for his time. Second, he conceived of ability in linear-metric terms, thus aligning himself with those who were revolting against the early localized-faculties argument of the phrenologists. Following Spencer, the brain was coming to be seen as a mass, and people would vary only in "circumference of head, size of brain, weight of grey matter, number of brain fibres, &c" (Galton 1892, p. 72). Further, the "furniture" of the mind included "associations," "recollections," and "bonds" (Galton 1883, p. 182). Galton was part of this growing tradition whose unilinear thrust is obvious. Third, Galton had an evolutionary base for his argument. Hereditary Genius built squarely upon the base that Darwin had laid only a decade previously. Finally, as mentioned, he conceived of human differences as quantitative and overlapping, which made his position congruent even with that of Boas and his students in the late nineteenth and early twentieth centuries (Stocking 1968, pp. 167-68).

Galton's specific impact on future conceptualizations of intellect was twofold. First, he treated human ability as a simple biological reality, much as had Spencer. Beyond this, however, Galton set the stage for the development of a methodology for demonstrating differences in this ability, by the example he set in his early testing laboratory (set up in 1883). Here, both a testing regimen and a statistical methodology developed (the latter will be discussed in Chapter 9). Such were his intellectual inputs. Galton's social inputs were equally important. Most important were his actions as mentor for other figures in social science at the time (for example, Cattell and Pearson), and his use of his abundant resources to fund favorite projects —for example, he helped establish the journal Biometrika, which for a number of years served as a vehicle for Galtonian thought. For the history of the testing movement, Galton's ultimate contribution comes from his commitment to the standardized test as a tool for stratification, a topic that will be explored in the next chapter. Thus, by 1890 the major portions of what has been termed the Galton paradigm in psychometrics (Daniels and Houghton 1972) were set. *

THE CONSTRUCTION OF MENTAL TESTS

From the above discussion, it becomes clear that ideas of human mental stratification developed in a period in which enormous social stratification existed. With Galton came the age of social Darwinism and the application of the belief that biological ideas could be directly applied to human systems.

One direct input came from the growing emphasis on efficiency in social concerns. Tied to the classical free-enterprise beliefs of the nineteenth century, efficiency gained intellectual support from the work of Malthus and of Spencer, with the idea of the survival of the

*This term appears in a very polemical paper by the authors cited. Similar terms have been employed by others in discussing modern psychometric psychology. These include capitalist paradigm, used by Riegel (1972, 1973); additive paradigm, used by Overton (1973); and psychometric consensus, used by Roth (1974).

fittest. Corresponding to the rise of scientific management in the industrial sector, testing was seen as a manner of quickly and concisely fitting one into the proper place in a complex and meritocratic social world (Callahan 1962; Buss 1976). Since a prime aspect of bureaucracy, and by extension, industrial society, is hierarchy (Weber 1946), a capitalist world view influenced the development of the ideas of both differentiation and worth (Riegel 1972, 1973). Differentiation became strikingly important to psychologists because the multitude of positions important for industrial output required such strikingly different skills. A quick and ready method of discovering the distributions of the various skills had a ready market. This is why the testing movement was so closely related to the eugenics movement (for example, MacKenzie 1976, p. 500). It was felt that mental testing also would be the quick and ready manner of determining who should breed. What was required was a simple indicator of a person's worth.

The Commitment to Simple Indicators

Granting the existence of this meritocratic view of society, the issue of the choice of measures remains to be investigated. If one wishes to place people in their proper societal slots, one obviously must first know where they best fit. But why did the early testers settle upon what are essentially quizzes for making such determinations? The fact that such a question is necessary at all indicates the strength of the testing movement at this time. So potent is it that a questioning aimed at paper-and-pencil testing is sometimes seen as an insult. In debate, this writer has been told (rather scathingly) that testing developed as a purely empirical attempt to see if tests could predict future performance. Likewise, the eminent psychologist Lee Cronbach (1975) has stated that testing developed as purely impartial scientific research. However, such responses leave the genesis of testing clouded in mystery.

The truth of the matter, as mentioned, is that a commitment to something akin to simple mental measurement developed long before any pragmatic usefulness of such measures had been demonstrated. The two common themes of the meritocracy idea operate here: measurements would be simple and they would be socially important.

Recall the development of cranial indicators in the early nineteenth century. At the time of early craniometry, two quite different traditions of research existed. The phrenological approach of Gall and Spurzheim considered the relationship of the brain to behavior to be complex. Thus, people could be qualitatively different in their brain patterns. According to David Krech (1962), "the immediate reaction of the scientific world to Gall's doctrine . . . was ridicule and abuse" (p. 34). However, the simpler measures of the brain (for example, cranial capacity, facial angle, and cephalic index) faced no such fate. The facial angle had a history that traced to Aristotle (Haller 1971, p. 9), and when Petras Camper reintroduced it in 1794, it was granted a cordial welcome. As mentioned earlier, the cephalic index and cranial capacity were so well thought of as measures that they continued to be used into the twentieth century, and to this day one occasionally encounters debates about the relationship of cranial capacity to intellect (for example, Tobias 1970). These simple measures of the head became immensely popular because they joined a number of important elements in nineteenth-century social thought.

First, simple indexes like the facial angle ranked people in a simple scalar arrangement, thus recapitulating both the Chain-of-Being idea and Descartes's belief in the "unity of spirit" (Krech 1962). Second, the chain idea applied not merely to mankind but to all of nature. It thus followed that facial angles could be applied to all animals. When this was done, a continuing decline of the angle became apparent. Here, apparently, was a law of all nature: superior beings had greater angles. This is demonstrated in Figure 4.

Third, the eighteenth and nineteenth centuries witnessed an explosion of interest concerning the brain as the seat of the mind. When measured in terms of the scaler indicators of the time, brain size (and, recalling Spencer, brain function), came to be seen as the criterion by which the secular chain was to be determined. Recalling that reason had, since Plato, been considered the highest of faculties, the interest in this particular faculty becomes self-evident: the correlates of reason would be the differentiators of peoples. In the nineteenth-century context, facial angle, position on the chain, and degree of intellect came to be synonymous.

Finally, the various cranial indicators employed by nineteenth-century researchers appeared to favor Anglo-American elites, thus justifying their station in life. To this end, schoolchildren were required to memorize both the characteristics of various races and their accepted places in the racial hierarchy. School books were explicit in the assignment of a superior position to whites and an inferior position to blacks (Elson 1975). Few could fail to be impressed by the economy with which beliefs in the secular scale of creation, the role of the brain in behavior (especially academic), the nature of human faculties, and the fact of human social stratification were joined in a single measure. This was especially the case when we consider that the social science of the day was largely the search for simple universal laws of society, as represented by Quetelet's social physics. Here, indeed, was a model for future conceptualization and empirical undertakings.

During the nineteenth century, the interest in simple indicators grew, but the indicator of choice gradually ceased to be any sort of

FIGURE 4

The Facial Angles of Various Human Races and Various Species
of Animals

Source: Ranson Dexter, "The Facial Angle," Popular Science
Monthly (1874).

direct physiological characteristic; and, instead, the relative standing on a written test became the indicator of choice. This was a great
change, for while written examinations had been employed by the
Chinese civil service over 4,000 years ago (Dubois 1966), and the
ancient Greeks had used testing as an adjunct to education (Doyle
1974), testing in the Western world had, until then, not followed those
earlier trends. Yet, apparently, European universities from the
Middle Ages onward had relied on formal exams in awarding degrees
and honors (Anastasi 1968, p. 5).

Here, we come upon a clue to why written tests came to be seen
as the most efficient ways of determining the quantity of one's intelligence. In that era one of the great markers of class was literacy,
and the elite members of society, aside from the hereditary royalty,
were the rare men of letters. When Galton wrote about hereditary
genius, he included only those categories of human achievement that

were associated with literate people. In their battles with the church over the issues of the day, those struggling to promulgate a secular view of the world relied on reason to rule the day, and this use of reason was demonstrated most clearly in closely worded written statements. When one compared the literate with the mob, it became clear that the degree of literacy to which one might aspire would serve as an index to his or her intelligence.

Thus, by 1869, Galton employed scores on exams for Cambridge's "senior Wranglers" (in mathematics) and for "senior classics" (in literature) in order to demonstrate the normal distribution of ability. Those who did well on these tests represented the brightest of the literate elite's children. In the same work, he used the distribution of scores on job tests, published in newspapers, in order to make the same points. Later, he would employ anthropomorphic tests in his early laboratory, but the reliance on written tests would remain to some extent. Then, when Binet and Simon produced their successful intelligence test, the test was in the form of a school exam because the two wished to make inferences about the chances of school achievement for the individual child.

Pragmatic Social Concerns of the Early Testers

While both general social concerns and the products of earlier intellectual endeavors played roles in the development of testing, those roles were mediated by the purposes of the early testers themselves. Those people worked within a general intellectual context, but they had specific ends in mind, which indeed required some specification. While discussion of such a specification will overlap with the content of the next two chapters to some extent, a brief look at the purposes of testers is still useful.

The general view of human intellectual functioning that came to a culmination toward the end of the nineteenth century led to certain beliefs regarding the measurement of the phenomenon. First, there should be strong associations among various mental measures, and between the measures and both independent estimates of brightness and such indicators of social success as income. Second (related to the first belief), mental measurements, indicators of success, and estimates of brightness should be related because they were all connected to a single underlying phenomenon. A simple isomorphism was considered to exist. Whatever caused one to do well on tests likewise caused success in the social world. This was not a hypothesis capable of being disproved in the normal sense. The common linkage was taken for granted long before tests were actually developed, and early testers were not as interested in developing a theory of intellectual functioning as they were in developing practical applications of what they already knew to exist. In the writings of these researchers, at least three areas of application appear.

The first application was in the determination of mental subnormality—the early detection of those who would eventually require treatment or special training programs. The second, related to the first, was in the efficient classification of people for placement in school settings. As mentioned earlier, this second general application stemmed from a Western interest in efficiency of operations, which grew with the enormous industrial growth of Western Europe and the United States in the closing decades of the century, and which drew its intellectual justification from economic Darwinism (where fittest was translated as most efficient). The third application was in political action, which will be discussed below.

This is not to say that no social factors other than race or class differentiation could lead people to attempt estimates of degrees of mental powers. Indeed, nineteenth-century pioneering works to this end included those of both Esquirol (1838) and Seguin (1966), who were specifically interested in mental retardation as a medical problem. Esquirol, who first noted the malady now known as Down's Syndrome, employed language use as a criterion of intellectual level, and noted degrees of retardation. * Seguin developed a sense-training and muscle-training treatment for retardation that is, to some extent, still used. Some of the late-nineteenth-century testers were also at least partially interested in the detection and treatment of mental retardation. Among these were de Sanctis (cited in Guilford 1967), Guicciardi and Ferrari (1896), and Binet (Binet and Simon 1905b).

Still, the issue of broader differences was clearly a major force. For example, in 1890, in the first article ever to use the term mental tests, Cattell tied the development of testing to practical use in training. Galton appended several comments to the article, nowhere disagreeing with his protege (see Cattell 1890; Galton 1890). Binet's program of testing was developed in a climate of academic efficiency. He was commissioned to find a way to determine which pupils would not perform well in the public schools. With the shift of the testing movement to the United States, issues of economic efficiency grew in emphasis. The very first sections of Terman's The Measurement of Intelligence dealt with the economic inefficiency resulting from the failure to determine the mental ability of schoolchildren. Following

---

*In the overtly racist nineteenth century, this malady came to be called Mongolism, when J. L. H. Down noted, in 1866, that sufferers had undoubtedly degenerated to a "lower" racial group. For a discussion, see Hirsch (1976).

a review of failure rates in the public schools, he concluded that "more than ten percent of the $400,000,000 annually expended in the United States for school instruction is devoted to re-teaching children what they have already been taught but have failed to learn" (Terman 1916, p. 3). Terman's solution to this vexing problem was massive use of intelligence tests, which "will ultimately result in curtailing the reproduction of feeble-mindedness and in the elimination of an enormous amount of crime, pauperism, and individual inefficiency" (Terman 1916, p. 7). * In this statement, efficiency was only one of the values of tests listed, but in later chapters Terman spelled out, at some length, the amount of money to be saved and the efficiency to be realized by large companies through the application of the tests.

The first reference to feeblemindedness in the above quotation reveals the third area of application of the tests and, therefore, underscores the political determinants of the testing movement. "Curtailing the reproduction of feeble-mindedness" is squarely a eugenic goal, one of two specifically political applications of tests, according to early testers. The other political application concerned immigration restriction, which in itself was seen as a eugenic practice (Karier 1976). In the United States the two were related aspects of a great racial hysteria that manifested itself most strongly in the early decades of the century, and that had its most explicit expression in Madison Grant's (1916) The Passing of the Great Race (see, for example, Higham 1971, pp. 250-52; Handlin 1957, chaps. 5-6).

As mentioned, almost all of the early testers in the United States were confirmed eugenicists and antiimmigrationists. Terman was instrumental in the passage of California's initial eugenics sterilization law—quite an accomplishment, given that as late as 1916 he was complaining that "there is no possibility at present of convincing society that [feebleminded Indians, Mexicans, and Negroes] should be allowed to reproduce" (Terman 1916, pp. 91-92).

Testing, then, did not develop in a social vacuum. Instead, it developed in the context of a set of widely shared beliefs in a hierarchy that had implications both for scientific conceptualization and for political practice. So many elements in social thought were linked to

---

*The first chapter of Terman's 1916 work shows astonishing similarities to Jensen's 1969 article, including comparisons of educational psychology with engineering (Terman 1916, pp. 4-5); a differentiation between intelligence and rote-learning ability (Terman 1916, p. 5; this corresponds to Jensen's Level I and Level II intelligence); and an assessment of compensatory education as having failed (Terman 1916, p. 3). The relationship of ideas is so direct as to almost make Jensen's article a restatement of Terman's ideas.

this general conceptualization that its denial would have been shatter-ing. Tests would justify the Zeitgeist or would show nothing. The 1890s were ripe for a testing movement, and proponents of the tests had utopian visions. So important did the tests already seem, that at least two committees were set up in the United States (one in the American Psychological Association [APA] and one in the American Association for the Advancement of Science [AAAS]) in the early 1890s to coordinate work on psychological tests (Peterson 1925, pp. 93-94). Yet by the early 1900s the testing movement had waned, a fact that, ironically, followed from the strength of the commitment to a simple meritocratic view of society.

Commitments and the Reaction to Anomalies

The decline of the early testing movement corresponded to an inability on the part of researchers to either demonstrate the fact of mental hierarchies or show a relationship between test scores and achievement. At the time of Cattell's article (1890), in which he in-troduced the term mental tests, numerous attempts were made to find correlates among tests, and between tests and such phenomena as school performance, almost inevitably with meager results. A re-view of some of the more widely cited studies follows:

In 1895, A. Oehrn investigated interrelationships among various tests (including counting letters, crossing letters, proofreading, memory, simple association, and a number of motor tasks), without discovering a common source of variance. * T. L. Bolton (1892), using data supplied by Boas, found little relationship between tests of mem-ory span and teachers' estimates of the intelligence of pupils. J. A. Gilbert (1894), working in the Yale psychological laboratory, found little or no relationship between teachers' ratings of intelligence and measures of "reaction time, simple memory, and various types of sensory discrimination." In Germany, Ebbinghaus (1897) gave tests of arithmetic computation, memory span, and sentence completion to children. Here, the latter test correlated with scholastic achievement, but the others did not.

Where relationships were found in the early years, they tended to be ephemeral. In one widely cited study, Stella Sharp (1899) found little consistency among schoolchildren as they moved from test to

---

*Freeman (1926, p. 53) stated that Spearman and Kruger later calculated correlations among the scores and found that a range of between 0.44 and 0.69 obtained "aside from the cases in which no cor-relation was found."

test, Likewise, Carl Seashore (1899) found no correlation between estimates of brightness and tests of keenness of hearing, discrimination of pitch, and time memory. * The next year, Binet (1900) compared children judged as bright with those judged as dull, on a wide array of tasks. This study requires more thorough discussion because it underscores both the atheoretical shotgun approach to the study of mental processes that marked the times, and the meagerness of the results obtained.

Binet compared the children on nine types of tests. First, there were three forms of tactual discrimination. On the first form, bright children excelled, but on the third form, after practice, Binet found little difference between the groups. Second, Binet studied reaction times, on which there was little difference between the groups. Third, he had the children count small points spaced closely together, and obtained small-to-nonexistent differences. Fourth, he had the children note the change in the rate of a beater, and found that the dull children excelled. (Binet rationalized that the bright children must paid no attention to the instructions given here.) Fifth, while bright children proved better at counting the beats of a metronome, dull children improved more with practice. Sixth, bright children were better at copying printed material. Seventh, they were also better at reproducing letters or numbers from memory. Eighth, they were also better at crossing A's in sentences, though the speed in hunting the A's did not differentiate the groups. Finally, Binet found no difference in the rate of reading and copying sentences. In all, there was a mix of results, the sum of which did not seem to offer a simple means of empirically determining those who would be considered dull.

As early as 1895, Binet had criticized the use of sensory tests in the determination of intelligence (Binet and Henri 1895). Here, however, he returned to some of those same sensory tests. His early criticism stemmed from a developing commitment to use more mental tests in opposition to the nonmental tests used by Galton and his followers. Binet's desire for prediction, however, outweighed his theoretical commitments, and at one time he even turned to cephalometry and palmistry in the search for correlates of brightness (Anastasi 1968, p. 10). Binet was ultimately to abandon theory almost altogether in his development of tests, a fact that reflects a basic discrepancy between testing as a scientific activity and testing as a pragmatic decision-making activity. This point will be discussed at greater length below.

---

*Freeman (1926, p. 41) reported that Spearman later recalculated Seashore's data by "a more elaborate method" probably correcting for unreliability), and in so doing, discovered a correlation of 0.20 between pitch discrimination and brightness.

No breakthroughs followed immediately from this study. Perhaps the strongest result to emerge in the next few years was W. C. Bagley's (1901) anomalous finding of a negative correlation between motor ability and class standing, a finding that has never been replicated and that has been ascribed to an artifact in Baglet's research design (Freeman 1926, pp. 41-43).

A final study, which proved a staggering blow to the testing movement, was performed by Clark Wissler (1901) at the Columbia University laboratories, then under the direction of Cattell. Wissler employed 21 different tests, an elaboration of the list of tests suggested by Cattell a decade previously. He then used Pearson's new method of correlation to determine the relationships among psychological tests, anthropometric measures, and college grades. The results were so dismal that they directly caused Cattell to end his own involvement with testing (Sokal 1972, chap. 7).

While grades in college courses tended to correlate with one another (with correlations ranging from 0.11 to 0.75), Wissler found very little relationship between physiological or psychological measures and grades. What is more, correlations among the various psychological tests were themselves vanishingly small, ranging from -0.28 to 0.39, with most in the range of plus or minus 0.20. Wissler considered this "little more than a mere chance variation."

It was with the Wissler study that testing entered its period of decline. R. D. Tuddenham (1962, p. 478) reports that by 1905 the academic movement was "moribund," so much so that Binet's later work almost did not revive it. The movement waned as a result of a decade of failure to discover important hierarchical mental differences. The negative findings of Sharp and Wissler are commonly cited as the crushing blows to the movement (for example, Peterson 1925, chap. 6; Tuddenham 1962, pp. 478-81), but their studies can better be seen as the culmination of a long line of studies that hardly ever produced the kinds of results expected. Be that as it may, the enthusiasm of testers declined markedly after 1901.

This simple decline of enthusiasm was one of three possible alternatives to anomalous findings. One might otherwise have continued research, in hopes of ultimately demonstrating the strength of one's theoretical position, or have capitulated to a rival view. The first of these alternatives was indeed followed for a decade before finally being abandoned. The second was unlikely, given that no rival position seemed viable. The hypothesis that underlying mental differences are not related to one another or to achievement (or to mental tests) could not be accepted without calling into question the concept of a hierarchy, which was central to the intellectual milieu of the day. Hence, testing simply declined.

Consider the potential effects of the results of the first decade of testing if the tests in fact had been merely neutral attempts at developing empirical generalizations, as so many psychometricians claim they were. First, human mental functioning would have come to be considered multifactorial, as consisting of some large number of independent functions. Second, school achievement (and judgments of brightness) could have come to be considered largely independent of purely mental traits. Other, perhaps social, determinants of school success would have had to be postulated. Third, the assumptions of a racial hierarchy and of meritocratic achievement would have required new scrutiny. These, largely, did not occur. The general assumptions remained, while the scientific activity was allowed to lag.

Ultimately, Binet and Simon demonstrated that it was possible to construct intelligence scales, and this demonstration saved the movement. Binet's accomplishment was hailed as a success because it appeared to rank people objectively in a hierarchy, and because it discriminated those who were normal students from those who were not (though the strength of the discrimination was never tested by Binet). The way Binet went about constructing his scales gives important clues about his tacit assumptions of hierarchy and meritocracy. In fact, these assumptions were built into his scales. An analysis of this appears in the next section.

Binet and the Development of Mental Tests

Binet's Assumption of a Hierarchy

In reading Binet's work, what we find is a conceptual problem very similar to that that marked Galton's work. On the one hand, he performed work that showed mental operations to consist of a bewildering array of separate processes. Yet he developed into a committed hierarchist by the end of the century. Throughout the 1890s Binet engaged in intensive qualitative research on different aspects of mentality. He performed Piaget-like studies of his two daughters' differences in habitual ways of thinking. He investigated the relationships among scores on various tests, and he investigated the various attributes of chess players, dramatists, and the like (for a review, see Wolf 1973, pp. 79-138.

The term bewildering array is important, for wherever Binet turned, he found a congeries of individual differences. Even regarding an apparently simple phenomenon such as memory, Binet's biographer states that he "provided evidence that people have memories, different kinds of memory, rather than a memory" (Wolf 1973, p. 131). What Binet did not find in that decade of research was evidence of a hierarchical intelligence. Where, then, did he develop the later commitment to the view of intelligence still widely held?

Tuddenham (1962) has claimed that the French tradition in psychology led Binet to a "clinical concern with the whole individual rather than with abstracted psychological dimensions" (p. 481), and Binet's qualitative research would seem to bear this out. Moreover, the intent behind the 1905 scale would seem to have followed from this holistic, rather than a reductionistic, tradition of thought, a point to which we will return in contrasting Binet with the U.S. testers. Yet Binet was also tied to the tradition of thought that was dominated by Galton. If he ultimately ceased to believe in the explicit units of the mind advanced by the English and German psychologists after 1890, he continued to think in terms of a measurable intellect. Though its definition might remain vague, it consisted of two general processes: "first, perceiving the external world, and second, reconsidering the perceptions in memory, recasting them, pondering them" (Binet 1890, p. 582, translated by Wolf 1973, p. 83). Here, perception indicates a tie to Galton's associationism, while the list of mental manipulations depicts mentality as consisting of a linear series of activities. This is much like the linear-time-series conceptualization of problem solving popular at the time and used by John Dewey (1910), in which one ran through such steps as "seeing the problem, analyzing or structuring the problem, generating solutions, and judging and selecting one of the solutions" (Guilford 1968, p. 40).

According to his biographer, as early as 1891, Binet's stress was on what he considered a "unity that existed within any of the diverse forms of conscious-unconscious activity" (Wolf 1973, p. 74). By the mid-1890s, he was ready to criticize the use of simple sensory tests in the determination of the nature of this "unity." He and Victor Henri wrote that the principles of the associationists did not account for the full range of mental phenomena; for this reason, they intended to show "the existence of an entirely different mental operation" (Binet and Henri 1895, p. 21, translated by Peterson 1925, pp. 122-23). The use of the singular term operation, rather than its plural, indicates the commitment to a single central process.

While Binet moved toward an ever more explicitly hierarchical view of the mind, his path was not straight. For example, in his 1895 article coauthored with Henri, he offered a string-of-beads view of intelligence in which it was considered to have as many as four different characteristics; and these were just the "higher" functions that he felt required study. Even as the century drew to a close, Binet's view of intelligence retained aspects of complexity, and perhaps even a mystical teleology. He held that while simple memory, reaction time, and discrimination tests could measure the "less interesting" functions, when one came to "intelligence, what method can we use? How can we measure the richness of inspiration, the accuracy of judgement, the ingenuity of the mind?" (Binet 1898, p. 113, translated by Peterson 1925, p. 136). However, by 1905, part of the reason for developing a mental scale was the demonstration of the possibility of scale construction. And by 1909 he was so committed to such a view that he flatly stated: "The mind is unitary, despite the multiplicity of its faculties" (Binet 1909, p. 117, translated by Peterson 1925, p. 263).

Yet Binet's theory of intelligence remained essentially unformed up to his death. One reviewer of his work (Varon 1935) indicated that he gave thorough discussions of his view in the period 1908-9, but an examination of his writings shows that the later explanations were only elaborations of the themes of the 1890s works. Even in 1909, the intelligence that separated the able from the less able consisted of the following (Binet 1909):

> A faculty of knowing, which is directed toward the external world, and which labors to reconstruct it as a whole by means of the small fragments of it which are given to us. . . . Comprehension, invention, direction, and censorship [self-criticism]—intelligence is contained in these four words. [Pp. 117-18]

This is little more than a listing of attributes that are considered to mark sophisticated thought, and at that, it is marked by a strong bias toward the inductive logic of the positivist philosophers. Moreover, a faculty "which labors" is a mystical, self-motivating entity, a teleological construct in the middle of a mechanistic argument. It is very similar to Galton's treatment of genius. So amorphous was Binet's idea of intelligence that it has been taken to be more than one thing by different writers. For example, Tuddenham (1962) has stated that Binet conceived of intelligence as "a shifting complex of interrelated functions" (p. 490). According to this, Binet's "general" intelligence might be seen as a general overview of intellectual processes, a "grand average" that might be useful for certain diagnostic purposes. According to Tuddenham, it was the U.S. eugenicist Goddard who wedded the idea of a strictly unitary function to Binet's methodology. Yet, while this position may have some merit, there is enough indication of a commitment to a single central process in Binet's own words to at least bring Tuddenham's statement into question. For example, in the articles announcing their scale, Binet and Simon (1916) listed judgement (poorly defined) as the central aspect of intelligence: "Indeed, the rest of the intellectual faculties seem of little importance in comparison with judgement" (pp. 42-43).

But, be that as it may, there was no particular reason for Binet to adopt even a quasi-unitary view of intelligence, except as such a view seemed intuitively obvious to one who lived in an era of growing emphasis on meritocracy and stratification. The precise determinants of his increasing turn toward a metric linear view of intellect must remain hidden for now. The self-evident nature of relative brightness may have influenced him, and his atheoretical positivism may have caused him to consider that intellect was only important to the extent that it specifically differentiated the bright from the dull. Also, the pragmatic issue of the determination of those who would not profit from schooling played a role, as will be shown shortly. But in any event, the search for a metric scale that would separate the intelligent from the unintelligent became his central topic of research from the mid-1890s on, and it was a task that would engage him for a decade before he prevailed.

The Construction of the 1905 Intelligence Scale

The construction of his intelligence scales reveals a dual commitment on Binet's part. First, he was interested in intelligence as a theoretical problem. Second, he was interested in intelligence as a pragmatic differentiator of schoolchildren. The two are related in that the second presupposes the first. That is, in order for schoolchildren to be differentiated along an intellectual hierarchy, such a hierarchy must be already supposed to exist. Of course, other characteristics besides intelligence could be used to differentiate. It was for this reason that Binet at one time turned to palmistry and handwriting analysis. But he remained convinced that intelligence was the prime operative agency, and the 1905 scale "was directly inspired by the desire to serve the interesting cause of the education of subnormals" (Binet and Simon 1916).

This point about a relationship between theoretical and pragmatic utility, and about a confusion between the two, must be stressed. On the one hand, Binet was simply interested in the development of a practical diagnostic tool that would be used along with other tools in the evaluation and treatment of particular learning problems. But on the other hand, he operated from a belief that learning abilities could be ranked according to a simple metric scale. He was convinced that "we shall be able to determine to what degrees of the scale idiocy, imbecility, and moronity correspond" (Binet and Simon 1916, pp. 40-41). All the various types of learning abilities and disabilities were ignored. From this it appears that Binet understood mental retardation to be a one-dimensional characteristic, though he was undoubtedly aware of the different syndromes of mental disability that were widely discussed at that time. By accepting the thesis of unidimensionality, Binet was able to treat the problem of retardation as basically one of method rather than of theory. Since the concept of intelligence was never fully delineated, the confusion between the measure and the entity was easily introduced.

Binet's problem of measurement proved almost too great for him, and more than once he almost gave up. By 1898, however, his pragmatic bent began to gain some success in his search for a measure, though it should be very clearly understood that this breakthrough occurred not through the analysis of new data.

In "La Mesure en Psychologie Individuelle" (1898), following a critique of the Cattell tests and of the APA committee on testing, Binet proposed a solution to the problem of developing a mental metric. In the following quotation from his article, note the roles of his presupposition concerning the nature of intelligence and of the atheoretical positivism marking his work and allowing him to believe that facts need only speak for themselves (Binet 1898, p. 113, translated by Wolf 1973, pp. 149-50):

> I bring no precise solution; any systematic measurement
> at the present time could be constructed only by means of
> a priori ideas, which probably would not be applicable to
> the immense variety of expressions of intelligence. We
> must proceed a posteriori; after collecting some facts.
> Forced to make some prescriptions, to give some coef-
> ficients, I have had recourse to empirical and provision-
> ary procedures that have come to me while collecting ob-
> servations or putting together some experiments. I will
> "force" two categories of measures [on the diversity].
> [Emphasis added in translation.]

Thus, he would force categories upon his data. At the same time, he disclaimed a priori ideas. The ingenuous character of the above passage is instructive for our purposes, especially in light of the categories he proposed for use. Binet's first criterion of categorization was constancy of tests. That is, all people would take the same tests in the same order—this is standardization of procedures. The second criterion was progressive difficulty. That is, tests would be grouped according to the number of subjects who successfully completed items. Implicit in this (a point that would become explicit in 1900) was the idea that only tests that discriminated those children who were judged to be generally bright, intellectually, from those judged dull would be maintained. The rest would be discarded.

The first criterion's usefulness depends upon one's purposes. Standardization of the test environment is absolutely essential if one is to maintain comparability of data. Any changes in test procedures, or in the choice of tests used, would decrease comparability. Now, were Binet solely interested in studies of differences in performance under strictly standardized conditions, then his stress on standardization would be exemplary. However, he was explicitly interested

in determining the competence of children for reference to nonstan-
dardized, everyday-life situations. His idea of the "unity of mind"
acted to make it seem obvious that differentiation in a rigidly controlled
and narrowly defined test situation would have direct relevance to a
broad range of activities. But if behavior were that homogeneous,
then it is unclear how standardization could make the tests much more
useful than a set of off-the-cuff measures of performance in any of a
number of different activities. The subtle confusion between testing
as a science and testing as a pragmatic activity appears here.

The second categorization criterion is much more immediately
important. The prescription to use tests that were graduated (and
that differentiated the bright from the dull) both presupposed a one-
dimensional intelligence and guaranteed that one would appear when
tests were employed. Since Binet considered tests to be pragmatic
diagnostic tools, there is no necessary problem with this (although,
again, it implicitly introduces the idea that behavior is homogeneous;
therefore the tests were not fully pragmatic). However, as regards
the use of tests as investigators of the nature of intellect, this prescription allowed Binet to disregard a primary canon of science: it
allowed him to exclude data that did not support the idea of a general
or one-dimensional intelligence. Since his own research had tended
to support a more multifaceted view of intelligence, this prescription
allowed him to force nature to obey the investigator. The confusion
between the two uses of tests enters again, for Binet and Simon (as
we have already seen) were convinced that their instruments measured intelligence and provided "a classification, a hierarchy among
diverse intelligences" (Binet and Simon 1916, pp. 40-41). Recall that
even various forms of retardation were to be represented by places
on the scale, a fact that exists to some extent to this day.

In their critique of other research on intelligence, Binet and
Simon (1916, p. 13) employed three specific criticisms. First, they
felt many researchers were simply ignorant of the phenomena in
question. Second, they noted that a great variability existed in the
terms used to describe maladies. Third, they noted a "lack of precision in the description of symptoms which reveal or which constitute a certain particular malady." Their third point is particularly
interesting, for the development of the mental scale was intended to
give precision to the terms used. Moronity, imbecility, and idiocy
would correspond to places on the scale and would find meaning in
terms of the scale itself. Thus, as noted earlier, greater or smaller
relationships were stressed.

Yet, while Binet and Simon recognized that "different physicians
do not examine the same patient in the same manner and do not give
the symptoms the same importance," they nowhere indicated recognition of the fact that the small typology of mental retardation that they

themselves employed might mask a large number of different symptoms. The idea of the scale guided their conceptions of retardation, and their commitment to this typological mode of analysis precluded the investigation of other forms of differences. In fact, it would be over two decades before retardation would be generally admitted to consist of a large number of different syndromes (for example, Fernald 1924; Goodard 1928).

Two years after his article appeared in which he described the categories that he would force on his data, Binet (1900) compared the test performances of the 5 most intelligent pupils and the 6 least intelligent from a class of 32. Discussed earlier, this study was one of those that cast doubt on the pragmatic usefulness of testing. Recall that on some tests the so-called bright children excelled; on some the differences were small to nonexistent; and on a few the dull children actually excelled. Finally, on some tests an initial advantage for the bright children narrowed after practice. Binet's response to this was that those tests that did not discriminate in favor of the bright children were poor tests, while those tests that did discriminate were good (for example, see Peterson 1925, pp. 142-43). *

To recapitulate the argument to this point, several phenomena were occurring simultaneously. First, there was a growing supposition on Binet's part of a unity of intelligence. Second, there was the development of a methodology that, if followed, would force the data thereby obtained into a linear arrangement. Third, there was a philosophical stance that allowed Binet to suppose that he had let facts lead him. Fourth, there was the existence of a subtle confusion between two different uses of tests. To the extent that Binet felt his scales to be instruments for measuring intelligence, we have a fifth occurrence. This was Binet's supposition that correlation indicates commonality. That is, those tests that correlated with a criterion were seen as measuring the same thing.

Despite all of this, the actual development of an intelligence scale eluded Binet for another half decade. As late as the First German Conference for Experimental Psychology, in 1904, Henri expressed disappointment at the meagerness of results up to that time. According to Spearman's (1904b) report on the conference:

> Henri enumerated the various tests that they had used for
> this purpose, following the pattern of the 1896 program;

---

*Interestingly, while Binet was clearly looking for an individual diagnostic technique, he concluded the paper by stating that group, rather than individual, differences could be determined by the successful tests. See Binet (1900) and Wolf (1973, p. 153).

all, however, had proved unsatisfactory, and now they
could only recommend long systematic investigations of
each person studied. [P. 448; see also, Wolf 1973, p.
140.]

This report came only 13 months before the publication of the articles
announcing the 1905 intelligence scale.

Obviously, Binet did not entirely give up in his quest for an intelligence scale, and when the French minister of public education ap-
pointed a commission (of which Binet was a member) to find a method
for identifying the subnormal children in school, there appeared "an
immediate and definite goal to Binet's work" (Varon 1935, p. 78).
Operating within the Galton framework of important individual differences, he assumed "without hesitation that the difference is one of
intelligence," even though he had "only a general idea of what he meant
by intelligence" (Varon 1935, pp. 78-81).

It is well known how Binet succeeded at this next attempt at
scale construction. He and Simon (Binet and Simon 1905b, 1908;
Binet 1911) developed a scale made from 30 subtests that crudely
ranked children. They added an age criterion to their procedures,
excluding tests that did not discriminate children by age. Finally,
they revised the scale twice, but in all of this, their definition of intelligence never went beyond that general speculation that has already
been discussed.

It must be stressed that this critique of Binet's work is not proffered in order to tag him as a bad scientist. To a considerable extent, the reverse is true. The critique is offered only to indicate that
he was inconsistent with regard to the relationship between what he
did and what he said he did. He claimed (and apparently believed) that
he let facts lead him. However, as this chapter shows, he actually
led the facts in his development of the scales. Disregarding this one
point, his work was truly exemplary. It was probably all but impossible for a researcher operating in the period 1890-1905 to consider
important mental differences to be anything but scalar. Accepting
this scalar view as central in psychological thought at that time, Binet
accomplished what numerous others had failed to do: he showed the
existence of an objectively determined scale. The role of presuppo-
sitions in scientific thought and methods finds a strong example here.

It can hardly be disputed that the Binet-Simon intelligence scales
came to be exemplars for future research, for the reasons cited above.
What Binet and Simon accomplished was the construction of a measuring instrument that (however crudely) ranked children in a hierarchy.
Later, it would be shown that one's position on the scale correlated,
to a moderate degree, with the grades one made in school. For the
limited aim of the detection of subnormals, the scale succeeded to an

extent that other series of tests had not even approximated. It was because the scale ranked people in an apparently objective manner that it was considered such a success.

While (as noted) there is some room for dispute over Binet's ultimate conception of intelligence, that conception became relatively unimportant. Once the tests had been transported to the United States, they were wedded to a strictly unitary view of intelligence. The tests were employed because they gave legitimacy to this position by virtue of the fact that they did rank people in intelligence. The pragmatic aspects of the tests came to be neglected as researchers came to employ the tests in their search for the core of merit that they knew to exist, while Binet's theoretical position was ignored. What was left was a methodology that was followed explicitly. Goddard patterned his tests directly on Binet's. Terman, who had ended an association with testing around 1905, was persuaded to renew work on it after the publication of the 1908 Binet-Simon revision, and his Stanford-Binet test was modeled closely on Binet's. Collectively, the tests were even called Binet tests. After Binet's death, IQ was given strong emphasis by Terman, and it acquired an aura of precision by which it appeared to place individuals in specified places in a hierarchy, no matter what their ages.

Now that the general ideas about the nature of intelligence had been given concrete form by means of Binet's tests, the testing movement could flourish again. No longer would mere speculation prevail. What was required now was the marshaling of evidence as to the role of this general intelligence in society.

7

HIERARCHICAL THOUGHT AND IQ

In the preceding chapter it was shown that a commitment to a poorly defined unitary intelligence developed in the absence of strong evidence for a unitary intelligence. Certainly, the evidence at that time was no more impressive than it is today, except for the brief period when Spearman's factor analysis seemed to demonstrate a general intelligence. Yet the belief in some sort of general entity was strong, at least in the context of discussions of social-policy issues.

In coming to understand the belief in a general intelligence, which appears to rule today, we must first analyze the expressed beliefs of the pioneers of testing, and we must see the way in which certain views of intellect came to be institutionalized in psychology. In this chapter we will first look at the beliefs of the early testers. It will be shown that major representatives of the testing movement (especially Terman, Thorndike, and Peterson) shared the dualistic view of intelligence that had marked the work of Galton and Binet. That is, they were aware of problems that beset a view of intelligence as being a general or unitary entity, but in the analysis of human problems they were ruled by the general idea that people may be readily stratified in terms of just an intelligence. The ways in which this inconsistency manifested itself will be shown.

Following this, it will be argued that the ultimate commitment to a single-value view of intelligence was part of a general phenomenon that swept science in the first part of the present century. This phenomenon made it extremely simple to assume that a unit score would give the major information needed for any given area of study. The chapter will focus on the views of early Binet-type testers regarding the general nature of intelligence. The more general belief in meritocracy will be mentioned only tangentially, in order to give context to the major topic of the chapter. This belief in a general merit will be discussed more fully in the following chapter. This is because the idea of merit is more closely associated with the issue of the social importance of intelligence, rather than merely with the structure of the entity.

Finally, the institutionalization of mental testing will be discussed. Here, it will be argued that the idea of a hierarchical ranking of people came to be ensconced in major textbooks written by the already mentioned major testers, and that those figures gained public support for their enterprise. In this manner, the idea of a hierarchy came to be presented to incoming psychology students as standard portions of their undergraduate and graduate educations. It thus became part of a well-developed tradition of research and therefore became all but impregnable to criticism.

EARLY TESTERS AND THE BINET TESTS

Three of the earliest major U.S. users of Binet-type tests were H. H. Goddard, Frederick Kuhlmann, and Lewis Terman, all of whom had studied under G. Stanley Hall at Clark University. Of these three, Goddard first translated and used the tests, and Terman developed the first true U.S. revision of the tests. The first test to compete with the Terman tests was developed by Robert M. Yerkes, who headed the massive army testing program during World War I. Finally, the first researcher to attempt to ascertain the importance of intelligence for nonacademic concerns was Edward Lee Thorndike, perhaps the leading theoretical educational psychologist in the United States for a period of 40 years. The views of Goddard, Terman, and Thorndike are especially interesting, since they had quite different theoretical positions but advocated similar social applications for the tests.

H. H. Goddard

Tuddenham (1962, p. 490) has stated that Goddard was responsible for the joining of Spearman's view of intelligence with Binet's tests. Whether this is completely true or not, it is definitely the case that Goddard's view of intelligence was very close to the view held by Spearman. In fact, Goddard reified the general-intelligence concept and presented intelligence as a unit character. Thus, he noted (1920):

> The chief determiner of human conduct is a unitary mental process which we call intelligence: . . . this process is conditioned by a nervous mechanism which is inborn; . . . the degree of efficiency to be attained by that nervous mechanism and the consequent grade of intelligence or mental level [are genetically inherited]. [P. 1]

Intelligence was a single thing, a process that involved a specific mechanism, which itself was a simple product of heredity. The mechanism could be rated by its degree of efficiency of operation, and the product of that operation was measured by its level or grade. The line from the chromosomes to the unit character is direct, and today the whole presentation seems somewhat simplistic. Yet it was the view of the first of the U.S. Binet testers, and it carried weight.

Goddard's position would undergo some changes over time, and by the late 1920s he would concede that mental retardation was a complex phenomenon, but by then more complex positions were in vogue. Especially important was the position of Terman, whose Stanford-Binet test was for 40 years the meter bar by which other tests were judged.

Lewis Terman

Terman's view is interesting because it did not necessarily support a hierarchical view of intelligence. Yet Terman spoke, almost without exception, in hierarchical terms.

In an article written a year after the publication of Binet's 1905 scale, Terman (1906) discussed a variety of tests he had given to seven bright boys and seven stupid ones. Like Binet, he found that not all tests discriminated the two groups of boys. In particular, tests of creative potential did not discriminate well. For the purposes of this study, what is interesting is that Terman decided to drop these tests from consideration, on the grounds that their correlations with other tests were low. Guilford (1968, p. 138) holds that it was Terman's pragmatic exclusion of test items that did not fit neatly on a scale that set the trend for future intelligence research in the United States. However, Binet had already used this tactic in France, and as we shall see, it was done elsewhere also.

Following his 1906 article, Terman withdrew from testing, but after the 1908 Binet-Simon revision, he was persuaded to reenter the field. After a series of articles, and the revision of Binet-type tests for the U.S. market, he made his most comprehensive statement on intelligence in his 1916 work, The Measurement of Intelligence. Here, Terman made various allusions to Binet's work, but ultimately provided the rationale for a simple mental metric.

Terman was aware of arguments for a multiplicity of mental functions, but praised Binet for having abandoned a multifaceted approach to the subject: "After many vain attempts to disentangle the various intellective functions, Binet decided to test their combined functional capacity without any pretense of measuring the exact contributions of each to the total product" (Terman 1916, p. 43). Of course, as we have seen, Binet did no such thing. To the extent that Binet wished to develop a diagnostic tool, he merely searched for a simple differentiator. Nowhere did he attempt to combine any specific group of mental functions, and he did not much care what he used to arrive at the differentiation, as long as he succeeded. That was why he tried palmistry, handwriting analysis, and craniometry in his early attempts at measurement. However, Terman's mention of "functional capacity" gives an indication of his own beliefs. He praised Binet for having undertaken "to ascertain the general level of intelligence" (Terman 1916, p. 43). Both capacity and level indicate quantity, in a metric sense. Thus, for Terman, one's intelligence might be multifaceted, but it could ultimately be summated. It had the characteristics of a metric scale. After that, Terman followed Stern (1904) in using the intelligence quotient in order to give precision to the hierarchical arrangement of persons.

In the United States, the aura of precision indeed took hold. As Brian MacKenzie (1976) has pointed out, psychology in the early part of the century had a strongly positivistic orientation, and modeled itself upon the physics of the time. For this reason, psychology's methodology rapidly became "restricted and codified" in terms of unit characters, which, it was felt, would be shown to follow simple physicslike laws. IQ was just such an entity. It rapidly came to be seen, and used, as the unit measure of intelligence. With the publication of The Measurement of Intelligence, IQ and intelligence came to be considered coequal and were regularly used interchangeably.

With respect to social stratification, it was well known that some people were bright and others were dull, and if the tests were not perfect, they at least tapped what was important in human affairs. Terman vacillated both between assessments of intelligence as a unitary and as a multiple thing, and between assessments of the tests as being crude and as being powerful. Thus, in several places he admitted the limitations of the Stanford–Binet test; he admitted that it was not designed to tap those attributes that led to success in specific fields, and that they could not act as a "detailed chart for the vocational guidance of children." But he continued to claim that they were "capable of bounding roughly the vocational territory in which an individual's intelligence will probably permit success" (Terman 1916, p. 49). And he used the scores in order to call for eugenic sterilizations. This dualistic treatment of intelligence and intelligence tests allowed him to accept the reality of a multiplicity of abilities without his simultaneously having to give up his belief in a hierarchy.

In this context, it is easy to see how Terman, in a single article, could state the following: first, that "recent criticism of current test methods on the grounds that these methods are usually based on the assumption that general intelligence can be expressed as a linear or one-dimensional function, was antedated some fifteen years ago by . . . Binet" (Terman 1921, p. 130); and then (1921):

> One may, of course, question our grounds for designating any kind of mental activity as "higher" or "lower" than another. Why, it may be asked, should certain types of mental processes be singled out for special worship? . . . The implication is that . . . two individuals differ merely in having different kinds of intelligence, neither of which is higher or better than the other.
>
> It is difficult to argue with anyone whose sense of psychological values is disturbed to this extent. . . .
>
> Many criticisms of the current methods of testing intelligence rest plainly on a psychology which fails to distinguish the levels of intellectual functioning or to assign to conceptual thinking the place that belongs to it in the hierarchy of intelligences. [Pp. 128-29]

In these two quotations, general intelligence is not strictly linear or one-dimensional, but it is expressed by levels. People are to be ranked as clearly higher or lower. Further, one specific attribute (conceptual thinking) is clearly seen as superior to other types of attributes, each of which is to stand as an intelligence. Terman's choice of the word values in the second paragraph (of the second quotation) is odd, for it suggests that the ranking of intelligence is to be a normative affair, while the rest of the quotation suggests that the discussion of intelligence is to be analytical. It takes an inferential leap to believe that this marks an acknowledgment on Terman's part that the use of intelligence tests in 1921 rested on a set of value assumptions rather than on purely empirical criteria. Yet such was the case, whether Terman recognized it or not. For him, the tests tapped some overriding aspect of psychoneural functioning that was superior to other human mental attributes. Ultimately, this attribute was so important that, even though he might admit that the tests were only crude devices, his educational and eugenic stands would be made largely on the basis of test scores. Finally, with the introduction of the intelligence quotient, the scores came to have at least an aura of precision in ranking; with this, any disclaimers regarding the nature of the entity in question became fully inconsistent with actual uses of the tests. Test scores were only interesting, or of social use, to the extent that they did treat people as differing in terms of a metric quantity.

Edward Lee Thorndike

Thorndike's position was as much removed from Terman's as the latter's was from Goddard's. Thorndike's statements reveal very

clearly the disjuncture that existed between discussions of the nature
of intelligence and discussions of individual and group differences in
the entity.

As early as 1902, Thorndike openly doubted the possibility of
the existence of a single, unitary intelligence (Aikins, Thorndike, and
Hubbell 1902):

> Any consideration of the nervous basis of mental life or the
> facts of human nature suggests a priori that it is more ra-
> tional to look on the mind as a multitude of particular ca-
> pacities, all of which may be highly independent of each
> other. [P. 374]

However, Thorndike was a lifelong eugenicist who ultimately saw a
strong correlation among those characteristics important in the social
world. Sometimes his statements on the connection of traits were of
the type that would appear to later generations to be merely silly:
"To him that hath a superior intellect is given also on the average a
superior character" (Thorndike 1920, p. 233). But other statements
fitted so well with meritocratic thought that they still make the rounds
today: "In the actual race of life, which is not to get ahead, but to get
ahead of somebody, the chief determining factor is heredity" (Thorndike 1905).

To some extent, this latter statement merely reflects Thorndike's genetics, rather than his psychometrics. However, note how
he forced a multitude of characteristics into play in the determination
of a linear form of success. His metaphor for competition, "race of
life," implies a simple scale of ultimate merit. Thus, he might be,
in Tuddenham's (1962, p. 505) phrase, "Spearman's perennial antag-
onist" with respect to the structure of the mind, but with respect to
social stratification, he and Goddard were one.

Thorndike's inconsistency was not limited to debates over the
nature of stratification, but extended to debates over the use of intelligence tests. At times, his view stressed the multiple nature of
mental elements, but at other times he could talk about the "higher
forms" of intellectual operations, which in their "deeper nature . . .
are identical with mere association or connection-forming, depending
upon the same sort of physiological connections but requiring many
more of them" (Thorndike 1925, p. 414). This shows clear connections with the positions of Spencer and Spearman, and it allowed him
to speak in terms of the "person whose intellect is greater or higher
or better." Thorndike insisted that this did not represent a "new sort
of physiological process," but, rather, a larger number of connections than in the case of duller people.

Yet, when he criticized mental tests, Thorndike returned to something of a multiple-factor approach to intelligence (Thorndike et al. 1927):

> The only sure statement of what [a test] measures is to show the test itself and its scoring plan. . . . Nobody has ever made an inventory of tasks, determined the correlation of each with intellect, selected an adequate battery of them, and found the proper weight to attach to each of these. [P. 2]

Here, an intellect is presupposed, but various tasks may not correlate with it—an important point. Later, he was more forceful on this (Thorndike et al. 1927):

> When we say that a man is found by measurement with the Army Alpha [an early major intelligence test] to have the intellect of an average recruit in the draft, all that is really asserted is that he does as well on that particular battery of tests scored and summated in a particular way, as the average recruit did. Just what the intelligence of recruits were and how closely their Alpha scores paralleled their intellects, we do not know. The measurement is one thing, the inference to intellect is a different thing. [P. 8]

Contrast this with Thorndike's earlier indication of a clear relationship between intellect and success, in a way that mimicked the existence of a g factor. But here he firmly stated his opinion that no clear relationship existed between the activities that led to success on various tests and this quasi-g factor. What we find is a slight difference in interpretation of information, but a difference that has crucial consequences. Thorndike as the foe of Spearman was not willing to grant the existence of a central mental function, but Thorndike the eugenicist was ready to posit what is, in effect, a central mental process leading to success in the social world.

There is no way for Thorndike to be completely consistent with respect to the above statements. He might simply state that the functions sampled in an IQ test, and those sampled naturally in economic striving, do not overlap with any degree of regularity. Thus, tests would be invalid. However, implied in this position would be the idea that any specified task or set of tasks would require specified samples of functions, and Thorndike's view of a simple hierarchy along which people could be ranked would be dealt a strong blow.

Alternatively, Thorndike could posit that intellect is a combined function of innumerable attributes coming into play at different times, and that tests sample too few functions to be really useful. This seems in line with his critique of the Army Alpha cited above. However, this is in conflict with his statement on multiple bonding, which he used to justify the idea of differential intelligence. If the bonding statement is to be believed, then one should expect a superior person to excel at almost anything intellectual, including intelligence tests. Further, this second tactic would imply a social structure in which success was caused by unnumbered elements added to one another, such that success was gained in an incremental fashion. An increment of intellect would lead to an increment of success. But it was already known, at the time Thorndike wrote these statements, that the relationship between standard scores and success was not strong, and Thorndike's own research was to bear this out (Thorndike et al. 1934). Yet Thorndike went to his death espousing a simple, genetically based intellectual hierarchy.

An Overview of Beliefs among the Early Testers

What is indicated by the brief looks at the three psychologists discussed above is that the great popularizers of the tests (and Thorndike was one of these, despite his criticisms of the army tests) all believed in a simple hierarchy of intelligence, when inferences to social processes were made. Whether, like Goddard, they simply declared the existence of a unitary trait by fiat, or whether, like Thorndike, they showed clear inconsistencies in their reasoning, the agreed-upon fact is clear. Ultimately, the underlying theoretical positions were unimportant, for the consensus was that whatever intelligence was, it was measured by the tests. This form of operationalism allowed tests to be employed and allowed an implicit theory of monolithic intelligence to reign, even while the psychometric community struggled over issues of the meaning of intelligence. We will return to this point.

Once the ratio of mental age to chronological age (IQ) was accepted as the proper measure of intelligence, the monolithic view had a ready numerical referent. So potent was this commitment to IQ that the great controversy in the years surrounding World War I concerned not the nature of intelligence but the question of whether age scales or point scales were better suited to its measurement. Age scales were Binet-type scales, in which different tests were designed for each age group. A scale that was successfully completed by about two-thirds of children of a given age was considered a proper measure of ability for that age group. Point scales, developed first by Yerkes (1917; Yerkes and Foster 1923), consisted of single or multiple tests taken by people of different ages, in which, very basically, the total

points obtained were summed. Scores were then age graded. According to Yerkes (1917), "the Binet is an age scale based upon the assumption of appearing functions; the point scale is a functional scale,
based upon the assumption of developing functions" (pp. 111-12).

Note the use of the plural term functions in Yerkes's statement.
This again illustrates the inconsistency of thought caused by the conflict between theory and methodology in the development of testing.
In the same passage as that quoted above, he mentioned that "all of
the important types of intellectual function are present in early childhood," yet he was a major participant in the development and use of
the Army Alpha and Beta tests (Yerkes 1921), by whose use individuals
and (later) groups were ranked along a single scale of merit. His own
commitment to the intelligence quotient was explicit; in the discussion
of the Yerkes-Foster Point Scale, he stated that "the IQ is obtained
in the usual manner by dividing mental by chronological age" (Yerkes
and Foster 1923, p. 8).

One point must be made here. It might not be inconsistent for
psychometricians like Terman and Yerkes to speak of something like
the total intelligence at the same time as they spoke of specific functions, under certain sets of circumstances. First, in the restricted
setting of the intelligence test, one's total score could represent one's
intelligence for that test (where intelligence was defined as test performance), as long as one did not make inferences to performance
outside the test setting. Second, if intelligence were considered to
be an additive (or perhaps a multiplicative) function of a series of
separate attributes (functions), then a survey of the attributes might
give an indication of ability over a broad spectrum of performances.
However, during the discussion in question, the additive nature of intelligence had not been demonstrated (it still has not been). Further,
as with Thorndike's critique of the army tests, there was no guarantee
that the tests in fact sampled a broad range of attributes, or that the
weighting given each was appropriate. It is common now to insist
that the tests sample a very narrow range of attributes. Finally, as
with Binet's reference to "judgement," it might be posited that a
small number of attributes are supremely important, and that only a
survey of these is necessary in assigning places in a hierarchy. But
the same criticisms hold here. In any event, the reification of IQ as
the index of intelligence occurred without evidence that it did indeed
represent what it was supposed to represent.

General Intelligence:
The Debate within the Discipline

This discussion is not intended to indicate that early psychometricians were unaware of problems in their treatment of intelli-

gence. In fact, there were so many problems visible to early practitioners that symposiums were put together in order that underlying
issues might be addressed. However, many of these discussions were
along the lines of "let's take stock and see where we go from here."
One of the first and most important symposiums on testing took place
in the March and April 1921 issues of the Journal of Educational Psychology. There, participants were asked, first, what they conceived
intelligence to be and how it could best be measured by group tests.
Second, they were asked what the most crucial next steps would be
in research.

This symposium had two major results. First, no consensus
as to the nature of intelligence emerged, though almost all participants
considered it to be essentially a unitary entity. Second, virtually
every participant urged that the methods that had been used in testing
up to that time be further employed to meet the problems that were
being faced.

Definitions of intelligence were as varied then as they had been
since the testing movement began (and as they remain to this day; see
Tuddenham 1962). One writer (Henmon 1921, p. 195) considered it
"native capacity for knowledge" plus knowledge. Peterson (1921, p.
198) considered it a biological mechanism revealed in a person's
"range of receptivity to stimuli and the consistency of his organization
of responses to them." Thurstone (1921) felt it to consist of an "in-
hibitory capacity," an "analytic capacity," and perseverance, while
another writer considered it a "capacity to acquire capacity" (Woodrow 1921, p. 208). Several writers merely mentioned an undifferentiated capacity or ability. Thorndike (1921), typically, considered it
"the power of good responses, from the point of view of truth or fact,"
while Terman (1921) considered it the ability "to carry on abstract
thinking." Other writers mirrored Peterson's belief in a mechanism
of adjustment, while one writer (Pressey 1921) announced that he was
simply not interested in the question at all.

A review of definitions of intelligence, begun in the late 1920s
(Schieffelin and Schwesinger 1930, pp. 11-12), revealed that the same
pattern of off-the-cuff statements existed at least up to 1926. The
terms power, or ability, or capacity were commonly employed. Other
definitions stressed the relative efficiency of those with high intellect,
or spoke of degrees of intelligence, and very few mentioned the possibility of a differentiated phenomenon. One writer considered it the
same thing as creativity.

That so many answers employing popular synonyms for intelligence could be given is surprising, given that testing had emerged
from its infancy by the early 1920s. That so many central figures in
the development of testing should speak in such undifferentiated and
undefined terms certainly shows the strength of the unstated assump-

tions about the meritocratic nature of human action. In fact, of all the participants in the 1921 symposium, only one (Ruml 1921) stated that the questions could not be answered, because of "the lack of precision in the terms and concepts that must form the basis for such a discussion and second, the absence of factual material on so many of the essential points" (p. 143).

Already, Binet's program for ranking schoolchildren was considered a measure of underlying capacity or ability. As will be shown in the next chapter, the problems raised in the course of research on test scores could conceivably have led to the breakdown of the whole testing program; but this was not to be. The vague conceptualizations and the methods would become institutionalized, and therefore would be passed on to students. When critical comments were made about aspects of the testing program, these assumptions were not at the heart of the criticisms.

As put (in a somewhat different context) by the anthropologist Marshall Sahlins (1976): "To be aware of something, however, to recognize it, is not the same thing as knowing the concept of it. It is not to put it in its right theoretical place" (p. 78). In this sense, full theoretical critiques of the unitary nature of test scores were seldom made. They could not be made without calling into question the basis of testing itself, the validity of group comparisons, or the meritocratic nature of the society within which testing flourished. When a psychologist compared racial or class groups, he or she tacitly accepted the existence of a stratified capacity. When one critized others' conceptions of intelligence, this critique did not extend to the question of its ultimate presence or importance. One example of this follows.

By the early 1920s, evidence was accumulating that challenged the view that intelligence constituted a metric quantity. Interrelations among higher-learning processes had been shown to be quite low (for example, Haught 1922, pp. 67-69). In the most important review of the development of testing up to that date (a work still considered a classic), Joseph Peterson (1925) admitted that "correlations among learning rates in different kinds of performance are not encouragingly high" (p. 268). Elsewhere, he admitted that "the combination of traits that make up what we call the highest intelligence in one vocation or line of endeavor is not the combination that gives the highest intelligence in another" (Peterson 1922, p. 378). Finally, he questioned the degree to which general intelligence "is a reality at all," and stated that he felt that "so far as production of group intelligence tests that will measure abilities making for success in many phases of practical life is concerned, we have not yet arrived at an entirely satisfactory solution" (Peterson 1921, p. 199).

Such critiques and queries as those presented by Peterson were met in a dualistic fashion. As statements of specific problems, they

were apparently granted polite receptions, and new work was undertaken in order to resolve them. As having real-world significance,
they were seldom recognized even by the people who made them. For
example, in the same period as the above works, Peterson published
a monograph titled <u>The Comparative Abilities of White and Negro Chil-
dren</u>. There, he concluded that "the intelligence of the negro race as
represented in America is about that which will give him an I.Q. of
approximately 0.75 to 0.80 when compared with whites" (Peterson
1923, p. 134).

It would be reasonable to suppose that Peterson would come to
doubt the social usefulness of test-score differences; but this is not
the case. Considering the case of blacks, he felt that the low average
IQ score would be a "great handicap" in competition with whites (Peterson 1923, p. 135). Further, he supported racialist conclusions
on the "practical problems regarding race differences" (Peterson
1925, p. 285).

It needs to be mentioned that Peterson was not antiblack. He
did not use his findings as support for a eugenics movement, even
though that movement was quite strong at the time he wrote. This
author has not found a mention of eugenics in any of Peterson's works.
Nor did he support "the contention by certain persons that the negro
as a class should have a different sort of education from that given
the white race" (Peterson 1923, p. 138). Further, he hedged very
slightly on the issue of innate racial differences, though he leaned
toward the hereditarian position. Finally, he was sympathetic to the
idea that the racist nature of the nation was responsible for the fact
that "the outlook for the bright and capable negro is dark, at the best"
(Peterson 1923, p. 135). Yet the lower scores of blacks were a source
of worry.

Peterson's inconsistency is apparent. While he felt that general intelligence might only be "a fiction of our thoughts" (Peterson
1922, p. 378), a hierarchical ordering was ultimately to be found in
the social realm. He was committed to the use of IQ-test scores in
the determination of that ordering, or else he would not have worried
so about the plight of low-scoring blacks. Yet, when social issues
were not at stake, he argued that psychologists were "falling into the
grave error of identifying the intelligence quotient . . . with intelligence" (Peterson 1922, p. 374), and that intelligence and ability to
learn had become conflated on the basis of very little evidence, especially considering that no one knew what that ability was.

Peterson treated the significance of unit-summary scores quite
differently in the two contexts, and he was hardly alone in this regard.
Recall the brief discussion of Thorndike, presented earlier. It seems
to have been common for major figures in the field to see little relationship between in-house discussions and occurrences in the external

world. It has been indicated here, and it will be argued at length in the following chapter, that a major source of this disjuncture was the presence of an ideology that gave to IQ scores a wealth of meaning independent of their empirical base. However, for now, trends within the scientific community will be stressed. Particularly important are the nature of science in the 1920s and the institutionalization of psychometrics.

SCALAR THOUGHT AS A GENERAL PHENOMENON

Psychometrics was not alone in its reliance on single-scale scores in the treatment of complex issues. The emerging sciences of the nineteenth and twentieth centuries relied heavily on physics as a model of all science, and to this end, practitioners attempted to develop simple, lawlike statements with which to explain the phenomena in their jurisdiction. In social science, Quetelet's social physics (see Chapter 6) was an early and major representative of this trend. Individual members of populations were treated as social atoms who varied only according to the characteristics under study. Employing this typological form of analysis, Quetelet attempted to develop strict laws of human action in which individual actions were merely representative of the actions of a class of persons. Thus, he employed the concept of the nonexistent average man, which he granted a real existence.

P. B. Medawar (1977) states that the same sort of phenomenon occurred in demography, soil geology, and economics. In demography, such writers as R. A. Fisher and A. J. Lotka devised the "Malthusian parameter," or "true rate of natural increase," as a way of measuring the degree of vitality of a nation. In an age worried about the dying out of the upper classes because of infertility, this simple index was seen as a way of determining not just the birth rate but also the vitality of a nation. In the study of soil, there were attempts to "epitomize in a single figure the field behavior of soil" (Nedawar 1977). Further, in economics the gross national product was developed and came to be seen as a "measure of national welfare, well-being, and almost . . . moral stature" (Medawar 1977), while the variety of influences on the quality of human life was neglected.

Intelligence testing, rather than standing alone, may be a special instance of this more general trend toward a model of science based on physics. In all these instances, there were attempts to discover a single underlying unity that would place all of the social (or economic or soil) world in perspective. For the community of intelligence testers, social processes ultimately were meritocratic, based upon simple comparisons of a general phenomenon that was ultimately genetic in origin. There was a straight causal line from gene frequencies to social position. Prior to the 1920s the primary variable in the social sciences was race (Haller 1968). After the 1920s, it increasingly came to be the individual, for psychometric psychology.

Closely related to the testing movement, eugenics treated people in the same typological manner as had Quetelet. Here, the attempt was to formulate a simple criterion by which one could determine who fell in the socially inadequate classes (and would thereby be subject to sterilization). A major figure here was H. H. Laughlin, who, as superintendent of the widely respected Eugenics Records Office (among whose members were C. B. Davenport, Goddard, Alexander Graham Bell, Thorndike, and Yerkes) and as coeditor of the Eugenics News, had an important role in the drafting of the compulsory-sterilization laws that several states passed in the first quarter of this century. In his influential book Eugenical Sterilization in the United States, Laughlin (1922, pp. 446–47) provided a ten-point list of those conditions that placed one in the inadequate classes. Those on this list included the feebleminded, the insane, the criminalistic, the epileptic, the diseased, the blind (including those with seriously impaired vision), the deaf (including those with seriously impaired hearing), the deformed, and the dependent (including orphans, ne'er-do-wells, the homeless, tramps, and paupers). People were placed on this list "regardless of etiology or prognosis."

This extensive list, rather than constituting a variety of human problems, was considered constitutive of the class (more strictly, the classes) requiring sterilization. The view of social action implied here is one in which the problems of a society are caused by a handful of specific, genetically related disorders whose elimination will yield social harmony. To take just one example from the list, the diverse sources and types of poor vision were lumped in a category of the blind, whose members, apparently, would be treated identically. It is not difficult to see how psychometrics, which dealt with the category of the feebleminded should treat that collection of disorders as one.

THE INSTITUTIONALIZATION OF MENTAL TESTING

The foregoing indicates the conceptual atmosphere at the time of the development of mental testing. Because of this, a method that necessarily depicted human differences in terms of a simple hierarchy came to dominate Anglo-American psychometry. The early leading figures in the field labored long and hard to show the relevance of their products to various social concerns, and, to this end, published a large number of books, pamphlets, and articles in popular publications. Recall that testing had been recognized and supported by the

AAAS and by the APA as far back as the 1890s. Now contacts were made with the Carnegie Institution and the Eugenics Records Office (which in turn was funded by Mrs. E. H. Harriman). The relationship with eugenics was important, for it gained audiences with a host of important figures. For example, the Second International Congress of Eugenics was convened at the American Museum of Natural History in 1921, and members included Madison Grant, Herbert Hoover, Gifford Pinchot (future governor of Pennsylvania), and the psychometricians Yerkes and Thorndike (see Chase 1977, pp. 277-78, 325-26); Winston Churchill had been a member of the First International Congress.

Perhaps the most important single event leading to the development of testing as a recognized form of scientific activity was World War I and the concurrent development of the Army Alpha and Beta tests of intelligence. Led by Yerkes, almost the entire body of leading testers in the United States was brought together for the task of determining the proper places of its new recruits in the military. This invisible college of psychometricians, who shared so many common elements of thought, worked closely in the preparation of the new tests, which were ultimately given to some 1.75 million soldiers.

The army tests generated a vast wealth of data, upon which much of the IQ research in the next decade was based. However, it also generated something even more important. Here was official governmental support for the testing movement as a recognized discipline dedicated to the scientific study of talent. Since the people involved in the army studies already were committed to the use of the intelligence quotient, a specific form of research into talent was recognized. Here was also the opportunity for the development of testing as an economic activity. The pioneer testers came to know one another, to become friends, and to share experiences (see the account in Seagoe 1975). They had access to the government's economic resources and to an overwhelming pool of subjects. Finally, their access to the popular media was enhanced, since they had governmental sanction.

At this point, who could argue against the place of IQ scores in the social world? Certainly, the students who flooded the programs of these men after the war, when U.S. psychology really boomed, were educated in a milieu in which this specific form of measurement of intelligence was taken for granted. From this point on, the manner of research could be passed on as scientific research tradition, and might be insulated from events outside the scientific community. (This is not to argue that it was so insulated; merely that once the tradition was formed, the social conditions leading to it were less essential to its continuance.)

From this point on, criticisms of the testing movement by those outside it were considered suspect (though, as it will be argued later, they could have impact). For example, two years after the publication of the results of the massive army testing program, Walter Lippmann published a six-part series of articles criticizing certain assumptions of the army testers. Despite Lippmann's use of some sarcastic barbs, the series was basically a warning against the misuse of tests. In no way did it amount to a radical attack on testing per se, and it did not question the idea of meritocracy on which the testing was based. Yet Terman replied to the series in a manner that left no doubt that he considered Lippmann antiscientific. In his article, titled "The Great Conspiracy: The Impulse Imperious of Intelligence Testers, Psychoanalyzed and Exposed by Mr. Lippmann," Terman (1922) began with the following:

> After Mr. Bryan had confounded the evolutionists, and
> Voliva the astronomers, it was only fitting that some
> equally fearless knight should stride forth in righteous
> wrath and annihilate that other group of pseudoscientists
> known as "intelligence testers." Mr. Walter Lippmann,
> alone and unaided, has performed just this service.
> That it took six rambling articles to do the job is unim-
> portant. It is done. The world is deeply in debt to Mr.
> Lippmann. So are the psychologists, if they only knew
> it, for henceforth, they should know better than to waste
> their lives monkeying with those silly little "puzzles" or
> juggling IQs and mental ages.

Apparently, at this time, Terman's response was seen as a masterpiece of "form, substance, and presentation" (Seagoe 1975, p. 117), though more recent reviewers have not been so kind (for example, Cronbach 1975; Medawar 1977). However, the important point is that Terman derided Lippmann mercilessly, despite the fact that such issues as the latter raised were at the same time making the rounds within the psychometric community. Some of the same points, indeed, had been discussed in the 1921 symposium.

According to Cronbach (1975, p. 10) Terman's virulence stemmed from the fact that he saw Lippmann as a "presumptuous lay-man to be routed." But the layman-practitioner distinction only holds where there is a recognized discipline within which people have specialized training. From this point on, criticism from outside the community was an attack on the community itself. The early testers had by now set up training programs in major universities like Stanford and Columbia; the testing industry was already entering its period of sustained growth; and mental testing had taken its place as a regular part of the U.S. culture. Testing was institutionalized, and a component part of its belief matrix was belief in the importance of differences in intellectual level.

8

MERITOCRACY IN THE IQ

In the two preceding chapters, it was shown how the idea of a unitary intelligence grew, and how that intelligence came to be conceived of as a general entity by means of which people could be stratified in a hierarchy. The dualistic treatment of intelligence by the pioneer testers, to which this conceptualization led, was also discussed. Now we must document how very important those early testers considered the entity in question to be. Following this, we will be able to understand how, to this day, IQ scores are considered indexes of an extremely important gradient of ability, despite a dearth of evidence to that effect. For this reason, this chapter is related to Chapter 4 in Part I.

In this chapter, we will first briefly review the ideas of hierarchical inequality that drove participants in the early days of testing; only we will concentrate not on beliefs about its structure, but on the sense of absolute importance that it came to have in the context of ethnic conflict at the turn of the century. That is, hierarchical stratification came to have global implications for the early testers. The denotation of intelligence may have been that intelligence is what the tests test, but the connotation included much, much more.

For this reason, we will next discuss the symbolic elements involved in testing, in order to ascertain just how those early testers did conceive of their tests. It will be shown that major figures of the day believed that an innate merit marked those who were bright, and this merit was a moral quality. It is from this sense of merit that the title of this chapter comes. By reversing the nouns in the title of Richard Herrnstein's influential book, IQ in the Meritocracy (1973), it is intended to show that, rather than IQ simply operating in a meritocracy, the belief in a universal merit guided IQ testing. It was built into the tests, and the tests therefore seemed to vindicate that belief.

With this in mind, we will end the chapter by examining the ways in which the early testers maintained their belief in the supreme importance of IQ-test scores, when the early results challenging that belief began emerging. By maintaining their belief in the face of negative evidence, these scientists were able to pass on to their students this sense of importance, which continues to exist.

SOURCES OF MERITOCRATIC THOUGHT

While the search for intelligence was the search for an individually located source of achievement, it was the search for much more as well. As mentioned, it occurred in the context of an emerging corporate industrial state marked by extensive economic inequality and hostility between racial and national groups. Moreover, the legitimacy of the state was being challenged by European socialists and by the fledgling labor movement. The United States was being figuratively invaded by southern and Eastern European immigrants as well as by immigrants from the Orient; and these were peoples who, in Gobineau's new racialism, had scores of inferior characteristics. In this context, intelligence was both the explanation of, and the rationalization for, social inequities.

With the development of the eugenics movement, and especially with the success of its more vociferous proponents, a wave of panic swept over the U.S. intellectual community. Were we, in fact, being outbred by inferior races? Just as two generations later, a fear of creeping communism would sweep the United States, now a fear of an undifferentiated inferiority appeared. At both times, the fear was that qualities destructive to our way of life, and residing within the minds of strange foreign peoples, were insidiously working their way into the fabric of U.S. life (Higham 1971; Handlin 1957). Mental testing in the United States was seen at least partly as a way of determining who had these inferior qualities, and who did not, in order that something could be done about the problem.

The above general societal conditions, which have been mentioned in several places, undoubtedly played a role. But how did these things operate directly upon the conceptualizations of testers? That is, what were their sources of justification for the positions they held? As a secondary source of meritocratic thought, secular Calvinism has been mentioned previously, and several testers seem to have been strongly influenced by such a phenomenon.* However, not

---

*Thorndike's biographer, Geraldine Joncich (1968) holds that his tendency to speak in terms of simple superiority and inferiority was a result of his rejection of his early Methodism, and its replacement with "a germ-plasm psychology of individualism, one which is,

all early testers would be so affected, or would come from backgrounds in which such a view held. Recent articles by several authors stress a third source of meritocratic thought: the growth of liberalism, democracy, and capitalism in Great Britain and the United States.

Best presented by Allan Buss (1976; see also Riegel 1972; Mac-Kenzie and Barnes 1974; Allen 1975), this position is held by several writers who wish to document the effects of sociohistorical conditions on intellectual ideas. According to this thesis, the development of testing coincided with the rise of the three elements listed above. The three were, to a considerable extent, reactions to the monarchical, feudalist conservatism marking previous states, and they posited individual accomplishment as an antithesis to the earlier commitment to class rule.

The classical view of progress was also at its zenith at this time, and progress in various sectors of society was encouraged, by means of "advances made in science, technology, and economics at the expense of a decline in religious beliefs" (Buss 1976, p. 49). Here, we see the switch from sacred to secular thought that characterized the late-nineteenth-century Zeitgeist. Buss's thesis is that the combined ascendance of liberalism, democracy, and capitalism "paved the way for the development of an integrated doctrine of individualism that permeated and served as a higher order integrator of diverse social spheres" (Buss 1976, p. 48). It is this emphasis on the individual that is most important to us here.

Society, at this time, was commonly conceived as consisting of numerous individuals who, using Quetelet's metaphor of the social atom, settled about the social sphere in a fashion determined by the nature of the individual units themselves. This view was antagonistic to the old class hierarchy, which had seemed so arbitrary. However, once the capitalist class had itself gained a measure of power, and the old order began to crumble, all had the (theoretical) chance to develop potential. Hence, "the existent class structure . . . must represent inherited individual differences in ability" (Buss 1976, p. 52). This

---

in effect, a secularized belief in the Elect and in Original Sin" (f. 332). For Thorndike, those who were bright were the secular equivalents of the saved, while those who were dull were the damned. Actually, several of the early testers had made early breaks with religion in the face of quite strong religious backgrounds. In an era that saw a strong conflict between religion and science, they saw science as the new source of the salvation of humanity. Galton, Cattell, and Terman all fit in this category. Galton was explicit in holding that eugenics would be a religious sort of phenomenon (Buss 1976, pp. 55-56).

belief was readily apparent in Galton's works, which is why he mentioned several times that anyone with natural ability would find an opportunity to express it, whatever the conditions of his background.

Social questions were to be conceived in terms of this doctrine of individualism. A mental (or biological) reductionism ruled social thought. Thus, races and classes each could be treated in terms of the individuals making up the groups in question. Classes consisted of those who, by chance, shared equivalent levels of ability. Races were those who, being biologically related, automatically shared the characteristics in question. In either case, the individual was representative of a given social type. Until the work of Boas and his students, social science was largely genetically oriented, and anthropology was, in effect, "race science" (see Harris 1968, chap. 4; Haller 1968). Elitism and individualism were closely related. *

The relationship between Spencerian evolution and the presupposition of differentiation by IQ score is readily apparent. Societies differed in the complexity of their social arrangements. According to Spencer (1898), "primarily we may arrange them according to their degrees of composition, as simple, compound, doubly-compound, trebly-compound" and the "great civilized nations" were all "trebly-compound" (pp. 550-54). With this being the case, it was not rational to suppose that those whose racial type was most suited to simple arrangements could adapt themselves well to modern industrial arrangements (see Spencer 1898, pp. 437, 459-60). At this point, all that was required for the development of a doctrine of intraracial differentiation was the insertion of emphasis on individual differences. This was accomplished by Galton, who, while not abandoning the thesis of racial inferiority, added to it the idea of normal variations within populations.

While Galton's work emphasized supremely eminent people, he also wrote about inferiority, and the same principles explained each phenomenon. Thus, society must, by principle, be hierarchically

---

*This relationship between individualism and elitism occurred in a context of stratification in a capitalist economy. For example, Galton used economic jargon metaphorically when speaking of the inheritance of ability. The same phenomenon occurred in the United States. Various testers spoke of the profit and loss associated with differential breeding. One researcher noted that sterilization should take place at the point where the costs of care would outweigh the wealth generated by an individual. Some interesting quotations appear in works by Kamin (1974) and, especially, Karier (1976), though neither of these writers speaks of the metaphorical use of such language.

stratified. It naturally followed that measurements of the characteristics of individuals, especially if these were of a central mental process, would mimic the differentiation of the greater society. Those
with a great amount of this ability would tend to rank high in each
case, while those with lesser ability would rank high in neither case.

SYMBOLIC ASPECTS OF INTELLIGENCE
IN THE WORKS OF PSYCHOMETRICIANS

This helps explain the source of the "merit" in meritocracy.
In Chomsky's (1974) critique of Herrnstein's (1971) article "IQ," he
has pointed out how tacit beliefs concerning those who are "deserving"
and those who are "not deserving" permeate the work. Quite apart
from probability statements about the relationship between a mental
attribute and success in a circumscribed set of activities, the idea of
merit indicates a more global sort of goodness or worth, something
operating within the individual, to which we should all give allegiance,
and that takes the place of the good-evil dichotomy of the freewill era.
It is analogous to the dichotomy of the saved and the damned of Calvinist Protestantism, except that now it is a continuous variable.
This is why genius had such mystical connotations for Galton.

For the early testers, intelligence came to be a catchall term
indicating what was good in human life. For example, Terman's (1917)
interest in eugenics was fueled not just by a worry about the decline
in an ability to perform certain mental gymnastics but by a fear of
"the increasing spawn of degeneracy" (p. 165). There existed the intelligent, who were usually good, and the dull, who were at least potentially destructive.

For example, Goddard (1923, pp. 2-3) explicitly felt that responsibility and intelligence were manifestations of the same underlying trait. He then readily shifted from responsibility to intelligence
to capacity, and in the same work charged that crime, pauperism,
epilepsy, and a host of other social problems were directly tied to this
trait. Morons were "the persons who make for us our social problems" (Goddard 1923, p. 5). These were themes present in the works
of both Gobineau and Grant (Gobineau 1970, pp. 108-34; Grant 1916),
but for Goddard they came to be symbolized by unitary test scores.

Intelligence was a catchall term, and a lack of it was seen as a
paramount cause of all that was bad in society; thus, for Goddard,
morons were the persons who caused social problems. Conditions
that were ugly, or disgusting, or evil were all tied to the lack of intelligence. Drunkenness, epilepsy, and prostitution (white slavery)
were all conditions that the intelligent could avoid, but that the stupid
could not. The research program of the testers grounded this princi-

ple of merit, and IQ became a symbolic representation that, to a considerable extent, stands today.

Goddard was hardly alone in these beliefs, as Galton had lumped together the various characteristics that it took to be a judge, and Thorndike had felt that morality, intellect, and other characteristics were linked: Terman also divided the world into two camps. Cronbach (1975) has indicated that Terman and other testers merely wanted to "open the doors" for the "talented poor" (see also, Seagoe 1975). However, this view of Terman as a benign benefactor of the bright child does not hold up when the context of his works is taken into account. Rather, he wanted to "preserve our state for a class of people worthy to possess it," and this would be done by curtailing the reproduction of "mental degenerates" (Terman 1917). Those who did not do well in school were not just dull, but "defective" (Terman 1916, p. xi).

Further, as with Goddard, Terman saw these defectives as responsible for most of the vice in society. Every "feeble-minded woman" was a "potential prostitute." And since vice and crime were costly, testing here had found perhaps one if its "richest" areas of application (Terman 1916, pp. 11–12). By psychological testing Terman meant IQ testing. This application was not just valuable, but also crucial, for not only individual life chances, but the "future welfare of the country," depended on the education of superior children (Terman 1916, p. 12).

Terman's concern for the gifted, then, was a function of his two-world view. There were the gifted, who were also upright, and the dull, who were neither. His special feelings toward the gifted were demonstrated throughout his career. Just as Galton had traced the family lines of prominent people in Hereditary Genius, Terman followed the lives of California schoolchildren with high test scores in the California Studies of Genius series, the last volume of which was published posthumously. Elsewhere, he attempted the rather wishful task of computing the IQ scores of the great men of history. The multiform accomplishments of these various people were encapsulated in metric scores for ready comparison. Galton earned an IQ of 200. Terman's idolization of the superintelligent was so evident that his biographer titled her work Terman and the Gifted (Seagoe 1975).

Other writers added human physiognomy to the traits that were related to intelligence or its absence. One writer (Hirsch 1926) indicated that the foreign born tended, as a group, to represent "a set of skew-molds discarded by the Creator." Among their characteristics were "narrow and sloping foreheads," "lips thick and mouth coarse," "chin poorly formed," "sugar loaf heads," and "goose-bill noses." Related to this, as late as the 1960 edition of the Stanford-Binet Intelligence Scale, children were counted as being incorrect if they considered sketches of people with broad noses, thick lips, large ears, loose hair, and ill-fitting clothes to be "pretty" (see Karier 1976, pp. 352-53).

Many other examples of such group representations can be readily found in the works of the early testers. For example, as late as 1940, Thorndike equated the inferior with the vicious (1940, p. 957). Again, as late as 1955, Henry Garrett's treatment of Martin Kallikak very specifically termed the descendants of Kallikak's dalliance as hundreds of the lowest types of human beings. Conversely, the descendants of his marriage to a "worthy Quakeress" were hundreds of the "highest" types of persons (Garrett 1955, p. 65). This is shown in Figure 5. So striking is the dichotomy that the high types all are dressed as pilgrims, and have demure and prayerful, somber expressions. The low types have evil looks on their faces, grin a lot, and are (when women) heavily made up (with lipstick and false eyelashes). Garrett's depiction may seem only silly to us now, but there is no doubt that he felt a general gradient of virtue to obtain. His election as president of the APA indicates that his views were at least not considered antithetical to those of the profession as a whole.

We have, here, the key to the problem of the dualistic treatment of IQ scores by the major psychometric figures. Intelligence could not be conceptually bounded, because it represented so many different things. To have strictly defined the word would have been to lose much of its usefulness as a metaphor for human worth. The testers knew that merit existed, and they knew that human behavior was somehow tied to mental activities. Boring's dictum allowed them to believe that they had tapped the connection between the two, without their ever having to make the relationship explicit. Either future research would make that clear, or else this was a problem for which there was no real answer (Jensen 1969a, pp. 5-6).

Intelligence was both the vague conceptual entity around which a large-scale research program developed, and a representation of the large constellation of beliefs about merit. To a considerable extent, the second explanation came to be embodied in the first. Since test scores represented degrees of merit, it made sense that they should predict success in the social world.

Recall that Terman recognized the lack of precision of the entity supposedly tapped by his tests. Yet he was adamant that "it would be desirable to make all [school] promotions on the basis chiefly of intellectual ability" (Terman 1916, pp. 16-17). To the extent that he meant measured ability, he indicated a very broad sweep of importance for the tests. Even to the extent that he merely meant real mental ability, he ran the risk of linking the indistinct concept with such things as learning, skills, and maturity. The statement is consistent

FIGURE 5

Henry Garrett's Dichotomy of Humans into "High" and "Low" Types
in the Story of Martin Kallikak

Source: Henry Garrett, General Psychology (New York: American Book Co., 1955). Copyright © 1955 by American Book Co. Reprinted by permission.

if we posit that Terman at least tacitly included a number of meritorious elements in his view of intelligence. This was apparently the case, for he was adamant that as the number of trained testers increases, "the information standard will have to give way to the criterion which merely asked that the child shall be able to do the work of the next higher grade" (Terman 1916, p. 17). But why should a child be excused from learning the content of a grade of school, especially on the basis of crude test scores? Terman apparently felt that the child deserved promotion on the basis of a quality distinct from effort or learning; some core of merit allowed the child to transcent such considerations.

THE PSYCHOMETRIC DEFENSE OF MERIT

This overwhelming commitment to an individualist, reductionist explanation of human achievement was what Imre Lakatos (1970) would call the "hard core" of a research program. It was the aspect of a program that was not at issue and was not really subject to investigation. When Kuhn (1962) states that scientific research, when successful, does not unearth new or startling information, he is speaking of the hard core of a research program. For the testers it was intuitively obvious that differences in achievement must be related to intelligence, and therefore to IQ. It was true that a handful of subsidiary characteristics might also affect success. For example, Freeman (1926, p. 381) mentioned chronological age, grade accomplishment in school work, application or industry, health, home environment, nationality and language difficulty, and "special or unusual conditions." But IQ was always the primary screening criterion. This view came to be ensconced in standard textbooks and was taught to new students. It might not be the case that, as has been suggested, once the decision had been made to stratify (for example, Lewis 1973), "the history of the last sixty years was inevitable" (Kagan 1974, p. 115); but it is certain that the continual use of a stratifying methodology made it seem that stratification mirrors nature. Yet how was the meritocratic position upheld when seeming counterevidence began accumulating?

What we find in the literature are at least four tactics employed to maintain a sense of legitimacy regarding the accepted position. The first of these, already discussed in the previous chapter, was the employment of different lines of reasoning when discussing the nature of intelligence and its social implications. This activity can be termed disjuncture. Yet even where discussions centered specifically on the nature or predictive strength of intelligence, problems developed. Here three other tactics were employed. Among these were, first, taking the presence of even a poor correlation as demonstrating the validity of tests, at least for scientific purposes. The second was that of considering a weak relationship between a test score and another criterion of ability as evidence of the invalidity of the other criterion. The third was the making of liberal use of ceteris paribus statements.

Correlation

The first of these three means of reconciliation of positions is a special case of what Berger and Luckman (1966, pp. 92-128) term legitimation in the maintenance of social reality. The specific form it took grew out of the radical positivism of the early twentieth century, where there existed a widespread belief that scientific explanation should be merely the demonstration of relationships between material entities (Sturtevant 1965, p. 58; see Pearson 1900; cf. Hogben 1957; Hamblin 1974). Since ultimate causation could not be determined, the goal of science would be the demonstration of immediate causation, where causation was determined by an inspection of sequences of action or, more weakly, by statistical correlation.

Statistically, almost any correlation, beyond some trivial amount, could thus be considered to show a causal relationship—a situation that invites the error of correlation entailing commonality (see Chapter 2). We will not dwell on the philosophical problems related to this assumption, as these are beyond the scope of this work. For our purposes, it is sufficient to be aware of the effect such a line of thought had on interpretations of the correlations among indicators found by early testers. A very early extreme to which this allowed theorists to go can be found in the work of Karl Pearson, who (before the advent of partial correlation techniques) defined heredity as the following (cited in MacKenzie 1974):

> Given any organ in a parent and the same or any other organ in its offspring, the mathematical measure of heredity is the correlation of those organs for pairs of parents and offspring. [P. 8]

Thus, for Pearson, any correlation between parent and offspring indicated biological inheritance.

Likewise, with testing, the fact of correlation was considered evidence of causality. Evidence in the development of testing consisted largely of tables of correlations. The presence of positive correlations was taken as evidence of the importance of the relationships found. For example, Terman (1916) took a correlation of 0.48 between Stanford-Binet scores and teachers' estimates of brightness as indicative of the validity of the Binet tests. In the same vein, correlations of about 0.50 between various types of tests were taken as evidence of a general learning capacity. Even a correlation range of -0.027 to 0.655 (average = 0.239) was taken as evidence of a unity of intellectual ability (Pyle 1921, pp. 161-66). Low positive correlations were seen as validating tests, though correlations much below 0.50 were viewed with increasing dissatisfaction.

This is not to say that all testers, by any means, held that small-to-moderate correlations adequately supported the use of mental tests to determine central mental faculties. For example, Peterson (1922) complained that testers had been forced to assume something of a perfect correlation between "degrees of ability to learn the habits and ideas on which the tests are based and degrees of intelligence" (p. 370), even though this was a problem that required investigation. Further, the view of learning capacity engendered by the tests, in which the mind "possessed certain powers though unitary in itself," then permitted "a jump from the _fact_ of 0.50 correlation to the _belief_ in perfect correlation" (Peterson 1922, p. 377). Recall that at this time, studies were emerging that often put real correlations at quite a bit lower than 0.50.

The important point here, however, is that moderate correlations were commonly taken to demonstrate the reality of a central mental construct, and the social importance of that construct. One way in which this was accomplished was through the denigration of competing modes of analysis of abilities.

Denigration

Denigration is similar to what Berger and Luckman (1966, p. 112) call _nihilation_, which is the action of denying legitimacy to a rival sense of reality. An example of nihilation is the denigration by Terman of Lippmann's stance on IQ testing, on the basis of the fact that Lippmann was not a psychometrician. Since he was not a member of the community, he was not allowed to question central precepts. Thomas Kuhn (1962) states that a sense of reality sometimes is upheld by means of the simple expedient of treating deviant members of a scientific community as marginal—not allowing them full membership or full participation in internal discussions. With IQ testing, denigration was aimed also at possible rival hypotheses.

In the work by Terman noted above, the quoted 0.48 correlation between Stanford-Binet scores and teachers' estimates of brightness corroborated the tests. But further, the fact that the correlation was not higher indicated that "either the teachers or the tests have made a good many mistakes" (Terman 1916, p. 75), though several alternative explanations can be proffered. Terman was convinced that the fault lay with the teachers, and he gave two reasons for this. First, teachers' estimates of brightness showed more variability than did test scores. Second, teachers used a variety of means to arrive at their estimates, while the tests were standardized. *

According to Terman, teachers' mistakes were made mostly among children who were over or under age for their grade, since students were judged on the quality of their work in the grade in which they were found, rather than by comparison with others of their own age. Thus, the disagreement between test scores and teachers' estimates "confirm[s] the validity of the test method rather than [bringing] it under suspicion" (Terman 1916, p. 76).

But is this what the comparisons showed? Recall Terman's reason for disparaging the efforts of teachers. The first is that teachers' methods are not standardized. But why should this invalidate their estimates? As mentioned in the discussion of Binet's treatment of alternative ways of dealing with retardation, the statement that there is a single valid way of measuring ability disallows the very body of information from which ideas of differential ability emerged —that is, common-sense agreement. Second, this assumes the very thing it attempts to demonstrate, the existence of a single undifferentiated brightness. Third, in making strict demands for standardization and reliability, it neatly substitutes reliability for validity. Fourth, if Terman was correct, then teachers' estimates were based on actual school performance (for example, Peterson, pp. 245-55), and should have predictive validity for that reason. To some extent, this argues in favor of teachers' estimates and against the use of the tests, since a primary source of their justification comes from their supposedly high predictive accuracy, an accuracy that Terman complained was lowered by teacher's refusals to follow his precepts. We will return to this type of complaint in the next section.

The critique of Terman's (and Binet's) denigration of teachers' estimates of brightness can easily be pushed too far. The main point to consider is that he did not really prove his case against teachers' estimates, or in favor of the estimates of the tests. He did make a point for reliability of measurement, though at the cost of eclecticism. In place of a variety of procedures, he substituted a restricted and codified method that depended for legitimacy upon some of the very assumptions it sought to demonstrate. More important, he used the lack of total correspondence between his and others' methods to validate his own method at the same time as he was invalidating the competition.

---

*In the passage just noted, Terman did not mention the second reason, but it appeared earlier in the same work in a discussion of Binet's experiments with teachers.

Ceteris Paribus Statements

The logic of the argument for the social importance of test scores requires, at the outset, that a strong relationship between scores and social achievement be found. A miniscule relationship, in a system in which a large number of factors could reasonably be considered to affect achievement, would, for all practical purposes, make test scores socially trivial phenomena. A social explanation could not be based upon score differences, unless it could be shown that the imposition of external factors acted to mask a relationship that was, in reality, quite strong—in essence, a ceteris paribus clause (see Nagel 1961, p. 560).

The role of ceteris paribus is a large one in the history of science, especially when one speaks of the quasi-general laws of the social sciences (Nagel 1961, p. 464). The term roughly translates as "other things being equal," and it indicates that a stated lawlike relationship would be apparent, were it not for the effect of extraneous events. Consider the following explanation of only a 0.50 correlation among different tests (Pyle 1921):

> But if learning ability is general, should not the correlation be unity? In the author's opinion, if the disturbing factors could be eliminated, the correlation would be unity. [P. 161]

Again (Pyle 1921):

> The disturbing factors are so many that we can never expect to get a very high correlation between any two mental functions. [T]he reliability of our measure [is] .608. . . . The average raw correlation in this table is .239. The average true correlation is about .40. [P. 166]

Here, the combination of "disturbing factors" was postulated as lowering the intertest correlation. After demonstrating a low test reliability, Pyle asserted that the disturbers lowered the observed correlations by 40 percent (roughly, lowering them from 0.40 to 0.24). Comment here centers on Pyle's reference to corrected correlations as "true" correlations. Statistical theory holds that unreliability of a true measure of a phenomenon will lower correlations between it and any phenomenon to which it should be related. Pyle's contention that true correlations are found by means of corrections made for unreliability rested on the assumption that a given test measured both an ability that should show a correlation with a criterion measure and a series of uncorrelated disturbers (that is, error measurement). As with Terman, this assumes that which it attempts to support, since it is by no means certain that a given instrument would not measure different things, especially on retests, which would each be positively related to the criterion measure. Again, a method based on problems of reliability is used to boost claims of validity. In this case, inter-correlations among various tests rose to an average of about 0.40, still a very low figure if one wishes to make a case for a general intellectual ability. Parenthetically, even the 0.40 was arrived at only after the active removal of tests that did not show strong correlations with other tests. Here, Pyle changed his mind regarding the degree to which all functions should correlate, and hedged that only functions that were "a part of general intelligence" should show such a correlation (Pyle 1921, p. 167). This circular methodology allows the deletion of any tests that do not seem to show a central function. Pyle deleted three in the same way as had Binet and Terman.

Pyle's defense of general learning ability rested on the same tactics chosen by Spearman (1927) for that purpose. Spearman had first proposed that the relationships among various tests could be explained on the basis of a general mental factor, and his early work seemed to bear out the contention (see Spearman 1904a). Later, he switched to the two-factor theory. However, studies by him and others tended to show that the single most important proof of the two-factor theory did not always hold. This proof had to do with tetrad differences in correlation matrixes, discussed in Chapter 3.

Recall that Thomson (1951) and Tryon (1932a) had demonstrated that, mathematically, tetrad differences equaling zero could be obtained even if no general factor were present at all, even if performance on various tests only overlapped to the extent determined by chance. This, however, did not make large inroads into Spearman's position, mostly, it appears, because this sampling did not generate new evidence, but only gave a different interpretation to already-known data. It might also be supposed that it gained little headway because of the general commitment to general intelligence that marked psychology at that time. A crucial attack on Spearman's position came when it was found that tetrad differences did not always yield zero. Spearman acknowledged this, but then postulated that the use of tests that overlapped excessively (such that group factors, instead of specific factors, appeared) would give the results found. Here was a generous use of ceteris paribus statements in support of a theory (Thomson 1951):

> Immediately, more problems arose: If such "disturbers"
> were found coexisting in the team of tests, the team had to
> be "purified" by the rejection of one or the other of the two.
> Later it became clear that this process involves the experi-
> menter in great difficulty, for it subjects him to the temp-

tation to discover "undue similarity" between tests <u>after</u>
he had found that their correlation breaks the hierarchy.
Moreover, whole groups of tests were found to fail to
conform; and so group factors were admitted, though
always by the experimenters trained in that school, with
reluctance and in as small a number as possible. [P. 63]

The above examples have dealt mainly with the handling of problems that occurred with conceptions of intelligence as a unitary thing.
The same type of response occurred when intelligence was posited to
have important social effects. Simply put, truly strong correlations
between test scores and various forms of achievement were lacking.
By the early 1920s, the general correlation of 0.50 between Stanford-
Binet scores and school grades was commonly acknowledged, but the
truly low correlations between test scores and out-of-school achievement had already been found.

Thorndike's anomalous findings with regard to nonacademic
achievement were especially annoying, in that his definition of the
value of a test score was "its value in prophesying how well a person
will do in other tasks" (Thorndike 1921, p. 125). In his 1934 study,
he rather lamely concluded that the scores he obtained would be more
accurate than an individual's personal opinion. Likewise, with various
tests of ability, intercorrelations were "high enough to make a measure of any one of them a better index of any other than the average
parental hope or teacher's opinion is likely to be" (Thorndike 1921,
p. 126).

Terman, more than Thorndike, expressed a need to treat the
low correlations found as of little consequence. Thus, he noted that
predictive validity was not the desired end in mind (Terman 1921):

A mistake that results from over-evaluation of a single criterion is seen in the effort to embody in a given intelligence
scale <u>every</u> kind of tests which will add to its correlation
with the criterion in question. This mistake is especially
likely to occur if one is interested in the predictive uses of
the test. The effect of this error may be to pervert grossly
the test as a measure of intelligence. If we wished to devise
a test which would give the most accurate possible prediction
of the class marks a given group of college students would
receive, we ought to include in it measures of personal
beauty, voice quality, bashfulness, willingness to cultivate
the good graces of the instructor, etc. . . . It should not
be the aim of an intelligence test to give us the <u>best possi-
ble</u> prediction of events of this kind. [P. 131]

Here, Terman explicitly excluded only items that would commonly be considered nonintellectual in his prescription, using the list in a partially sarcastic sense in order to indicate that only <u>real</u> measures of intelligence should be bothered with. However, earlier we found that he had excluded tests that definitely were of an intellectual nature, in his study of seven bright and seven stupid boys (1906). Later, he and Maud Merrill deliberately included in Stanford-Binet revisions only those items that correlated highly enough with mental age on the earlier form. Further, items that otherwise seemed good were excluded from revisions of the Stanford-Binet if they did not correlate well with the overall test score. Also, recall Terman's earlier comments on the inability of Chicano, Indian, and black children with low scores to compete successfully in life. Here, correlation was strongly implied. So, correlation was important to Terman, despite assertions to the contrary, and the quote above can reasonably be seen as an attempt to belittle the impact of an only-modest correlation.

To state that early testers made use of ceteris paribus statements in order to preserve a certain view of mental processes is not to claim that those scientists were guilty of bad science. Such statements are used widely in science. In fact, much of scientific research consists of claims that an anomalous finding is caused by the presence of a variable X, and of attempts to demonstrate the truth of the assertion. The point here is that a quite different view of intellectual functioning could reasonably have been offered on the basis of the same body of data, and claims made consistently operated to negate the alternative view. In this way, such discrepancies that did emerge were made manageable. They came to be seen as not terribly important, and the respected view of mental functioning was maintained.

SUMMARY

In sum, the early popularizers of intelligence tests in the United States were committed to a view of intelligence by which it was considered a crucial variable in human social life. So strong was this commitment that intelligence became conflated with various other qualities. It came to symbolize that which was good in modern civilization, and lack of it symbolized that which was not good. When, ultimately, research findings consistently showed only modest correlations among the tests and real-world achievements, testers were forced to use considerable ingenuity to uphold the thesis of importance. For, how crucial can a phenomenon be if it does not even show a statistical relationship to the various forms of achievement in society? This problem will be discussed further in Chapter 10.

9

NATURE AGAINST NURTURE

Now we must turn to an issue that is conceptually distinct from that of meritocracy. One reasonably can believe that the basis of social stratification is the differential distribution of intelligence, without simultaneously believing that the expression of that intelligence is innate. Indeed, on the whole, hereditarians and environmentalists disagree in this regard only on the issue of genetic causation.

As was demonstrated in Chapter 5, despite their disagreements over reasons for black-white or middle-class/lower-class IQ-score differences, both hereditarians and environmentalists tend to agree on the methodology to be used in determining the genetic character of traits. This entails the use of heritability estimates—nature-nurture balance sheets—that are supposed to determine the relative strengths of nature and nurture. As was shown earlier, the reliance on such techniques leads to a nature-versus-nurture approach to the discussion of traits. This occurs because the techniques artificially divide the two. Policy discussions then come to be directed at attempts to determine if a trait difference is natural, rather than being directed at a determination of the causes of the trait difference, such that social amelioration can take place.

In the early twentieth century, psychology was dominated by hereditarianism, but unlike the cases with the other conceptual elements discussed here, the majority opinion regarding the development of traits changed in favor of environmentalism. Yet, the manner of viewing the development of traits, as being made up of separate environmental and hereditary components, did not change. This is important, for it is the simple view of heredity depicted by this manner of studying it that gives the hereditarian position its obvious influence.

In the present chapter, the genesis of the idea of hereditary simplicity will be sketched first. It will be shown how this general idea was given operational meaning through the work of Galton and the biometric school of biology. Following this, the early history of genetics will be traced, and it will be shown how a sense of the amassed complexity of inheritance replaced the idea of simplicity in the minds of experimental geneticists.

Second, the close ties of psychology to the biometric school will be discussed. It will be shown, for example, that the general reliance of psychologists on least-square statistical techniques made it easy for them to adopt a nature-versus-nurture approach to inheritance; indeed, it will be shown that such an approach fits quite well with the prevailing hereditarianism of the day. Further, it will be shown that the dominance of certain powerful hereditarian-research programs (specifically at Stanford) supported this line of thought.

Finally, the determinants of psychology's shift to environmentalism will be discussed. Most important here is the effect of a growing experimental tradition that developed at the universities of Chicago and Iowa, but also important are the findings that emerged when the static approach of Stanford was traded for more dynamic approaches in the study of heredity. It will be shown that a tension between experimental and heritability approaches to inheritance continues to mark psychological work.

Since this chapter deals with a different set of issues than did any of the three earlier chapters of Part II, it will require a more thorough analysis. Therefore, a considerable portion of the chapter will be devoted to the historical development of trends in conceptualization. It is only in this manner that the present state of hereditarian thought in psychology can come to be clearly understood.

NATURE AND NURTURE PRIOR TO GENETICS

The tradition of dissension over nature and nurture can perhaps be traced to the earliest monogenesis-polygenesis debates. At that time, debates centered on whether the Christian God had made humanity in its myriad forms during the six-day Creation, or whether different peoples had metamorphosed over time. Even at that early date, practical implications followed from the positions that people held, for a feeling of many monogenesists was that the enslaved Africans could ultimately take on the attributes of whites.

Monogenesists ultimately came to posit rapid Lamarckian evolution, a stand quite at variance with that of the polygenesists, who felt that human traits were "fixed in nature" (for example, Jefferson 1955, p. 138). Concerning the faculties, debate tended to center on whether the enslaved Africans could ever hope to attain the level of their masters. While monogenesists used such examples as black poet Phyllis Wheatley, to demonstrate the liberating effects of civilized residence, such polygenesists as Thomas Jefferson (1955, pp. 140-43) felt that the evidence supported the claim that the slaves' lower "rank in the scale of beings" was an immutable fact of nature. The similarity between that early debate and today's IQ controversy is obvious.

Whatever the specific elements of given arguments, by the early nineteenth century the source of human differences was alternatively considered to be nature or nurture, and the two were commonly considered mutually exclusive terms. Polygenesists' arguments, as precursors of today's hereditarianism, were grounded at least partially in Calvinist predeterminism. With the development of a secular natural history, they came to be based on Spencerian laws of evolution. Whatever the basis of support, the word that best describes either position is simplicity. These were basically single, variable approaches to trait expression. In biology, this sense of predeterminism was best exemplified by the debate over preformationism, in which it was claimed that beings were created fully formed, as homunculi (see Chase 1977, pp. 87-89). In this regard, Quetelet (1842) had held that "at birth, man is possessed of the germs of all [his] qualities" (p. 74). This led him to propose racial theories of such characteristics as criminality.

In practical matters, the growing hereditarian position was the one that received the greatest amount of support. It was not known what one might do in order to effect changes in personal characteristics by environmental intervention, but there was good evidence that one could breed for traits. In the area of animal husbandry, this was routinely accomplished without any conception of what led to the similarity among relatives. In fact, with respect to breeding, two simple aphorisms were commonly followed: "like begets like" and "breed from the best" (Rosenberg 1967).

The Hereditarian Influence of Francis Galton

Galton's influence on biological and social science is often overlooked today, but the importance of his influence can hardly be overestimated. It was Galton who first applied purely probabilistic approaches to the treatment of biological issues. In the course of accomplishing this, he discovered the principles of correlation and regression, the two most widely employed statistical tools in biometry and psychometry. One issue in which these techniques play telling roles is that of nature and nurture, an issue in which Galton was extremely interested for much of his life. For Galton, the issue was nature versus nurture, and he clearly took the side of nature, long before any evidence had been obtained that would tend to support one position over its rival. Recent papers, in fact, indicate that Galton's development of statistical procedures was done in order to demonstrate the primacy of heredity in human ability and to help map eugenic attacks on problems of ability (see, for instance, Cowan 1968, 1972a, 1972b; MacKenzie 1974; MacKenzie and Barnes 1974). Policy ideas led to scientific ideas, rather than the reverse.

As early as 1865 (six years after the publication of Origin of Species, and four years before the publication of his own Hereditary Genius), Galton counted entries in biographical dictionaries and, finding that the number of relatives on the lists appeared in greater numbers than would be supposed on the basis of population averages, concluded that genius must be hereditary (Galton 1865; see Cowan 1972b). Even at this early date he accepted this as evidence of the priority of nature in the determination of traits. Already, he called for eugenic reform, stating that if "a twentieth" part of the effort spent breeding animals were spent on human breeding, then "what a galaxy of genius might not we create!" (Galton 1865, pp. 165-66). Issues of human breeding were to occupy his life for the next 46 years.

As mentioned above, several writers have argued that Galton's development of statistics was undertaken in order that he might be able to make eugenic applications of the laws of inheritance. He believed that "natural laws were only comprehensible when mathematicized," and he spent his life pursuing such laws "so that he could use heredity to elevate men" (Cowan 1972b, p. 511). By 1869 he had produced hypothetical probability distributions of human ability, so that he could make estimates of the number of truly bright people and truly dull ones in a population at a given time.

Galton extended his researches to a great many phenomena (for example, various human faculties such as the ability to visualize scenes), and found in each case that heredity played the greatest role in the development of these characteristics. Galton's feeling that either nature or nurture must be predominant in the development of a trait is of some importance, because of a degree of ambiguity that had existed regarding the genesis of similarities and differences among relatives, prior to his work. With Darwin (and others who came before him), inheritance had been conceived of as a force, and variation and reversion (later, regression) had been considered to be the results of different forces. Since both similarities and differences among relatives always existed, these coexisting forces of inheritance, variation, and reversion must exist in varied amounts, in unique tangles that were difficult to deal with effectively.

Galton changed this multiple conception by considering heredity to be a relationship, rather than a force. Thus operationalized, it could be quantified and measured. Heredity came to be seen as the degree of resemblance between relatives of successive generations. What is more, heredity operated probabilistically. Galton, very early, considered familial resemblance to result from the action of particles of hereditary information that one gained in a chance fashion from one's ancestors. One received a given percentage of one's makeup from each ancestor representing a given degree of remoteness. Thus, in Galton's law of ancestral heredity, one received one-fourth of one's makeup from each parent, one-sixteenth from each grandparent, one sixty-fourth from each great-grandparent, and so forth. Inheritance, variation, and regression all came to be part of a single model of heredity (see Cowan 1972a, 1972b). This gave operational meaning to the nature-versus-nurture conceptualization, in which nature represented a unitary whole that operated according to the laws of chance.

For Galton, any similarity between generations, especially where the distribution of a trait approximated a normal curve, represented the effects of nature, while only discontinuous variation, or generational differences within populations, represented the working of nurture. Where the normal curve held, it was considered that the various small effects of nurture were canceling one another out. What was left was the original distribution, which would have been present without environmental differences, and which would be reproduced from generation to generation (Cowan 1972a). Nurture was largely impotent.

By dividing causation into two opposing groups, Galton gave clear definition to issues of the genesis of traits. Accepting the presence of two general causative agents, it was theoretically possible to parcel out the independent effects of each. In fact, this was the goal of Galton and his followers, especially Pearson. While Galton had first discovered the presence of regression to the mean, his grasp of applied mathematics was too weak for him to undertake sophisticated statistical studies; consequently, he "farmed out" mathematical problems to others (Cowan 1972b).

His greatest disciple was Pearson, an engineer who once worked on applications of Hooke's law of the spring (see Hogben 1957; MacKenzie 1974). When Pearson read Natural Inheritance, he came to accept Galton's view of heredity and its importance. At that point, he turned from engineering to the analysis of the inheritance of traits, and worked closely with the aging Galton. An exceptional mathematician, Pearson noticed a formal resemblance between the action of springs and the phenomenon of regression, and he developed regression equations through which the analogy of spring tension was applied to biological phenomena. *

---

*Hooke's law is an empirical generalization in which, within prescribed limits, the length of a spring will be proportionate to the force applied to the spring: $y = kx + C$, in which k and C are constants. Likewise, in the law of ancestral heredity, the amount of influence an

In this manner, the idea that "like begets like" gained formal mathematical expression. Following the popularization of Galton's work, it came to be widely accepted in scientific circles that the relative effects of nature and nurture could be readily determined. While Galton's formal theory of heredity (the law of ancestral heredity) gave a conceptual framework within which such determinations could be pursued, the fact is that any particulate (or even fluid) theory of heredity could produce the same results; the mathematics simply were not limited by any specific theory (Hogben 1957). Thus, in the main, the idea of simplicity of causation remained; only its application changed.

Biometrics, Mendelism, and Eugenics

While Galton developed his biological methods in order to support eugenic action, he was far from alone in this regard. In fact, with the rediscovery of Mendel in 1900, a rival to the Galtonian position developed, but there was at first no difference with regard to eugenics between the two camps. While Galton's proteges were eugenicists, so were such prominent Mendelians as William Bateson, Fisher, and C. B. Davenport (MacKenzie 1976; Rosenberg 1961, 1967). The striking differences between proponents had to do with questions of the mechanisms of inheritance and evolution, and with the methods employed in the study of inheritance. W. F. R. Weldon and Pearson had worked out the mathematics of biometry on the basis of a cumulative, accretionary theory of evolution, and these methods were well suited to that theoretical position. Mendelians, on the other hand, led by Bateson in England, were inclined against biometric analysis and in favor of experimental methods. *

---

ancestor has on the determination of an individual's trait depends on the degree of distance separating the ancestor from the individual. In borrowing from engineering, Pearson developed the mathematics of all future correlational analysis. For a detailed and critical review of this, see Hogben 1957, pp. 210-31).

*While Dunn (1965) and Sturtevant (1965) have somewhat played down the degree to which the debate between Mendelians and biometricians was tied to the preferred methodologies of each group, there is considerable evidence that such differences were very important. Even though certain of the Mendelians (for example, Johanssen) employed statistical techniques to a considerable degree, others (like Bateson) were mathematically unsophisticated and considered a biometric approach to the study of inheritance to obscure the phenomena studied (for reviews, see Farrall 1975; MacKenzie and Barnes 1974).

Both groups considered heredity to be a simple phenomenon. The biometricians would claim that correlations between relatives on a trait indicated that the first fundamental principle of practical eugenics was: "It is five to ten times as advantageous to improve the condition of the race through parentage as through environment" (Pearson 1912, p. 8). Meanwhile, the earlier Mendelians, building on Mendel's work with dominant and recessive single-gene effects, felt that such problems as feeblemindedness, alcoholism, and epilepsy were caused by the presence or absence of single Mendelian factors. If biometricians could claim to have developed techniques for determining the degree of resemblance of relatives, the Mendelians could claim to have discovered the causes of resemblance. If, in 1912, Pearson could continue to state that a few trained field workers could soon solve the problems of mental retardation (Rosenberg 1967, p. 36), Davenport went to his death in the 1940s still proclaiming the importance of unit gene actions (Rosenberg 1961). Further, well into the 1940s, Thorndike continued to consider the environment of cities to be a direct expression of the genetic character of its citizens (Pastore 1949).

Any possible complexities of nature and nurture were largely ignored in the climate of optimism that guided research. As put by Rosenberg (1967), "in the minds of most students of human genetics, social and utopian aspects were foremost" (p. 36).

Despite this seeming consensus regarding the amenability of human character to proper breeding, by the end of World War I a split had appeared between geneticists and eugenicists (for example, Allen 1975; MacKenzie 1976; Farrall 1970); and eugenic thought began a decline, from which it did not reemerge, outside Germany. MacKenzie (1976, p. 517) holds that, in Britain at least, the combined effects of World War I and world economic depression, and the emergence of German fascism were telling points against eugenics. Buss (1976, p. 57) states that the development of liberalism, itself paradoxically tied to Galton's thought, led to the decline of eugenics policy.

While these arguments are compelling as regards the political nature of the eugenics movement in Britain, they are not sufficient to

---

After Fisher's (1918) seminal paper showing a natural relationship between biometry and Mendelism, the two camps generally ceased hostilities (though there remains a split between experimentalists and statisticians in biology to this day); but publication of Fisher's paper was delayed because both Pearson and Bateson, acting as referees for the British Royal Society, refused to publish it, and it was subsequently published in a less prestigious journal. For more on this, see the account and citations in Farrall (1975, pp. 96-98).

account for the decline in eugenic thought among active scientists.
For example, as demonstrated by Allen (1975, pp. 32-33), geneticists
began withdrawing support from the eugenics movement several years
prior to the end of the war, for reasons that were, to a considerable
extent, independent of political events—that is, for reasons internal
to experimental genetics.

Some treatment of the decline of eugenic thought among geneticists is necessary, because it will show the ultimate differences that
prevailed between biometric and experimental modes of investigation
in the area of human differences. It was the difference between mathematical and experimental approaches that ultimately caused a falling
away from eugenics on the part of experimentalists. Biometricians
(even Mendelian biometricians like Fisher) did not immediately follow experimentalists, probably because techniques of variance analysis served to mask, rather than reveal, the underlying complexities
that experimental investigation revealed.

EXPERIMENTAL GENETICS AND
THE PROBLEM OF COMPLEXITY

What were the events within genetics that led to the disaffection
for eugenics that geneticists increasingly felt following the first two
decades of the twentieth century? A number of events must be mentioned, no one of which stands alone (see the list in Allen 1975, p. 32).
First, we must mention two publications of 1909. In that year, the
Danish botanist Johanssen introduced the terms gene, genotype, and
phenotype. Gene indicated the fundamental Mendelian unit, or factor,
while the genotype-phenotype distinction indicated the basic genetic
makeup of the organism, as opposed to the expressed characteristics
of the developed organism. The distinction may have been made before (for example, by Galton; see Sturtevant 1965, p. 59), but it was
Johanssen who made explicit the fact that the phenotype was a developmental phenomenon that required interaction of genetic and environmental factors. It was Johanssen's experiments that showed, apparently for the first time, that inherited variations could be slight, and
environmentally produced variations large. Further, only experiments
could distinguish the sources of the variations.

Johanssen's studies were made with beans, among which he
found a previously unreported event. Among beans that were not of
a pure line, he could breed for differences in traits. However, among
beans that self-fertilized (that is, were homozygous), selection on the
basis of expression of a characteristic did not yield population changes
in the expression of the trait. The inference, clearly, was that whatever differences obtained here were strictly functions of environmental

differences among bean plants. Therefore, the phenotype was the result of an interaction of the genotype and environment.

At the same time as the publication of Johanssen's work, Richard Woltereck was developing the concept of the norm of reaction (Reaktionsnorm), discussed in Chapter 5, by which he meant the curve of the expression of a trait in a purebred species (see the more thorough account in Dunn 1965, pp. 95-97). The specific trait expression was relative to the given environment, in which variations could be unlimited. What was inherited, then, was not a specific trait, as had usually been assumed, but the "total norm of reaction with all its countless relations" (quoted in Dunn 1965, p. 97).

A third finding occurred a year prior to Johanssen's and Woltereck's works, but it was not to have a great deal of influence until the 1930s. This was the phenomenon that came to be known as the Hardy-Weinberg law of equilibrium. Independently reported by Hardy (in Britain) and by Weinberg (in Germany) in 1908, the law of equilibrium, by reference to classical probability theory, predicts the relative frequencies of different genes in a population at equilibrium. Where the alternative genes I (dominant) and i (recessive) exist in proportions p and q (where $p + q = 1$), the relative proportions of possible genotypes will be generated by $(p + q)^2$. Given a homogeneous environment, and $p = q$, the relative frequencies of II, Ii, and ii will be of the order 1-2-1, and there will be three times as many I-traits expressed as i-traits. *

The Hardy-Weinberg law may seem prosaic enough, and for a long time it was not fully appreciated (for example, Allen [1975] mentions the "slow penetration of the idea of genetic equilibrium" p. 32); but ultimately, it was responsible for the realization among geneticists that it would be immensely difficult to select undesirable genes out of a population. If one was interested in a phenomenon more complex than is shown in the simple model mentioned above (for example, where inheritance was polygenic, where norms of reaction were great, and where p and q were not equal in frequency) then artificial selection became enormously difficult, and any change in the relative frequency of the genes in question in a population could be accomplished only very slowly. The acceptance of the principle of genetic equilibrium was simply not compatible with the utopian eugenics of the early twentieth century.

A fourth event—or rather a series of ongoing events—occurred in the second decade of the twentieth century, and further developed understanding of the complexity of genetic analysis. This was the on-

---

*The specific terms used here are from Dobzhansky (1962, pp. 140-41).

going research done by T. H. Morgan and his students into the genetics of the fruitfly, drosophila. The premier group of geneticists in the first part of the twentieth century, these researchers not only mapped parameters of norms of reaction for various traits and various genotypes, but actually developed the chromosome theory of heredity (Allen 1969; Carlson 1966). In doing so, they discovered the mechanistic basis for the complexity of gene action.

For example, in 1912, Morgan performed the first major work showing the complexity of phylogenetic results of the phenomenon of crossing over of genes, and ties aspects of crossing over to the concept of recessive lethal genes. In 1913, A. H. Sturtevant drew the first gene-linkage map, and proposed the theory of multiple allelic action that ultimately shattered the presence-absence theory then almost universally held. That same year, C. B. Bridges, in a study of crisscross inheritance in drosophila, showed the complexity of gene effect for traits tied to a single chromosome (the X chromosome). The work of these two graduate students continued in 1914, when Sturtevant demonstrated the independent segregation of linkage groups, and found, for example, that even though a single gene substitution might lead to the suppression of a trait, there might still be multiple genes working in the expression of the trait. In 1916, H. J. Muller's doctoral thesis dealt with the complexity of crossing over among genes, and proposed the idea of multiple crossovers. *

Thus was born the classical gene, the concept that ultimately paved the way for the double helix. In the period from 1912 to 1917, Morgan's group of researchers redefined the study of heredity, tied it strictly to the mechanical model of multiple alleles, and demonstrated the amassed complexity of gene action (Carlson 1966, p. 66). It was largely here that the simple conceptions of inheritance so in vogue at the time met their sharpest challenge. However, social effects of this work did not immediately manifest themselves, partially because the leader of the group, Morgan, preferred to remain apolitical. He recognized the inadmissibility of much eugenicist doctrine, but preferred not to embroil himself in a debate with that group—some of them were his personal friends, and others controlled funding agencies (Allen 1975). Thus, eugenics's political successes were still to come, though the biological basis for the policies advocated was already being undermined.

Most of the comment on the problem of eugenics remained internal until the mid-1920s. Still, some comment had emerged earlier, though most of this came from people outside theoretical biology: for

---

*An excellent review of the abovementioned research can be found in Carlson (1966, chaps. 9-11).

example, Franz Boas in anthropology, E. B. Titchener and Livingston Farrand in psychology, Burt Green Wilder and F. P. Mall in anatomy, and Frances Kellor and R. E. Park in sociology (Beardsley 1973; Paynter 1971). These writers tended to aim their writings at the specific issues of the immigration and black questions so widely debated at the time, rather than at the general issues of eugenic action that the drosophila studies helped to resolve. However, within biology, the cytogeneticist A. F. Blakeslee (1914) wrote, as early as 1914, that "in the garden of human life as in the garden of corn, success is the resultant complex of the two factors, environment and heredity" (p. 518). In the same article, Blakeslee warned that too great a willingness to legislate eugenics would blind people to the power of environmental manipulation (for a summary, see Ludmerer 1972, p. 79). By 1919, Lancelot Hogben (1919) could maintain, in view of the complex interactionist nature of organismic development, that "between biological science and economic determinism there is no conflict" (p. 153). *

The Changing Meaning of Heredity

It is clear that a fundamental difference came to exist between the biometric and Mendelian (later, genetic) views of the process of biological inheritance. In part this was caused by the various biases of early proponents of each position, and in part it was caused by methodological differences. Whatever the sources, after the work of Morgan and his students, the social implications of one's accepted position came to be considerable.

Recall the discussion of conservative and liberal thought in Chapter 1. The biometric tradition began in an atmosphere that can be characterized as "bourgeois liberal." Here was a concern for the quantitative and continuous, a preference for abstraction and theory, and the insistence on a universal application of principles. Among others, Galton, Pearson, and Weldon were convinced of the universal applicability of statistical designs for the solution of human social problems. The highly abstract law of ancestral heredity accounted for the presence of these problems, and once various aspects of reproduction and inheritance had been given purely mathematical defi-

---

*However, it cannot be said that Hogben was, at that time, completely opposed to the legislation of eugenics. In the article just cited, he held that certain classes of people should be sterilized. Here he included "the feebleminded, epileptic, or homicidal maniac" (Hogben 1919, p. 154).

nitions, they could be treated as givens. Little attention needed to be given to more basic mechanistic reasons for phenomena.

Mendelian thought was conservative in nature. Here the stress was on discontinuity, and there was a preference for the particular and the concrete. Especially with Mendel's most vociferous English proponent, Bateson, discontinuity and the concrete instance were of paramount importance. In fact, Bateson apparently found Mendel's rediscovered paper compelling precisely because it gave a mechanistic basis for the idea of discontinuous variation, an idea that he had propounded for some time, and that was an anathema to the biometricians (see Coleman 1970; also, the account in Carlson 1966, pp. 1-8). For Bateson, morphology and experimental research were central to biology because "that part of biology was concrete." If he had an axiom, it was that one should savor one's exceptions.

This vast difference in emphasis led researchers to look for different things. While the biometricians looked for correlations among relatives, with a mind toward the pragmatic application of any findings, the Mendelians began experimental work in order to isolate the precise causes of particular instances of continuity and discontinuity. Even after Fisher had shown that Mendelian inheritance could yield biometric results, this difference did not change. Rather, biometricians still sought average representations of relationships in a population, only now these were compared with a given Mendelian model. This was still a massed-action view of environment and heredity, and it still portrayed inheritance as a linear affair where both genetic and environmental elements were added incrementally to a trait (though an interaction component could be added to the tail end of a linear model, in order to account for variations in the distribution of a population as a whole).

From such a view, it seems reasonable to generate nature-nurture ratios, or balance sheets, with which to answer questions of the causation of traits. If, for example, 80 percent of a trait is genetically determined, then is not breeding the most feasible way of changing the expression of the trait in the population? As mentioned earlier, the experimentalist must say no, or at least "not necessarily."*

---

*While his choice of examples differed, Lewontin's critique of Jensen's use of heritability estimates followed the same logical path as had Hogben's criticism of Fisher's use of balance sheets 37 years earlier. In this as well as other respects, the IQ controversy resembles nothing else as much as an instant replay of the earlier nature-nurture controversy. The same arguments are used, and similar data are contrasted. For more on this, see Paynter (1971).

The Analysis of Data

The importance of these differences in approach to issues of heredity becomes clear when we examine the responses of members of the rival camps to identical sets of data. We will view a single example here, and then develop a case for the relationship between biometrics and psychometrics, which will shed some light on the influence heritability estimation has had on social scientists.

The body of evidence at hand is a series of studies performed by Frank N. Freeman and his associates (for example, Newman, Freeman, and Holzinger 1937; Freeman, Holzinger, and Mitchell 1928), dealing with adopted children raised in a single home, and identical twins raised together and apart. Consider the study of monozygotic twins. The correlation of IQ scores for such persons, raised together, was 0.88, and even those raised apart showed a higher correlation than did those of dizygotic twins raised together (0.67 versus 0.63). However, among a set of 19 monozygotic twin pairs, 9 pairs differed in obtained scores by 6 or fewer points, 6 pairs differed by 7-to-12 points, and 4 pairs differed by 15-to-24 points. On basically this set of data, Frederick Osborn (1951, pp. 89-96), in his Preface to Eugenics, considered the study strong evidence for the importance of heredity in the determination of intelligence; further, he considered it supportive of a eugenics program. Muller, on the other hand, primarily because the IQ-score differences among "genetically identical twins who were reared apart are considerable," considered this a strong indicator of the importance of environment in the determination of intelligence (see the account in Pastore 1949, pp. 153-55).

Now, these differences are partially functions of the desires of the different interpreters. Osborn was a eugenicist, Muller a Marxist. However, Osborn was also interpreting the data in terms of a general correlation among twins, while Muller concentrated on the fact of wide variation in the magnitude of score differences. Significantly, Muller also took the evidence from Barbara Burk's famous adoption study (often cited by hereditarians) to be evidence for the importance of environmental differences in the development of intelligence, because genetically diverse adoptees came to resemble their adoptive parents to a moderate degree. The fact that genetically diverse individuals could be made relatively similar, on the basis of control of crude social variables, impressed him more than did the fact that genetically homogeneous people generally resembled one another; the latter merely represented the generally acknowledged fact that relatives tended to resemble one another, while the former indicated something of the dynamics of trait expression.

With the successes of experimental genetics, the scientific backing of the eugenics movement began to fade. All sources consulted by this author mention a split between genetics and eugenics that had opened by the end of World War I. With certain exceptions (for example, E. M. East), those conducting genetic research ultimately came to repudiate eugenics. Included here are Morgan, who had toyed with the idea of eugenics actions, and who had been a member of some organizations linked to eugenics activities, but who ultimately called for "a little goodwill" in the handling of intergroup problems. Other workers in genetics who left the eugenics movement and became either public or private critics of it included W. E. Castle, H. S. Jennings, Raymond Pearl, Vernon Kellogg, E. Carlton Mac-Dowell, and S. J. Holmes (see Allen 1975; Provine 1973; Ludmerer 1972; Haller 1963). According to Charles Rosenberg (1967), the early enthusiasm gave way to "a collective skepticism, a kind of intellectual bad taste, in the profession, especially among younger, research-oriented men" (p. 37). This led to a growing abandonment of even legitimate applications of human genetics, which has only recently begun to abate.

HEREDITARIAN THOUGHT IN PSYCHOLOGY

The drawing away from eugenics that occurred within biology, with the growing realization of the complex nature of genetic inheritance, did not occur among psychologists. Rather, the simpler nature-nurture approach to the development of traits remained, and the vestiges of this line of thought have marked nature-nurture debates in psychology to this day.

This does not mean that psychologists did not, on the whole, abandon eugenics. Actually, they did do so. But the general psychological split from eugenics did not occur until a decade or so after the genetics-eugenics split, and it was not as complete. While the excesses of the early 1900s may have left an "intellectual bad taste" for geneticists, they did not do so for psychology, where various protagonists have continuously debated issues of nature and nurture in what has become a kind of traditional dissensus. For example, in 1928, the yearbook of the National Society for the Study of Education was entirely devoted to issues of the nature and nurture of intelligence and achievement. It was here that the famous Burks (1928) and Freeman, Holzinger, and Mitchell (1928) studies of foster children appeared. In all, 862 pages were devoted to the issue, and a hereditarian stance prevailed. Again, in 1940, the entire issue of the yearbook was devoted to studies of the nature and nurture of intelligence, this time covering a span of 890 pages. It was in this yearbook that the final summary of the Tryon (1940) rat studies was presented, as well as the controversial work on environmental influences on IQ that was done by Stoddard and Wellman (1940). Finally, in the modern debate the proponents of innate class or race inferiority have been largely psychologists. * There are at least four reasons for this difference between biologists and psychologists, and all are somehow related to this line of simple hereditarian thought.

Psychology and Least-Squares Techniques

First is the fact that psychology's primary methodology is least-squares analysis. In the early part of the twentieth century, statistical analysis of the least-squares variety was transferred to U.S. psychology, to some extent through the efforts of Thorndike, who held that this new quantitative approach to the discipline would be its salvation (see Joncich 1968).

This technique had the power to elucidate relationships that would have been otherwise difficult to spot. At the same time, it had the effect of causing users of the technique to generally view causality in terms of undefined, massed effects. That is, the methods used could show effects, but could not show the material occurrences that generated those effects. Theoretical postulation of underlying phenomena was necessary here.

Generally, this may not be a very great problem. However, recall that in biometrics, causation was seen in terms of an elabora-

---

*As mentioned in Chapter 4, a general social-science bias toward environmentalism has been noted by several writers, as has a general biological-science bias toward hereditarianism (for example, Halsey 1968; Pastore 1949; Harwood 1976, p. 371). However, this writer believes these biases to be minor when one views the actual social pronouncements of members of the various disciplines and subdisciplines. Of the major proponents of the hereditarian position since the mid-1950s (Jensen, Eysenck, Cattell, Ingle, Herrnstein, Burt, Eckland, Shuey, Garrett, Shockley, W. C. George, C. P. Armstrong, A. J. Gregor, and Ernest van den Haag), only George, van den Haag, Ingle, Eckland, and Shockley are not psychologists. Of these, Shockley is a physicist and Eckland, whose position is actually more interactionist than hereditarian, is a sociologist. Of the biology specialists, George was professor emeritus at the University of North Carolina from 1949 on, and he wrote a book on biology and race for the governor of Alabama in 1962. Van den Haag was a professor of social philosophy at New York University, and only Ingle was an active researcher. Among active environmentalists, however (including Hunt, Deutsch, J. Kagan, E. Gordan, Dobzhansky, Bodmer, Montagu, Brace, Livingstone, Hirsch, Steven Rose, Lewontin, Kamin, B. Simon, Jencks, A. Halsey, Layzer, and Bronfenbrenner), the sampling

tion of the old "like-begets-like" idea. When biometricians (later, psychometricians) claimed that some 80 percent of the variation in a trait was genetically caused (and when they showed data that seemed to bear out this claim), psychologists respected the claims because the claims were made in this statistical context. Psychometry's bread and butter was the descriptive statistic, and it would be difficult for psychologists to reject such data out-of-hand without attacking the very methods to which they had become so committed.

Later, we will return to this point, and review some experiments in psychology that brought about a shift from hereditarian thought in the 1930s.

The Isolation of Psychology from Genetics

The second reason why psychologists were late to recognize the weakness of the eugenicists' case was that these scientists were not in the forefront of genetic research. To some extent, this is merely a function of specialization in science. People in one field can certainly not be expected to follow developments in another field. Such concepts as the norm of reaction, crossing over, and epistasis were not part of their working vocabulary, and while individual psychologists might be familiar with the terms and understand their definitions, there was little reason for the theoretical significance of the concepts to become widely known. After all, Fisher (1918) had just recently shown that biometric techniques could be used whatever the underlying process of genetic causation happened to be. Since biometric and

---

of specialties is broader. For example, Dobzhansky, Bodmer, Hirsch, and Lewontin are geneticists, Rose is a neurobiologist, and Layzer is a physicist. The other writers specialize in psychology, sociology, anthropology, and education. (For listings of names, see Harwood 1976, 1977; Cartwright and Burtis 1968.) These lists are, of course, by no means exhaustive, but in the absence of more thorough data, we can take them as suggestive.

It is interesting that so few biologists have been willing to take public stands in favor of the Jensen thesis, while a fairly large number of psychologists have taken such stands. Of course, many psychologists have taken a stand against the Jensen thesis, but it is evident that many of them have felt torn in doing so. The point is merely that elements exist in psychological thought that made a hereditarian position on human achievement seem more reasonable to members of the discipline, in the aggregate, than is the case for biology. A general survey of the beliefs of members of disciplines would be very helpful in testing this hypothesis.

psychometric analyses were so similar, the temptation must have been
very great to borrow heavily from the one area of genetic analysis that
was readily comprehensible to psychologically trained researchers.

As a single example of this tendency, let us review two studies
by Burks (1928a, 1928b) in the 27th Yearbook of the National Society
for the Study of Education. Burks, an associate of Terman at Stanford, wrote the first article, "Statistical Hazards in Nature-Nurture
Investigations," in order to make explicit some pitfalls awaiting the
unwary investigator, and (one supposes) to set the stage for the second article: "The Relative Influence of Nature and Nurture upon Mental Development: A Comparative Study of Foster Parent-Foster Child
Resemblance and True Parent-True Child Resemblance."

In the initial article, Burks developed a very thorough assessment of statistical pitfalls, including sample selection, the tendency
to impute causality when correlation is found, problems of inextricable
causation, problems in a priori assumptions, problems of partial correlation, problems of causality in the use of partial regression, restriction and extension of range, incommensurability of various findings, and spuriousness of relationships. What emerged appeared to
be a hard-nosed look at research procedures, and a detailed look at
complexities of statistical evaluation. So many hazards were detailed
(14 major sections, and often more than one problem to a section), that
the article could well be used to challenge the usefulness of statistical
studies of nature-nurture problems.

However, this was not the case, for Burks began her second
article by stating that attempts to study nature and nurture must isolate the various effects of the two, and that this could be done either
experimentally or statistically. She concluded (Burks 1928b):

> The second method offers us more than the first, ulti-
> mately, for in addition to isolating nature-nurture effects,
> it promises to yield an explanation of the actual mechanics
> underlying mental heredity. A start has been made towards
> developing such a scheme of mathematical analysis in the
> work of R. A. Fisher. [P. 221]

Burks's debt to the biometric tradition is indicated by her reference to the development of Mendelian biometrics by Fisher. References to Yule, Spearman, Wright, and Kelley also underscored this
tradition. Nowhere did she discuss the use of true experimental procedures in the study of nature and nurture, even for purposes of sup-
plementing a study. In fact, in the passage just quoted, she denigrated
the explanatory power of direct manipulation, and implied (counter-
factually) that it did not yield an explanation of the actual mechanics
of mental heredity. But recall that it had been known from the early

1900s that biometric analysis gave little insight into the mechanisms of heredity.

Burks's view of inheritance was not the simplistic one that often made the rounds, in which nature or nurture was considered the primary cause of the development of a trait. She merely wished to determine which of the two was more efficacious in explaining the variance of a trait in a population, where social background was considered to be the environment. However, the fact that she was not thoroughly aware of the experimental basis of modern genetics was made apparent by the way in which she concluded that a change in environment would not have as great an effect on measured IQ as would a change in breeding. It is also shown in her insistence on the presence of some "innate intelligence," which she admitted might be somewhat affected by environmental variations (see Burks 1928b, pp. 308-9). Such a phrase was a throwback to the Galton era, in that it gave a trait a fixed status independent of a given environment.

Another bit of evidence of the fact that psychometricians like Burks were operating outside an experimental tradition of research is given by the fact that, though her study was generally experimental in design, she neglected the analysis of true experimental effects of adoption placement. That is, even though her study demonstrated that an average IQ gain of about five points (over what one would reasonably expect to find, given the conditions of the study) obtained when children were raised in somewhat superior adoptive homes, her study dealt almost wholly with what would later be termed heritability, that is, nature-nurture ratios. Her major finding, mentioned twice in the study, was that about 17 percent of the variance in IQ scores was related to differences in environment, a conclusion that others have found wanting.* When another adoption study in the same volume

---

*Hogben (1932), Muller (1933), Wright (1931), and Goldberger (1974b) have all indicated that the figure of 17 percent must be a very conservative figure, for a number of reasons. Most important is the fact that, despite assertions to the contrary, her sample was very homogeneous, with an overabundance of upper-middle-class homes. Further, she had no blacks, Chicanos, or Jews in her sample. Also, 59 percent of her sample was not contacted, and of those that were, data on 24 percent were unavailable, mostly for a variety of reasons, which, it is reasonable to assume, would have environmental impacts (reasons given for unavailability included: a "dead parent," "divorced parents," "sickness," "living in an inaccessible region," "field worke told by organization secretaries not to visit case" [why?], "working mother," "deafness of a foster parent"). Another 9 percent refused cooperation, and 8 percent gave only partial cooperation. Since en-

(Freemen, Holzinger, and Mitchell 1928) appeared to grant a greater role to environment in the determination of IQ, Burks (1928c), instead of concentrating on the great similarity of the two studies (both esti- mated that adoption led to an IQ increase in the neighborhood of five points), attacked the methodology of the other study, while neglecting methodological problems in her own study. We will return to this point.

Psychology and Social Action

A third reason for the hereditarian proclivities of psychologists is that from the first, they were interested in the social application of the idea of heredity. As shown, even such even-handed investiga- tors as Binet were at least as interested in the possibility of pragmatic application of psychological technique as they were in the generation of knowledge about the nature of intelligence and about nature and nur- ture. Since humans were extremely difficult animals to work with ex- perimentally, other methods, which had been developed in the course of the eugenics movement, were employed. What is important here is that to a considerable extent, psychology was policy oriented, and the studies done were assumed to have policy implications. Since one of the major issues of the time had to do with class and race differ- ences in intelligence (this was indeed seen by many as the leading is- sue of the day; hence, the viability of the eugenics movement), it is small wonder that so many psychological studies had to do with this topic. Given the complexity of the issues at hand, and the impossibil- ity of demonstrating the paramount importance of either heredity or environment, many articles could be generated without exhausting the field. If genetic studies were undertaken to determine the mechanisms of inheritance, psychological studies were performed (if we may exag-

---

vironmental variance was so strongly constricted, heritability was in- creased, and the effect of social environment was almost certainly underestimated. Further, recall (from Chapter 5) that when Wright (1931) reanalyzed Burks's data by means of path analysis, he found that heritability included more than just heredity. Wright obtained two overall estimates of heritability for the Burks data, 0.81 and 0.49, which he took to be the best upper and lower estimates of heredity. When Goldgerger (1974, pp. 18-19) substituted, for the simple index of environment used by Wright, a more complex index also found in the Burks study, the upper limit of heritability fell to 0.68. Goldber- ger suspects that were more refined indicators of environment used, heritability would fall still more. Interestingly, Jensen uses the 0.81 figure as the heritability estimate resulting from the Burks study.

gerate) to determine who was smarter. The social implications were always present, which brings us to the fourth reason for the strength of hereditarian thought in psychology.

Psychology and Hereditarian-Research Traditions

Precisely, a predisposition to accept the nature side of debates was a constituent element of psychological thought in the early twentieth century. This has to do not only with policy orientation but also with the specific issues of genetic causation. Both testing and psychometric analysis began with Galton, and his influence on each was pervasive. In the normal passing of traditions from professor to student, those who pursued nature-nurture investigations tended to be those who either were oriented toward a nature-versus-nurture position in the first place, or who came to agree with their professors over time. Hereditarian schools dominated psychology. As has been shown, the early testers were almost all hereditarians, as their students tended to be. Inspection of their writings, as done in previous chapters, reveals that, from the first, they felt that they were on to the secret of human achievement, and that the tests would ultimately allow them to determine who had worth and who did not. As Paynter (1971) has pointed out, they "shared the prejudices of their time. They 'knew' that the races differed in mental capacity; they wanted to determine, in a scientific way, how much" (p. 26). Especially at Stanford, where Terman wielded enormous influence, the bias toward a nature-oriented explanation of human differences prevailed. And since Stanford became the premier school of psychometry, its influence was pervasive. If the psychologists there were not well versed in genetics, this did not halt their enthusiasm; rather, their enthusiasm was enhanced, for such selective ignorance allowed them to disregard the enormous complexity of inheritance, and hence to offer simple models of heredity.

Thus, the results that lent too great a weight to the environment as a factor in the determination of traits were viewed skeptically, while those that showed that heredity dwarfed all other causes were viewed as almost self-evidently true. Thus, Burks (1928b), in the conclusion to her second study, exuberantly quoted Galton to the effect that "heredity is a force in the determination of mental ability by the side of which all other forces are 'dwarfed in comparison'" (p. 309).

The importance of tradition, and especially of the political weight of proponents in a controversy, is demonstrated by the already mentioned 27th Yearbook of the National Society for the Study of Education. In that work, as mentioned, the findings of Burks and of Freeman, Holzinger, and Mitchell were somewhat similar. Both studies found a moderate boost in IQ scores following adoption. However, the Freeman study had a much more environmentalist flavor, and appeared to show that environment had a much greater overall impact than Burks was willing to grant it (Freeman, Holzinger, and Mitchell 1928, pp. 209-11). This study is one of the first that was to emerge from the environmentalist schools that developed at the universities of Chicago and Iowa. What is important here is the reaction to the study.

In compiling the yearbook, the two articles were placed back to back, with Burks's coming second. Following that, a third article appeared, also by Burks (1928c), which compared and contrasted the two. What is important is that Burks was specifically requested by the chairman of the society's yearbook committee to prepare this article (Burks 1928c, p. 317), which pointed out a number of methodological weaknesses in the Chicago study, while mentioning none in the Stanford study. It is of course more difficult to spot errors in one's own reasoning than in another's, but it is even more difficult to understand why the Chicago group was not also given a chance to compare the articles.

The chairman of the committee was Terman. This does not suggest any kind of a conspiracy theory as an explanation of the decision on Terman's part to choose Burks to review the two articles. His decision was not hidden. Terman evidently decided that the two earlier articles required a comparison, and decided that his methodologically sophisticated colleague at Stanford would be the best person for the job. However, it is evident that he would not have chosen her had he not found her results compelling, in line with his own hereditarian beliefs. Also, she was his research and secretarial assistant in the preparation of the yearbook (Terman 1928, p. xiii).

What occurred here was dominance by a single institutional group. Not only was Terman the chairman of the society's Yearbook Committee on the Possibilities and Limitations of Training, but Terman's associates at Stanford dominated the yearbook, in the sense that the Stanford group had by far the most articles therein. In part I, 8 of 22 articles had authors who were either listed as being at Stanford or were well-known students of Terman. It is not known how many might have been less well known Stanford Ph.D.'s. In part II, at least 4 of 16 articles came from the Stanford group, including a fourth article by Burks (1928d).

The pervasive influence of the Stanford group did not stop there, but continued with the chapter prefaces included with the various studies. In his introduction, Terman (1928) indicated that all viewpoints had been sought, yet the chapter prefaces (added by "the committee" for the benefit of the "lay reader" [see Whipple 1928, p. ix]) were of a rather hereditarian posture. In some cases, the prefaces were simply signed "Editor" (G. M. Whipple), but in other cases they were signed "L. M. T." (Lewis Madison Terman); and in most cases they were not signed at all, though the language in them was very similar to Terman's. The comments in several instances tended to downgrade environmental results and to upgrade hereditarian results. Thus, when Thorndike showed that home environment tended to raise the IQ correlations of siblings, an unsigned preface noted that the inference was not "thoroughly established." However, when an article by Gladys Tallman indicated that the degree of intellectual resemblance increased with an increase in degree of genetic relationship, any possible environmental explanation of such a fact was ruled to be "too far-fetched to be taken very seriously" (National Society for the Study of Education 1928, pt. I, p. 82). A study of the degree of resemblance in maze running among white rats was faulted for showing correlations that were too low (for example, 0.31 versus the expected 0.50, by Mendelian theory alone). In any event, the evidence of the study was such that, if correct, "an enormous weight of evidence immediately falls in the direction of heredity in the human domain" (pt. I, p. 88), though this is demonstrably not the case. It was indicated that a study by Peterson on interracial comparisons in learning "carries the implication (though it does not prove) that differences . . . are due to a more elemental difference than can be produced by mere differences in educational opportunities" (pt. I, p. 332). A study that indicated that mental age was more important for school achievement than grade in school was commended for "pointing which way the wind blows" (pt. II, p. 112).

CHANGING ORIENTATIONS WITHIN PSYCHOLOGY

Even granting the correctness of the argument that psychology, as a whole, remained more hospitable to nature-versus-nurture arguments than did other disciplines, change still occurred in the beliefs expressed by major psychologists, regarding at least the specific issues of black-white intellectual differences. From the early 1920s, when something of a consensus existed regarding the genetic explanation of racial test-score differences, the beliefs expressed by psychologists later followed the general trend of becoming more "agnostic," to use George Stocking's (1960) phrase.

According to Yoder (1928), by 1928 there were "three distinct viewpoints" on this specific issue: There was a group that accepted racial superiority as a proved fact; a group that accepted racial superiority as an unproved possibility; and a group that was highly skeptical of the evidence on racial differences, and that tended to insist on the doctrine of racial equality. By 1930, Carl C. Brigham had repudiated the thesis of racial differences, at least as portrayed in his A Study of American Intelligence; and even such stalwarts as Goddard (1928) expressed increasing skepticism about the results of the tests.

The only study of the day, of which this author is aware, that attempted to survey the racial beliefs of various social scientists appeared in a special issue of the Journal of Negro Education in 1934 (Thompson 1934). For the study, the author interviewed a nonrandom sample of 77 psychologists, 30 educationists, and 22 sociologists and anthropologists. Among replies received, sociologists and anthropologists tended to take an equalitarian position, psychologists tended to take a more hereditarian position, and educationists tended to fall in between. For example, 25 percent of psychologists, 14 percent of educationists, and only 5 percent of anthropologists and sociologists indicated that the evidence demonstrated black inferiority. The percentages were reversed regarding those who felt that the evidence indicated general equality (11 percent versus 15 percent versus 38 percent). What is more, when summaries of the replies of various writers were printed, it turned out that even many of those who held to a belief in inequality tended to hedge their answers, to indicate that "inferior" did not mean "inherently" inferior, or to state that different groups might be inferior in some ways and superior in others (see Thompson 1934, pp. 511-12).

For psychologists specifically, 75 percent felt either that the evidence indicated equality or that the data were inconclusive. This percentage can be compared with Friedrichs's (1973) cross-sectional sample of members of the APA, of whom 68 percent either disagreed or tended to disagree with the Jensen thesis. Granting the possibility of real selection biases in the 1934 sample, it still seems that a rapid change in opinion had occurred in the 1920s and early 1930s, a change that was represented in Friedrichs's more professionally drawn sample, 36 years later. *

This growing agnosticism among psychologists can be traced to at least four types of events. First were findings by early testers that were difficult to square with the genetic fatalism that marked the movement. Second were criticisms of testing made by people from other professions, which claimed expertise on some of the major issues. Especially significant was the cultural-determinist school of thought of Boas and his students (see Paynter 1971). Third was the

---

*Thompson included, in his article, the names of all of the 1934 sample respondents, though he did not indicate the beliefs of specific persons (the reader is thus referred to Thompson 1934, pp. 495-97).

appearance of experimentally oriented studies, within psychology, that appeared to demonstrate a degree of malleability in IQ scores. Fourth was the development of environmentalist-research programs, especially at Chicago and Iowa, which tended to promote environmentalist doctrine in response to the hereditarian doctrine promoted at Stanford.

Research by Psychologists and Hereditarianism

In the first category listed above, the first, and probably most important, studies were performed by Cattell, after he had abandoned testing to become what has been termed the organizer of science. In his earlier writing, according to Nicholas Pastore (1949, p. 134), Cattell leaned toward a hereditarian and eugenicist position in discussions of scientific talent (Cattell 1903). By 1914, however, his studies of the backgrounds of U.S. men of science had convinced him that environmental variations played crucial roles in the development of talent. Among his findings were these facts: there existed wide sectional variations in the production of scientists; cities tended to produce the largest numbers of such persons; over a period of years, southern states increased their representation among U.S. scientists; and blacks and mulattoes were almost unrepresented here (see Pastore 1949, p. 130; also, Cattell 1914, 1915, 1917). Challenged on his interpretations by such hereditarians as F. A. Woods, Cattell retained at least a modified environmentalist approach (which appears initially to have been made in opposition to hereditarian theorists), as he noted that the position "approached by men with so much authority as Sir Francis Galton, Professor Karl Pearson, Dr. F. A. Woods, Dr. C. B. Davenport and Professor E. L. Thorndike, is untenable" (Cattell 1914, p. 510).* Cattell's position was that fairly rapid changes in the output of eminent persons could not be explained in biological terms, and made more sense if one construed social environment as having an important effect on human achievement. In the 1920s and 1930s, studies followed that supported this interpretation. Some of these will be discussed below.

---

*It is interesting that Cattell's environmentalism grew after he left the testing movement, took over the editorship of Science, and became the organizer of science. In that position, he was subject to the influence of scientists in a wide variety of disciplines, including experimental genetics and Boasian anthropology, and was relatively free from the provincialism that marks people in isolated subdisciplines. This author is inclined to speculate that this influence was important in Cattell's turn from eugenics, but, at least for now, this must remain unsubstantiated.

Criticism from Outside Psychology

The criticism of testing by people outside psychology is important because it forced a focus of attention, within psychology, on the problems discussed. One major attack was the already mentioned famous criticism of the army studies, and of the work of Cyril Burt, by Walter Lippmann. Specifically, Lippmann attacked problems of mental age (especially as related to the numerous announcements at the time that the average mental age of people in the United States was only 14), the use of tests for judgments of relative talent, the assumption that test scores represented levels of intelligence, and so forth. Following this was Lippmann's vigorous exchange with Terman (noted previously), in the same magazine.

The importance of Lippmann's criticisms lies not so much in the fact that they were brand new, but that they were presented publicly, were made by an influential writer, and acted as a stimulus to the methodological critiques within psychology that ultimately led to such occurrences as Brigham's repudiation (and others) of earlier work. By themselves, of course, Lippmann's articles could not be very effective in this regard, but they were joined by cultural anthropology's criticism of testing, which had more profound results. Made by Boas and his major students, this attack stressed the idea that biological differences among peoples were not worthy of serious study. This was because of the impossibility of removing cultural content from human action. The important anthropological task, for Boas, was the description of culture; because the effect of culture was so omnipresent, a codified method of ranking mental powers was met with a measure of distrust. It was partly for this reason that Boas had been a defender of racial minorities since at least 1896 (Beardsley 1973), though he was not totally convinced of the presence of human intellectual equality (Boas 1901).

A significant portion of Boas's influence came through his position in the American Anthropological Association. After a decade of intense political infighting, Boas and his associates gained active control of the association, and were able to propound an antiracialist cultural anthropology and give it institutional support. That the association was not more active is probably associated with the fact that a number of marginal participants (like Grant and Davenport) were active racialists (see Stocking 1968, chap. 11). Apparently in response to the association's refusal to investigate biological differences among peoples—a primary goal of physical anthropology at that time—the National Research Council set up a Division of Anthropology and Psychology, the avowed purpose of which was to investigate "the racial characters, mental and physical, of groups within the American population" (Stocking 1968, p. 298). Again after a period of infighting, this division was taken over by Boas's associates. Two of these, A. L. Kroeber and Clark Wissler (who had performed the studies that drove Cattell from the testing movement) chaired the committee successively.

Here, a direct link was forged to the testing community. Kroeber, who had felt in 1915 that absolute equality of all human races must be assumed, was ready by 1920 to consider that the topic must be investigated. Wissler got him in contact with Terman, and the two collaborated on the first attempt to produce a culture-free intelligence scale in the fall of 1920. In the same year, Wissler (1920) issued a plea for a rapprochement between psychology and anthropology.

Stocking characterizes Wissler as neutral in the disputes between psychology and anthropology (Stocking 1968, p. 297), a term that seems apt. Wissler was actually a member of the Galton Society, and during his tenure as chair of the Division of Anthropology and Psychology, it was almost completely composed of members of the eugenics and immigration-restriction movements, a majority that reached a peak in 1923, the year of the Immigration Restriction Law. However, he was also culturally oriented, and his book Man and Culture (1923), while heavily Nordic in tone, had a great deal of influence on psychologists in terms of presenting the anthropological idea of culture (Stocking 1968, p. 301).

By the mid-1920s, Boas had secured a major role in the National Research Council and secured fellowships for Melville, Herskovits, Margaret Mead, and Otto Klineberg, which were used to pursue research directed by Boas. From these students came several of the studies that directly challenged the conclusions of Brigham's analysis of the army studies. Brigham's study, in fact, can be seen as, ironically, helping to establish the anthropological view of culture and bring about the downfall of the simplistic racial explanations of psychologists of the early 1920s. This is because the work of Boas's students was directed at Brigham's study and at those that mirrored it.

By 1925, the first full critique of the army studies had been made by William Bagley, (1925) a student of Titchener. Bagley reanalyzed the army data, and found a relationship between test scores and the amount of educational spending in various states. In 1928, Truman Kelley (1928), actually a strong hereditarian, criticized the tests on methodological grounds, and suggested that they demonstrated that neither a unilinear, nor a two-factor, theory of intellect was sufficient to account for the variance in scores obtained. * Of Boas's stu-

---

*It was Kelley's critique that apparently proved overwhelming to Brigham, whose 1930 repudiation leaned heavily on it for documentation (see Brigham 1930, pp. 160-62).

dents, the one whose studies have become most famous was Klineberg, whose decade-long research into racial differences demonstrated that IQ scores changed with the length of residence of blacks in the North (Klineberg 1931, 1935a, 1935b). Especially interesting is the fact that his study of changing IQs was directly modeled on Boas's earlier studies of changing head forms among immigrants. One of his findings was that of a tendency (mentioned in Chapter 5) for blacks in the North to gain higher IQ scores than did whites in the South, a finding that was extended by Ruth Benedict and Gene Weltfish (1943) in a book that was partially suppressed (see Montagu 1963).

Of the other students, Mead studied socialization in Samoa, at least partially in order to demonstrate the extreme plasticity of human behavior. More specific to the issue of racial differences, she played a role through her critique of testing methods, where she complained that though a writer might recognize that testing methods were in "swaddling clothes," "he is not so conscious [of the fact] that a methodology adequate to deal with racial and nationality testing has not even been born" (Mead 1926, p. 658). Mead's empirical work demonstrated that massive changes in social behavior accompanied cultural change, and this became part of a general criticism of the nativist views of psychologists. The hereditarian hypothesis was contrasted with the fact of widespread environmental effects on behavior.

Of Boas's other students, the most important was Herskovits (1926, 1928) who examined the "mulatto hypothesis" in some detail. This hypothesis was that the children of mixed marriages would have average intellects roughly halfway between those of the two parent races. Herskovits used various anthropometric indicators to determine the degree of racial mixture of black subjects and correlated these with scores on the Thorndike College Entrance Examination. What obtained were low correlations, so low that Herskovits (1926) concluded that they could be "of no value in drawing conclusions as to the comparative ability of the Negro when compared to the White" (p. 41).

The influence of this growing number of critics of the early testers was considerable. When they were joined by psychologists from the emerging environmentalist schools (for example, Frank Freeman), their side gained enough influence to lead to the growing degree of agnosticism first noted in the Yoder (1928) article.

Still, any evidence of a growing environmentalist consensus is absent. For example, at Stanford a staunch hereditarianism prevailed for quite some time. Thus, though her study in the 1928 yearbook indicated an environmental impact on IQ scores, Burks scarcely mentioned this fact. So strong was her hereditarian bent that she stated that Boas's (1911) The Mind of Primitive Man had no direct relevance to issues of nature and nurture (Burks 1928d). In contrast,

Boas saw his studies, and those of his students, "as part of a coordinated attack on the problem of the cultural factor in racial differences" (Stocking 1968, p. 300). It may be that Kroeber's attempt to "introduce some anthropological sophistication" into Terman's research program (Stocking 1968, p. 301), had failed. It is certain that many years would pass before Terman admitted, even in private, any doubts as to black inferiority. When the leadership of The 39th Yearbook (National Society for the Study of Education 1940) gave strongly environmentalist interpretations to a series of findings, Terman and his supporters responded with a scathing rebuke of those writers. This will be detailed below.

In any event, the critical reaction to the early Brigham study, to a considerable extent coming from cultural anthropologists, was instrumental in bringing about the agnosticism that still generally reigns regarding at least the specific issue of black-white differences in intelligence. Along with Brigham, Terman's student Florence Goodenough (Goodenough and Harris 1950) eventually gave a public apology for early nativist interpretations of some test findings, and Peterson (1934) came to express great caution in his analysis of racial differences. The debate of the 1920s was instrumental in turning E. G. Boring and Freeman in a direction opposing the hereditarian camp (see the account in Marks 1975). Among others, T. R. Garth (1931, 1934), who began as a strong eugenicist, ultimately decided, on methodological grounds, that the worth of different peoples had never been established. At least by 1927, Boas was convinced that "all our best psychologists" recognized the lack of proof of the differing mental functioning across groups (Boas 1927, p. 681; see also Gossett 1963, chap. 16). The superlative used in the quoted remark may indicate that Boas felt anyone who did not recognize the lack of proof would, ipso facto, not be one of the "best" psychologists. However, as an indicator of the general direction in which psychologists were to go, the statement is essentially correct.

Experimental Research in Psychology:
The 39th Yearbook

By the publication date of The 39th Yearbook (National Society for the Study of Education 1940), the greater proportion of psychologists had abandoned the view that black-white differences in test scores were necessarily genetic in origin. While much of this change can be attributed to the events already described, a portion of it is doubtless related to a changing mode of conceptualization within psychology. Specifically, psychologists moved away from the use of mere nature-nurture ratios, and toward experimental design. If this tendency was never to become fully dominant in the discipline, it at

least served to undercut some of the more extreme views of hereditarians. Nowhere is this more clearly demonstrated than in The 39th
Yearbook, for which operations were chaired by George Stoddard of
the University of Iowa. So different was the leadership for this yearbook from that for the 1928 yearbook that the editor (Whipple 1940,
p. xvii) termed the two, respectively, the Terman yearbook and the
Stoddard yearbook.

In his introduction to the 1940 yearbook, Stoddard made no bones
about the difference in perspective between it and its predecessor.
The difference was to be one of experimentation versus statistical
manipulation (Stoddard 1940):

> In the 1928 Yearbook, as in most studies on heredity and
> environment, an answer was sought to the question: What
> are the relative weights of the factors, nature and nurture,
> in the mental growth of the child? This question led to sta-
> tistical approaches based largely upon correlational tech-
> niques and the analysis of variability. Studies of twins af-
> forded the classic examples.
>
> Increasingly, it seems important to ask this question:
> Regardless of the proportionate weights of nature and
> nurture (something never to be satisfactorily answered),
> what are the limits of environmental impact in producing
> demonstrable effects upon mental growth? Following this
> lead, research-workers are basing their programs upon
> attempts to give the young child favorable growing facili-
> ties. [P. 40]

In the same volume, a colleague (Carter 1940) admitted "the futility
and artificiality of the idea of untangling nature and nurture influences
in the sense of ascertaining the percentage contributions of each in
any general sense" (p. 248).

From the above, it appears that the experimental critique of
nature-nurture estimation had had a telling effect by 1940; indeed, the
yearbook was filled largely with experimental studies. However, implied in Stoddard's comment is the idea that the 1940 work was completely experimental, while that of 1928 had been completely statistical, an idea that is not totally true. Later comment by Stoddard and
Wellman (1940) implied that experimental research supported an environmentalist position, a point that, again, is not totally true. In
fact, studies of adoptive children almost universally showed some
gains associated with adoption, but studies of educational enrichment
tended to show little or no IQ gain. The studies that showed the greatest gains tended to be those that were done by the Iowa researchers,
and these studies were scathingly rebuked by both Goodenough (1940)

and Terman (1940). This brought a sharp rejoinder from Wellman (1940). *

The truth of the matter is that both yearbooks had a mix of studies, and differences tended to be ones of emphasis. Still, the differences were real, and they underscored the differences in argumentation of hereditarians and environmentalists. Those who created the earlier work were apt to conceive of issues of nature and nurture in terms of balance sheets, while those who put together the later work were more interested in experimental results. A prime example of this is found in the studies of the maze-running behavior in rats, which appeared in both issues. In the Terman yearbook, the rat study focused on the correlation of error scores for related rats (Burlingame and Stone 1928). This sibling resemblance was considered to be an important proof of the hereditary nature of general intelligence, and the preface to the study (written either by Terman or under his direction) indicated that the results had crucial implications for the study of human intelligence. In the Stoddard yearbook, a study of rats was included, but this was the summary of the Tryon (1940) studies of maze-running behavior of inbred strains. The results showed that, at least with rats, quickness in the running of a specified maze could be bred with relative ease, but that the superiority of the maze-bright strain was specific to both the task and the environmental conditions involved (see Tryon 1940, p. 118).

The difference, here, was that in the earlier yearbook, the presence of correlations was seen as sufficient warrant for making broad statements about the effects of nature and nurture on phenotype. Since correlations always obtained between relatives, and because these could be fitted within a genetic model of inheritance, nature was considered to be supreme. In the 1940 work, that supremacy was not granted.

---

*This exchange was part of a much greater conflict between the Stanford and Iowa groups, which became quite polemical at times. For example, in his review of the 1940 yearbook, Terman (1940) stated that Goodenough's hereditarian reviews were characterized by "critical insight, scientific caution, and just appraisal of others' work," while the Stoddard and Wellman environmentalist work "impresses me as biased and uncritical" (pp. 460-61). Further, he felt that it was "characteristic of the Iowa group of workers that they so often find difficulty in reporting accurately either the data of others or their own." Stoddard (1943) responded that "over the years, the Stanford revisions have offered not very reliable measurements of functions not very close to intelligence" (p. 116). In the same work, Stoddard reanalyzed the studies reviewed by Goodenough and, not surprisingly, found an environmentalist hypothesis to be substantiated by them.

What had occurred in the previous 12 years, both inside and out-side psychology, had had telling effects. By 1940, the newer research groups at Chicago and Iowa were strong enough to challenge the group at Stanford directly. It was now that the major adoption studies still widely discussed (for example, those by Skeels and his associates) began emerging. However, the temptation remained strong to use a balance-sheet approach to the analysis of heredity, and just three years after publication of the yearbook, a new debate arose over the useful-ness of such methods (for example, Loevinger 1943). Then, in the 1950s, Burt reintroduced heritability to IQ study, and provided the main body of literature and main theoretical foundation upon which Jensen's article would depend in 1969.

SUMMARY

What has been attempted in this chapter is a tracing of social and scientific thought on the subject of the sources of traits. The tra-ditional conception of nature versus nurture (which drew much of its power from the politically motivated discussions about the sources of black-white differences), came to be a constituent part of biometric analysis, such that those who used biometric techniques would tend to continue to see issues of heredity in such terms. Since the devel-opment of experimental methods in genetics, biometric analysis has not had the field alone; however, it remains strong, particularly strong in psychology, and nature-nurture has become a sort of traditional source of dissension within the field. Thus, nature-nurture debates are likely to continue to arise.

10

CONCLUSION: MERITOCRACY AND MODERN SOCIAL SCIENCE

While this study is complex in nature, its overriding thesis can be stated quite simply. First, the evidence for the hereditarian position in the modern IQ controversy is extremely weak. Despite this weakness, the position seems strong because a number of issues in the controversy have been allowed to lie largely unexamined. That is, both hereditarians and environmentalists generally have assumed (at least tacitly) that the hereditarian position with respect to the measurement, structure, and importance of intelligence is proved. A historical examination of the development of mental testing shows that these assumptions were commonly held at the time of the institutionalization of mental testing, and for this reason they were worked into the fabric of psychometric research.

Part I of this study documented the weakness of the set of assumptions at issue. Part II of the study documented the existence of the assumptions at the time that mental testing first developed. Now, it may be useful to discuss, in more detail, the relationship between the two parts. First, we will document the existence of the assumptions in modern psychometrics, among prominent psychometricians. Then, the nature of scientific-research traditions will be discussed in more detail than was previously done, in order to make clear how once-popular ideas continue to dominate research. Finally, a number of concrete ways in which the assumptions have been maintained in modern psychometrics will be presented.

THE ROLES OF THE ASSUMPTIONS
IN THE NEW CONTROVERSY

Part II of this study is important because it supplies explanations for the hereditarian assumptions discussed in Part I. It can be shown that a number of important psychometricians (including several important environmentalists) treat intelligence in the same ways that the early psychometricians treated it. This similarity exists with respect to the imprecise use of the term itself, the reluctance to dispose of the idea of a general intelligence, and the common, almost unquestioning acceptance of IQ as functionally important in human affairs.

A major source of evidence for this is the fact that nature and nurture have been the central issues in the controversy, for most commentators. Since the genetic determination of IQ is clearly the least resolvable issue in the controversy, its centrality as an issue is prima facie evidence that the other issues are considered largely settled. This centrality is aptly demonstrated by the "Comment on Behavior and Heredity" (Page 1972). Signed by 50 eminent behavioral, social, and biological scientists, this comment supported research into "the possible role of inheritance in human abilities and behaviors" (Page 1972, p. 660), and called for academic freedom regarding such research. The important point is that preliminary statements in the comment make it obvious that it was written in response to the numerous attacks on Jensen, Herrnstein, and Shockley. For both attackers and defenders, the central point was heredity. However, for heredity to operate, there must exist something upon which it may operate; this something was the core of merit about which the three writers mentioned above had hoped to demonstrate a substantial heritability.

The Imprecise Treatment of Intelligence

The first assumption, that intelligence tests measure intelligence, is closely tied to the inconsistent use of the term intelligence when social concerns are discussed. That is, intelligence is at once the entity the psychometrician studies and the core of merit that operates in the social world. In Part II, it has been shown that this dualism strongly marked the work of the early testers. The same happens at the present time.

The dualistic use of the term intelligence has been commented upon by others. According to Block and Dworkin (1976, pp. 429-32), many psychometricians state that lay critics err in confusing the technical term intelligence with commonsensical, everyday conceptions of intellect, much in the same way that seventeenth-century commenters confused Newton's technical use of the term mass with common notions of mass. Block and Dworkin hold that many of those same psychometricians then inconsistently use common words like smart, stupid, bright, dull, intelligent, and unintelligent as what are essentially stylistic variations of the terms high-low IQ (Block and Dworkin 1976, p. 429). Their point is that such mixing of technical and nontechnical terms leads to just the sorts of misunderstandings that psychometricians deplore. Thus, a given writer will offer descriptions of test construction in considerable detail, to let the reader understand what is meant by the technical use of intelligence, only to go on to the use of everyday synonyms like <u>bright</u> and <u>dull</u> in discussing test results.

Block and Dworkin's discussion is offered as a criticism of sloppy word usage on the part of a group of scientists who supposedly understand what they (the scientists) intend when they use various words interchangeably. However, the Block and Dworkin criticism does not go far enough. The important point is that the dualistic meaning of intelligence operates not only between the professional and lay communities, but within the professional community itself. Indeed, the almost complete lack of consensus regarding the meaning of intelligence, among psychometricians, indicates that a single technical meaning of the term has not been developed. Rather, as shown in the Chapter 2 discussion of operationalism, common expectations about the nature of intellect mark much research. Further, as shown in the brief look at the development of testing, these common expectations correspond to important elements of social thought in the nineteenth century, which then became constituent parts of the early testing programs. This becomes especially important when one contrasts the social implications of differential test scores drawn by testers, to the rather meager data provided by the tests themselves.

Were the psychometric community truly wedded to a technical sense of intelligence, then one of three definitions of intelligence could legitimately be used. First, since intelligence testing was designed to determine the likelihood of success in school and in the economy, one could, following O. D. Duncan et al. (1968), consider it to be something akin to a pure disposition to succeed. However, use of such a definition would allow a host of nonintellective factors to be considered part of intelligence, since anything that increases the correlation with success (for example, parents' SES, years of schooling, personality characteristics) would be part of that disposition (Block and Dworkin 1976, p. 431). Of course, inclusion of such data would indicate that intelligence was not strictly an intellectual phenomenon, or even necessarily a characteristic of the individual. Further, the relationship between test scores and intelligence would then become problematic. To the extent that test scores did not correlate with success (however measured), they would not measure intelligence, and strong social pronouncements would not be possible on the basis of such scores.

Second, one could operationally define intelligence as Boring did (1923): intelligence is what the tests test. However, in that case the relationship between intelligence and success would be suspect. Moreover, such a definition would exclude from consideration all the intellectual processes that do not appear on standard intelligence tests. In this sense tests would be intellectually and conceptually sterile,

though as handy instruments for the empirical study of certain processes, they might still be useful. Finally, this definition of intelligence would necessitate the removal from use of most tests, since
they do not intercorrelate perfectly and cannot be considered to measure precisely the same thing; this, despite the fact that new tests
are usually considered valid to the degree that they correlate with
other standard tests (in the past, the Stanford-Binet).

Third, one might define intelligence in terms of cognitive functioning. This would have the advantage of a reference to the class of
phenomena that is generally indicated by the term. This position
would require research on intelligence to be directed at its nature,
and questions of the social importance of the subject matter would
necessarily be of secondary importance. Unless one, from the start,
restricted the number of cognitive elements that one would consider
to be constitutive of intelligence (which would generate the same problems as those generated by Boring's dictum), then the structure of intelligence would become an open question. One could not legitimately
treat it as a linear variable. In fact, one would have no a priori reason for treating intelligence as a single variable at all (see Kagan
1974). Concern with cognitive functioning would lead researchers
away from attempts to determine the general level or degree of an undefined capacity—so loosely conceptualized that it may ultimately come
to take a place alongside vital force and ether as scientific concepts—
and toward attempts to map out the parameters of such functioning,
to discover what cognitive functioning entails. Such a position would
necessarily require a research program largely oriented to behavior-
genetic, neurophysiological, and interactional (that is, Piaget-like)
research, though standardized tests would probably continue to play
some role.

None of the above paths has been followed. Rather, it is apparent that elements from each of them has been used, in a haphazard
fashion. Intelligence is considered a general cognitive capacity that
is deeply implicated in social standing and is properly represented by
test scores. As such a global concept, it can simultaneously be employed in the design of research and in the making of social pronouncements. The slippery nature of the term allows one to slide from one
meaning to another without ever quite realizing that the concept in use
has changed. Using Peterson's (1922) criticism, the belief in this
universal capacity allows one to posit, in the place of a correlation of
0.50 (or 0.20 or 0.10) between test scores and achievement, a real
relationship of unity, or thereabouts, between intelligence and achievement. This is only possible if one already presupposes some sort of
universal merit that attaches to cognitive functioning of a specific sort.
Apparently, this is what occurs in the case of Jensen. Jensen (1969a)
comments that "troubles occur only when we attribute more to 'intel-

ligence' and to our measurements of it than do the psychologists who use the concept in its proper sense" (p. 8); yet he himself reifies the concept of a general ability factor making of it much more than merely a mathematical factor emerging in the statistical treatment of a given body of data. It is, he admits, "only a hypothetical construct intended to explain covariation among tests. It is a hypothetical source of variance (individual difference) in test scores" (Jensen 1969a, p. 9). Yet a general factor quickly becomes translated as a measure of "the processes of abstraction and conceptualization," a "central symbolic or 'cognitive' processing mechanism" (Jensen 1969a, p. 11), and then of "the probability of acceptable performance" in occupations (Jensen 1969a, p. 14).

He reminds the reader that intelligence should not be considered the totality of mental ability, but just "the particular constellation of abilities" that has been "singled out . . . as being especially important in our society" (Jensen 1969a, p. 19). Later, however, he speaks of "intellectual resources, especially at the levels of intelligence required for complex problem solving, invention, and scientific and technological innovation" (Jensen 1969a, p. 36), as if the mental processes supposedly not tapped by IQ tests are not involved in such activities. Still later, he states that no study has been performed that equalizes black and white children in intellectual ability through statistical controls of environment and education (Jensen 1969a, p. 83); and he then calls for what is in essence a eugenics program directed specifically at the black population (Jensen 1969a, pp. 91-95). The call for eugenics is based totally on differences in test scores, and demonstrates the overriding importance he grants them.

The above is significant because Jensen is, by and large, extremely careful to speak in terms of IQ differentials, and to shy away from such terms as bright and dull and their synonyms. Despite this restraint, he still comes to give his hypothetical construct a global significance that is simply not called for on the basis of any extant data. He does this despite the fact that he reports studies that show that even where IQ scores remain relatively low, children can be taught matrixes of learning skills that lead them to a level of scholastic performance "commensurate with that of children 10 or 20 points higher in IQ" (Jensen 1969a, p. 106). If this is the case, then one might ask: What is the basis for the call for eugenics? There can be little basis for such a call unless the linear score is itself seen as having a degree of significance that is not reflected in mere achievement scores. It is this sense of universal importance that has guided intelligence research since its inception, thereby leading to inconsistencies in the discussion of the structure and importance of intelligence.

The Structure of Intelligence

With respect to the structure of intelligence, we have a situation very similar to that that existed in the 1920s. Numerous writers admit the diverse nature of intelligence in principle, but ignore it in practice.

Consider the case of Steven G. Vandenberg, who has been a major figure in the development of behavior genetics, through his factor analyses of test scores. In one widely cited series of such analyses, he found that the degrees of both unilinearity and heritability of scores varied widely with both the specific tests employed and the populations sampled. Here, his conclusion was that one would find "a general factor of low, moderate, or high importance and one or more factors that tend to be limited to one or more abilities" (Vandenberg 1968b, pp. 155-56). This would depend upon whether the variables studied measured different abilities, or rather, more related abilities. Moreover, the hereditary variance one found could be either overlapping or independent, and large or small, depending on these same conditions.

While Vandenberg's findings would appear to support the idea of a radically multifactorial cognitive functioning (in that the factors discovered, their relationship to one another, and the overlapping heredity variance all vary widely from study to study), he did not conclude this. Instead, he simply affirmed Spearman's position that "there may prove to be a number of independent hereditary abilities as well as a general hereditary ability factor" (Vandenberg 1968b, p. 157). Elsewhere, Vandenberg (1968a) has simply termed his research an investigation of "the nature and nurture of intelligence," without differentiating that intelligence.

Other writers also follow this trend. One example is Sandra Scarr-Salapatek (1971a, 1971b), a firm critic of Jensen, who consistently uses the term IQ in her discussion of human differences, and who performs her empirical analyses specifically in terms of IQ (or other unit-score) differences. For her the IQ score is clearly the important datum, and she uses a reliance on it to support, in principle, Herrnstein's view that society will necessarily be genetically stratified to the extent that heritability of IQ is high.

Note the treatment of intelligence by John C. Loehlin, Gardner Lindzey, and J. N. Spuhler (1975). These writers allude to a multiple-factor view of intelligence, noting that "we will usually find it useful to deal with a fairly small number of broad abilities" (Loehlin, Lindzey, and Spuhler 1975, p. 54). However, whether they stick with a single general ability, with a small number of factors, or with a multitude of factors, is called "merely a matter of convenience, not of basic theoretical commitment." But where else in science is the theoretical nature of the subject matter not supremely important?

These writers then use some 380 pages in attempting to determine the various genetic and environmental effects on IQ test scores (though occasionally on Thurstone Primary Mental Abilities scores), and only late in their study do they inform the reader that such scores do not have much consequence in most people's lives (Loehlin, Lindzey, and Spuhler 1975, pp. 245-57). To their credit, these authors explicitly state that their interest lies in test scores rather than in more general aspects of intelligence (p. vii), but they still title the book Race Differences in Intelligence, apparently in order to have a concise title.

The most striking clue as to the conception of intelligence and test scores in modern psychology comes from the response to Jensen's original article. It is well known that his thesis is painful to many members of the psychological community. The sense of affront that apparently stemmed from his work cannot be attributed to discussions of ungrounded test scores. Instead, the perception of his critics was that his thesis dealt with more concrete social issues, and responses to him had just these issues in mind. That he was not immediately called to task for his use of IQ scores in his analysis (though a few writers mocked his assessment of a general factor as the "rock of Gibraltar") indicates the level of tacit agreement on the idea that a hierarchy is clearly present. The controversy is about the existence of a general superiority and inferiority, and the literature coming from it has been extensive precisely because such a paramount topic is at issue.

The Social Importance of Intelligence

As with the idea of a hierarchy, the idea of social importance has grown without a substantial empirical underpinning. Its acceptance is best illustrated by the number of attacks on Jensen that simply did not mention the statistical relationship between test scores and human achievements. So often taken for granted is the predictive power of IQ scores that Jensen (1969a, pp. 13-16, 74-78) devoted only a few scattered pages to its demonstration in his original article, and even there he cited statistics indicating a low correlation for such relationships as that between IQ and job performance. In his monograph on IQ and meritocracy, Herrnstein (1973, pp. 111-39) devoted only 29 pages to the topic of the importance of intelligence. This space was devoted almost wholly to demonstrations that upper-class people tend to have higher IQ scores than do those from the lower classes, and that people with extremely high IQ scores tend to do very well in school and in the economy. Herrnstein relied heavily on the Terman studies of genius, and he did not discuss the very extensive literature that shows that IQ scores are not predictive of achievement, despite the fact that he had collaborated with Boring on a sourcebook on testing and must have been aware of this line of research.

Again, it must be the case that something more basic is at issue than just test scores. When we speak of intelligence, it is with a certain reverence; we understand that a critical element in our way of life is under discussion. It must be in such a context that a half century of research negating the belief that IQ scores were closely tied to achievement could be blithely ignored when the controversy began. For the record, the greatest part of that research appeared in the late 1950s and the 1960s, and a major part of it had been generated by projects performed for major testing associations (for example, the American College Testing Program). By 1969, all of the major points noted in Chapter 4 had received documentation. For the writers cited here, whatever is important about intelligence must be something not reflected in the data; either this is the case, or the few major studies that did appear to show IQ scores to be important (for example, Terman's genius studies), in conjunction with the general moderate relationship between such scores and schooling, could bring about the general acceptance of the importance of IQ scores, but only if the belief in the importance of test scores preceded those findings. That is, only if the belief in the importance of IQ scores were a function of the meritocratic tradition in psychological research.

ON SCIENCE AND SOCIETY

This study has focused on the determinants of a certain view of intellectual functioning, and on the ways in which that view came to gain prominence within U.S. psychology. As such a study, it takes for granted that scientific knowledge is a social product. However, as revealed by Ben-David's quotation noted in the first chapter, this is very much a minority position in sociology. To the extent that sociologists study science as an institutionalized activity, they generally analyze the determinants of scientific output or of group structure (for example, Ben-David 1971; Price 1963; Crane 1972), without focusing on the determinants of specific theoretical positions. Why this is the case is a complex issue beyond the scope of the present study; it suffices to note that this is the case.

This is not to state that there have been no attempts to develop theoretical positions with regard to the social determination of scientific knowledge. A major spokesperson in this regard is Thomas Kuhn (1962, 1970a, 1970b, 1974), whose paradigm, or exemplar, concept of the nature of scientific inquiry has provoked wide comment (for a review, see Eckberg and Hill 1976). Basically, Kuhn takes a tightrope position with regard to the nature of scientific knowledge. On the one hand, he acknowledges that one may not take just any position with respect to subject matter. Nature sets limits to conceptualizations by constantly presenting the researcher with discrepancies between theoretical predictions and the actual outcomes of research. On the other hand, Kuhn stresses that within a scientific-research community, a specific mode of conceptualization will be granted credence and be maintained even in the face of a certain amount of counterevidence. This is the most general meaning of the term paradigm.

More generally, Kuhn and those sympathetic to his position (for example, Masterman 1970) hold that general metaphysical ideas directly shape the mode of conceptualization within a scientific community, and that such conceptualizations play major roles in the concrete management of research. This is parallel to Parson's (1968, p. 6) contention that theories serve to "canalize" thought. However, Kuhn is somewhat more concrete than is Parsons, for he holds that it is through the pragmatic modeling of new research on older research that traditions of thought are passed on in science. Thus, his primary contribution to the study of the social determination of scientific knowledge comes via his exemplar concept, where an exemplar is defined as an exemplary piece of research upon which other research is modeled. By virtue of its prestige within the community, the exemplar directly shapes the expectations of research scientists. Though this point has not been clearly discussed by Kuhn until quite recently (1974), exemplar is the most fundamental meaning of paradigm for him.

The importance of concrete accomplishment must be stressed. Far too often, the development and maintenance of conceptual categories are treated in a semimystical fashion that reminds this author of some humorous statements by high-school friends that they learned by osmosis. That is, by some semivisceral process, knowledge would seep into them. With respect to problems in the sociology of knowledge, it may be this lack of concreteness that makes the position of subjectivists unpalatable to so many U. S. social scientists.

Kuhn's sociology of science is largely limited to happenings within a scientific community. That is, he is largely an internalist rather than an externalist in his choice of phenomena to analyze. * However, even if a scientific community is somewhat insulated from the greater society, it is not totally insulated, and this is especially the case with human sciences.

---

*For discussions of internalism and externalism in the study of science, see Kuhn (1968) and Allen (1976). While Kuhn's own work stresses events internal to the community of practitioners, he has admitted the importance of external events. Thus, in his extended discussion of the Copernican Revolution in astronomy, he admits that "nonastronomical beliefs were fundamental first in postponing and then in shaping the Copernican Revolution" (Kuhn 1957, p. viii).

Here is where the link to societal conditions arises, and it is this link that has been exploited in the present study. Specifically, it is denied here that a scientific community is fully insulated from the greater community, especially in the early phases of the institutionalization of the discipline in question. With the social and behavioral sciences, insulation may never be great. With this in mind, the present study has focused on the institutionalization phase of the development of mental testing, in order to find out why a simple meritocratic position came to be granted allegiance in the absence of strong supporting evidence.

What we have seen is that the relationship between society and social sciences may not be direct, but it nonetheless exists. While it is hazardous to make too many generalizations from what is, in essence, a case study, certain important aspects of scientific work stand out and seem worthy of at least a brief discussion.

IMPORTANT ELEMENTS IN THE SCIENCE-AND-SOCIETY RELATIONSHIP

In the following discussion, a total of five areas of inquiry that seem, particularly, to offer insights into the relationship between science and society will be presented briefly. Each of these can stand as a specific topic of research, but together they stand as a body of interrelated topics that promises to lend insight to the processes occurring in the formation and support of theoretical positions.

Specificity of the Issue

What the analysis presented here shows, first, is that social influences on scientific conceptualization are strongest where general ideas are involved. That is, where specific issues develop, it appears that points of dissension develop. Information will be marshaled here in order to make cases and to disprove rival positions. As was shown in Chapter 1, the specific position one takes regarding the sources of intellectual differences or other topics can be predicted to some extent on the basis of social characteristics. But the important fact is that different positions are taken. Thus, nature-nurture disputes have at least a 500-year history.

However, when the issues are general, then something approaching consensus can reign. It is the idea of a meritocracy that spurs the first three assumptions we have discussed. Looking at each of these three assumptions in detail, we find that strong disagreements exist regarding it: that is, it stands as an issue. We have seen in several places just how much disagreement exists with regard to the structure of intellect. Yet, when the issue of human worth arises, this disagreement disappears, and almost all concerned parties marshal IQ scores in order to determine the relative amount of worth owned by different parties. Here, the idea of a simple metric difference acts as a substrate upon which other arguments are based. We do not concentrate on it, but accept it tacitly, in Polanyi's (1966) sense of the word: "In an act of tacit knowing we attend from something for attending to something else; namely, from the first term to the second term of the tacit relation" (p. 10).

When we argue nature-nurture issues, the general idea of a meritocracy underlies our arguments. Because we are tacitly aware of this, the specific issue of nature and nurture has meaning for us. But because we are only tacitly aware of this, the component parts of the idea of meritocracy do not come under critical scrutiny. When any one of these components is itself critically discussed, the general idea of a meritocracy does not enter into the discussion because we are involved with technical details. A relationship may be seen between the technical discussion and the general idea, but as we have seen already, it need not be seen.

One reason a relationship need not be seen is that the general idea can have support from other areas than just its specific technical underpinnings. For example, in U.S. social science the idea of a meritocracy is represented in mainstream thought in both sociology and economics. Within sociology, the functional theory of stratification holds, as a matter of principle, that a properly organized social collectivity will stratify people on the basis of talent (for example, Davis and Moore 1945). Likewise, the orthodox position within economics on the distribution of income, with its stress on marginal productivity, is based on the idea that talent is scarce at the top (for example, Leftwich 1973). With this general commitment to a meritocracy within modern social and behavioral science, consideration of certain technical aspects of the position need not affect that position in the main.

The Social Nature of the Issue

Somewhat related to the above issue is the degree of social importance of a position. Technical issues, puzzles, using Kuhn's (1962) term, can be studied without taking into account social implications. That is, the context of technical puzzle solving is quite narrow. The puzzle exists for the researcher in its own right, and he or she can attack it as a technical issue. On the other hand, to the extent that the issue is seen to have social consequences, general social ideas will permeate the work. This is illustrated most clearly in the discussion of the work of experimental geneticists presented in Chapter 9. Because they were interested in a full determination of the technical nature of trait transmission, they were led on a path that ulti-

mately revealed the complexity of such transmission. The biometricians (and then the psychometricians), however, were interested
in social applications of the general idea of heredity, and so they were
not open to ideas of complexity. Rather, they became committed to a
quite simple view of heredity, as being made up of heredity and environmental components. By use of this simple dichotomy, they hoped
to solve the problem of intellectual differences. It is instructive that
geneticists turned away from eugenics earlier than did psychologists
(as a group), and that the break was cleaner.

The Nature of Methodology

The difference between correlational and experimental studies
has already been mentioned. This is important, for correlation is
intended strictly to demonstrate only a relationship, not specific causation. In discussing broad and socially volatile issues like nature
and nurture, it becomes easy to lose sight of this fact, even for the
sophisticated researcher. Because the issue is seen as encompassing
only two broad causative factors, a methodology is employed that pro-
duces ratios that show the relative importance of the two factors.
Then, because the methodology neatly divides causation, the initial
presumption is given credence.

The same is true with the construction of mental scales. Because a unitary intellectual difference is considered to underlie human
differences in performance, scales are produced that both lead to a
simple hierarchical ranking and load strongly onto a single factor.
It is for reasons like these that methodology must not be considered
neutral with respect to scientific issues. Methods themselves canalize
thoughts (for example, Carroll 1972; Douglas 1971; Kaplan 1964, pp.
28-29).

The Role of Practical Accomplishment

As the exemplar concept indicates, it is the active work of research scientists that maintains conceptual categories. Two general
means of accomplishing this maintenance of categories can (at the risk
of oversimplification) be termed words and deeds.

Words. By words is meant the way in which one talks about a given
phenomenon. From structural anthropology, we have the idea that
language shapes perceptions. What is important in linguistic determinism is the common, banal way in which events are discussed.
Banality is important. The political sociolinguist Murray Edelman
(1977) notes:

> In politics, as in religion, whatever is ceremonial or
> banal strengthens reassuring beliefs regardless of their

validity and discourages skeptical inquiry about disturbing
issues. . . . If political language both excites and molli-
fies fears, language is an integral facet of the political
scene: not simply an instrument for describing events but
itself a part of events, shaping their meaning and helping
to shape the political role officials and the general public
play. [Pp. 3-4]

The same phenomenon occurs in science. Recall the manner in
which the early testers referred to brightness and dullness. Common
terms were employed in recurrent fashion in order to assure one and
all of the monumental importance of this intelligence they were measuring.

When psychometricians steadfastly refused to acknowledge the
meagerness of the evidence for the importance of test scores, it was
because they knew that there existed two categories of people, and
that their job was to determine who fell in which class. They had always talked in this way, and thus their expectations were shaped.
The same thing occurs today, when we hear that social stratification
is a way of husbanding intellectual resources (Herrnstein 1971).
Moreover, it is still often said that the salvation of the nation will
come through the education of our gifted children. Those phrases
common when Terman used his very expressive language in 1916, to
a considerable extent, make the rounds today. We may no longer call
dull people defective, but we retain a category of dullness that every-
body understands. And this dullness exists in terms of IQ, a word
that often takes the place of the word intelligence in conversations.

Banality is important both for shaping perceptions and for dis-
couraging critical inquiry. To a considerable extent, it is because
IQ and its related connotations are such common parts of our way of
dealing with the world that psychometricians can come to see IQ scores
as representative of a global sort of merit. When such scores are
employed in settling disputes about the distribution of intelligence,
the descriptive category employed is that that anyone would use. Why
should someone want to inquire about something that is so universally
understood? Indeed, how could one do so?

Deeds. By deeds is meant the practical ways in which research scientists deal with a stubborn world in order to make their ideas prevail. Recall that for a very long period of time, it seemed imprac-
ticable for psychologists to construct mental scales. The reaction
to this was not to abandon the idea of a unitary intelligence, but to
give up on testing. Once Binet and Simon had shown that scales could
be constructed, testing bloomed once again. When the established position then faced difficulties, it could be maintained by one of at least

four activities. First, one could focus selectively on either technical problems or social concerns, without ever noticing the connection between the two. In Chapter 8 this was termed disjunction, but it is similar to what Schegloff (1972) indicates when he states that we "focus on" and "focus off" areas of a field. This refers to selective cognizance and implies a tacit relationship.

Second, one could employ even poor evidence to support the accepted position. Thus, any correlation between IQ scores and achievement is indicative of a causal relationship. What occurs here is that the criteria for inclusion of a set of data as evidence for the existence of a presupposed phenomenon are less rigid that are the criteria for inclusion of data as evidence against the phenomenon.

Third, and related to the second tactic, is the tactic of using a poor correspondence between the indicator in question and a different type of indicator as evidence of the lack of usefulness of the different indicator. We saw how Terman did this with respect to IQ scores and teachers' evaluations of students. More recently, when one researcher (Harmon 1963) found a very poor correlation between a complex criterion of scientific competence and standard measures of ability, he concluded that the criterion must be at fault.

Fourth, one could make liberal use of ceteris paribus-type clauses in order to lessen the impact of weak empirical support of a position. This is essentially what Garfinkel (1967) meant in his discussion of the et cetera clause. There, such phrases as "let it pass" and "for all practical purposes" are used in order to allow one to gloss over potentially troublesome features of a conceptual field, thus allowing one to continue with a problem at hand without being distracted. Several examples of this were presented in Chapter 8.

The Institutionalization of Knowledge

What is required here is an analysis of the ways in which a specified position comes to be accepted as dogma. Since only that knowledge that has some sort of institutional base can stand as real knowledge, we need to address such issues as the following. First, what general ideas are present in a society at the time a specialty is institutionalized? Especially important here is the set of ideas granted credence by elite groups. This topic overlaps with that of the words category above, but it is more specifically political in its intent. A common position will not only be perceived as commonsensically true, but it will also gain active support. If it is congruent with the beliefs of elite groups, then its financial support is assured. Recall the co-membership of important politicians and psychometricians on major eugenics councils. Obviously, an overlapping of interests existed. Further, such nonpolitical ideas as the Chain of Being strongly affected the development of testing.

Second, what are the general structures of social relationships in the society? This includes the nature of the means of production, as in the Marxist sense. It has already been mentioned how several writers have commented on the capitalist nature of mental testing in the United States (for example, Riegel 1972; Daniels and Houghton, 1972; Bowles and Gintis 1976). It seems no coincidence that a direct relationship appears to exist between an economic system and a system of thought. By virtue of its importance, the economic system tends to affect our mode of speech, and this in turn affects our categorizations. Thus, as mentioned earlier, many early psychometricians (and some to this day) used the language of classical economics metaphorically when discussing intelligence, thus using the concepts of the former as models for the understanding of the latter.

Third, what positions are granted economic and institutional support? Here, we can find direct intervention of interested parties in the outcomes of disputes, and in the direction of continuing research. In a truly pluralist society, a variety of theoretical positions should find support, but if certain groups have anything approaching a monopoly of economic access, or if certain positions have truly widespread acceptance, then only a narrow range of research will be funded. Hence, the findings that eventually emerge will be necessarily biased. As an example of this, the biology historian Garland Allen (1975) has documented how eugenicists like Davenport had little trouble obtaining funding from wealthy benefactors during the early twentieth century, while antieugenicists like Boas were turned down flatly.

It is not the contention here that the outcomes of specific disputes are simple functions of the allocation of resources, though the issue may require some investigation. Rather, the argument is that all three of the above issues may act in a more subtle fashion to shape the manner of conceptualization of scientists. This position is based upon the idea that the meaning of our words has an embedded quality. That is, a communication contains more information than appears on the surface to strangers. More information may exist without being explicitly recognized by participants in a communication, or without the participants even being able to explicate fully that information. Using Polanyi's (1966) phrase, "We know more than we can say" (p. 4). The bulk of information is only tacitly recognized, yet it is recognized by those who share linguistic frameworks.

That being the case, the shaping of conceptualizations can occur through recognition and support of positions that are explicitly neutral with regard to, say, a political position, but that are tacitly congruent with other conceptualizations and commitments. Thus, it requires no conspiracy theory to explain the support of certain lines of research by interest groups. The strongly positive governmental support of early mental scaling is offered as an example of such subtle shaping.

The explicit interest was the purely empirical investigation of talent. But tacitly, the idea of a mental hierarchy was given official governmental sanction.

This focus on the institutional support of a position, and on the institutionalization of the position, is important. What we are specifically analyzing in this study is the development and maintenance of part of the scientific racism that at one time permeated social science. While individual and class characteristics have been discussed, these are not really the issues of interest. Rather, we are interested in analyzing the ways in which ideas came to be embedded in institutional practice, such that almost anyone filling a role in the institutional context would behave in a predictable manner with respect to the issues at hand. That being the case, this study can be considered to be part of the institutional-discrimination literature (for example, Feagin and Feagin 1978). The importance of all of the factors and practices mentioned in the preceding sections of this chapter, for the purposes of this study, is that they represent those ways in which the institutionalization of knowledge occurs.

TOWARD A NONMERITOCRATIC SOCIAL SCIENCE

The gist of the previous discussion is that a large number of interrelated processes and actions work together in affecting the outcome of scientific research. In the context of this writer's position on the IQ controversy, the question arises: What can be done to lessen the influence of the meritocratic position in today's social science? Even asking such a question implies that the outcome of scientific research is not fully societally determined. But in practical terms, what is to be done?

Given the fact that scientific knowledge is institutionalized knowledge, one must work within the context of such institutionalization. Specifically, elements in the science-society relationship discussed above can work in more than one direction. One can make explicit underlying assumptions, and can show the relationship between technical aspects of discussions and the more general phenomena in which we are interested. In this way, by making cases in terms of parameters that scientists respect, minds can be changed. Such has been the tactic employed in this study.

But this is a limited form of activity; for, if a given social structure continues to exist, then those positions that are congruent with that structure will continue to find support. In terms of banal language, if we continue to talk in terms of a meritocracy, then the idea will continue to bear real consequences. Thus, at most, this tactic will lead to a healthy dissension, the outcome of which is difficult to predict. However, the alternative to this is a reliance on major, revolutionary social change, the prospects of which do not appear to be great.

It appears likely that there will continue to be a major emphasis on unilinear human merit in the analysis of social stratification, especially income stratification. However, it could be that discussions of stratification as, on the one hand, a product of underlying individual differences, and on the other hand, a product of institutional arrangements, may come to be a traditional source of dissension, in much the same way that nature and nurture are the source of a traditional disagreement. Indeed, to some extent, this is the case now, at least in social science. In psychology, this is not the case, probably because of the focus of the discipline on the individual.

It is easy to be cynical with regard to the possibilities of such issues. With nature and nurture, the issue was settled in the past, only to be reopened in 1969. One might ask, regarding the idea of a simple meritocracy, when the next great hereditarian will emerge. Still, if one does not enter the battle, then it will be lost by default. As a matter of faith, one must assume that "truth will out," and that one has the truth. One can make institutional links and can work for legislative and judicial change. But one should never forget that either a conceptual or a political victory will be a long time coming.

BIBLIOGRAPHY

Abelson, A. R. 1911. "The Measurement of Mental Ability of 'Backward' Children." British Journal of Psychology 4: 268-314.

Adams, B., M. Ghodesian, and K. Richardson. 1976. "Evidence for a Lower Upper Limit of Heritability of Mental Test Performance in a National Sample of Twins." Nature 263 (September 23): 314-16.

Aikens, H. A., E. L. Thorndike, and Elizabeth A. Hubbell. 1902. "Correlations among Perceptive and Associative Processes." Psychological Review 9: 374-82.

Allen, Garland E. 1976. "Genetics, Eugenics, and Society: Internalists and Externalists in Contemporary History of Science." Social Studies of Science 6 (February): 105-22.

_____. 1975. "Genetics, Eugenics and Class Struggle." Genetics 79 (Supplement, June): 29-45.

_____. 1969. "T. H. Morgan and the Emergence of a New American Biology." Quarterly Review of Biology 44:168-88.

American Heritage Dictionary of the English Language. 1976. Boston: Houghton Mifflin.

American Psychologist. 1965. Special Issue, vol. 20 (November).

Anandalkshmy, S., and J. F. Adams. 1969. "An Alternative Heritability Estimate." Harvard Educational Review 39 (Summer): 585-87.

Anastasi, Anne. 1968. Psychological Testing. New York: Macmillan.

_____. 1958. Differential Psychology. 3d ed. New York: Macmillan.

Astin, Alexander W. 1968. "Undergraduate Achievement and Institutional 'Excellence.'" Science 161 (August 16): 661-68.

Astin, Alexander W., and Jack Rossman. 1973. "The Case for Open Admissions: A Status Report." Change, vol. 5 (Summer).

Averch, Harvey, et al. 1972. How Effective Is Schooling? A Critical Review and Synthesis of Research Findings. Santa Monica, Calif.: Rand.

Axelrod, Joseph. 1968. "The Creative Student and the Grading System." In The Creative College Student: An Unmet Challenge, edited by Paul Heist, pp. 117-43. San Francisco: Jossey-Bass.

Bagley, William C. 1925. Determinism in Education. Baltimore: Warwick and York.

_____. 1901. "Mental and Motor Ability." American Journal of Psychology 12:193.

Banton, Michael. 1967. Race Relations. New York: Basic Books.

Banton, Michael, and Jonathan Harwood. 1975. The Race Concept. New York: Praeger.

Barzun, Jacques. 1937. Race: A Study in Modern Superstition. New York: Harcourt, Brace.

Beardsley, E. H. 1973. "The American Social Scientist as Social Activist; Franz Boas, Burt G. Wilder, and the Cause of Racial Justice, 1900-1915." Isis 64:50-66.

Ben-David, Joseph. 1971. The Scientist's Role in Society. Englewood Cliffs, N.J.: Prentice-Hall.

Benedict, Ruth, and Gene Weltfish. 1943. The Races of Mankind. New York: Public Affairs Committee.

Bennett, Lerone, Jr. 1961. Before the Mayflower. Baltimore: Penguin.

Bereiter, Carl. 1976. "Genetics and Educability: Educational Implications of the Jensen Debate." In The IQ Controversy, edited by N. J. Block and Gerald Dworkin, pp. 383-407. New York: Random House.

Bereiter, Carl, and S. Engelmann. 1966. Teaching Disadvantaged Children. Englewood Cliffs, N.J.: Prentice-Hall.

Berelson, Bernard, and Gary Steiner. 1964. Human Behavior. New York: Harcourt, Brace and World.

Berg, Ivar. 1970. Education and Jobs: The Great Training Robbery. New York: Praeger.

Berger, Peter L., and Thomas Luckmann. 1966. The Social Construction of Reality. New York: Anchor-Doubleday.

Bijou, Sidney W. 1971. "Environment and Intelligence: A Behavioral Analysis." In Intelligence: Genetic and Environmental Influences, edited by Robert Cancro, pp. 221-39. New York: Grune and Stratton.

Binet, Alfred. 1911. "Nouvelles recherches sur la mesure du niveau intellectuel chez les enfants d'école." L'Année psychologique 17:145-201.

_____. 1909. Les idées modernes sur les enfants. Paris: Flammarion.

_____. 1900. "Attention et adaptation." L'Année psychologique 6: 248-404.

_____. 1898. "La mesure en psychologie individuelle." Revue philosophique 46:113-23.

_____. 1890. "Perceptions d'enfants." Revue philosophique 30:582-611.

Binet, Alfred, and Victor Henri. 1895. "La mémoire des mots." L'Année psychologique 1:1-23.

Binet, Alfred, and Theodore Simon. 1916. The Development of Intelligence in Children. Translated by E. S. Kite. Baltimore: Williams and Wilkins.

_____. 1908. "Le développement de l'intelligence chez le enfants." L'Année psychologique 14:1-94.

_____. 1905a. "Sur la necessité d'établir un diagnostic scientifique des états inférieurs de l'intelligence." L'Année psychologique 11:163-90.

_____. 1905b. "Methodes nouvelles pour le diagnostic du niveau intellectuel des anormauz." L'Année psychologique 11:191-244.

Blakeslee, Alberg F. 1914. "Corn and Men." Journal of Heredity 5:518.

Blau, Peter, and Otis Dudley Duncan. 1967. The American Occupational Structure. New York: John Wiley.

Block, N. J., and Gerald Dworkin. 1976. "IQ, Heritability, and Inequality." In The IQ Controversy, edited by N. J. Block and Gerald Dworkin, pp. 410-540. New York: Random House.

Bloom, Benjamin S. 1969. "Letter to the Editor." Harvard Educational Review 39:419-21.

_____. 1963a. "Testing Cognitive Ability and Achievement." In Handbook of Research on Testing, edited by N. L. Gage. Chicago: Rand McNally.

_____. 1963b. "Report on Creativity Research by the Examiner's Office of the University of Chicago." In Scientific Creativity, edited by C. W. Taylor and F. Barron, pp. 251-64. New York: John Wiley.

Blum, Jeffrey M. 1978. Pseudoscience and Mental Ability. New York: Monthly Review Press.

Boas, Franz. 1927. "Fallacies of Racial Inferiority." Current History 25 (February): 618f.

_____. 1911. The Mind of Primitive Man. New York: Macmillan.

_____. 1901. "The Mind of Primitive Man." In Annual Report of the Smithsonian Institution, pp. 451-60. Washington, D.C.: Government Printing Office.

Bodmer, W. F., and L. L. Cavalli-Sforza. 1970. "Intelligence and Race." Scientific American 223 (October): 19-29.

Bolton, T. L. 1892. "The Growth of Memory in School Children." American Journal of Psychology 4:362-80.

Boring, E. G. 1923. "Intelligence as the Test Tests It." New Republic 35:35-37.

Bowles, Samuel, and Herbert Gintis. 1976. Schooling in Capitalist America. New York: Basic Books.

_____. 1974. "IQ in the United States Class Structure." In The New Assault on Equality, edited by Alan Gartner, Colin Greer, and Frank Riessman, pp. 7-84. New York: Harper & Row.

Bowles, Samuel, Herbert Gintis, and Peter Meyer. 1975. "The Long Shadow of Work: Education, the Family and the Reproduction of the Social Division of Labor." Insurgent Sociologist 5 (Summer): 3-22.

Bowles, Samuel, and Valerie Nelson. 1974. "The 'Inheritance of IQ' and the Intergenerational Reproduction of Economic Inequality." Review of Economics and Statistics 56 (February): 39-51.

Brenner, Marshall H. 1968. "The Use of High School Data to Predict Work Performance." Journal of Applied Psychology, vol. 52 (January).

Bridgeman, P. W. 1927. Logic of Modern Physics. New York: Macmillan.

Brigham, Carl C. 1930. "Intelligence Tests of Immigrant Groups." Psychological Review 37:158-65.

Bronfenbrenner, Urie. 1975a. "Is Early Intervention Effective? Some Studies of Early Education in Familial and Extra-Familial Settings." In Race and IQ, edited by Ashley Montagu, pp. 287-322. New York: Oxford University Press.

_____. 1975b. "Nature with Nurture: A Reinterpretation of the Evidence." In Race and IQ, edited by Ashley Montagu, pp. 114-44. New York: Oxford University Press.

Burks, Barbara Stoddard. 1928a. "Statistical Hazards in Nature-Nurture Investigations." In The 27th Yearbook, of the National Society for the Study of Education, pt. 1, pp. 9-38.

_____. 1928b. "The Relative Influence of Nature and Nurture upon Mental Development: A Comparative Study of Foster Parent-Foster Child Resemblance and True Parent-True Child Resemblance." In The 27th Yearbook, of the National Society for the Study of Education, pt. 1, pp. 219-316.

_____. 1928c. "Comments on the Chicago and Stanford Studies of Foster Children." In The 27th Yearbook, of the National Society for the Study of Education, pt. 1, pp. 317-21.

_____. 1928d. "A Summary of the Literature on the Determiners of the Intelligence Quotient and the Educational Quotient." In The 27th Yearbook, of the National Society for the Study of Education, pt. 2, pp. 248-353.

Burlingame, Mildred, and Calvin P. Stone. 1928. "Family Resemblance in Maze-Learning Ability in White Rats." In The 27th Yearbook, of the National Society for the Study of Education, pt. 1, pp. 89-99.

Burt, Cyril. 1966. "The Genetic Determination of Differences in Intelligence: A Study of Monozygotic Twins Reared Together and Apart." British Journal of Psychology 57:137-53.

Buss, Allan R. 1976. "Galton and the Birth of Differential Psychology and Eugenics: Social, Political, and Economic Forces." Journal of the History of the Behavioral Sciences 12 (January): 47-58.

Butler, J. S. 1976. "Inequality in the Military: An Examination of Promotion Times for Black and White Enlisted Men." American Sociological Review 41 (October): 807-18.

Callahan, Raymond E. 1962. Education and the Cult of Efficiency. Chicago: University of Chicago Press.

Campbell, David P. 1971. "Admissions Policies: Side Effects and Their Implications." American Psychologist 26 (July): 636-47.

Carlson, Elof Axel. 1966. The Gene: A Critical History. Philadelphia: Saunders.

Carroll, Michael. 1972. "Considerations on the Analysis of Variance Paradigm." Pacific Sociological Review 15:443-59.

Carter, Harold D. 1940. "Ten Years of Research on Twins: Contributions to the Nature-Nurture Problem." In The 39th Yearbook, of the National Society for the Study of Education, pt. 1, pp. 235-55.

Cartwright, Walter J., and Thomas R. Burtis. 1968. "Race and Intelligence: Changing Opinions in Social Science." Social Science Quarterly 49 (December): 603-18.

Cattell, James McKeen. 1917. "Families of American Men of Science." Scientific Monthly 4:248-62.

_____. 1915. "Families of American Men of Science." Popular Science Monthly 86:504-15.

_____. 1914. "Science, Education, and Democracy." Science 39: 154-64.

_____. 1903. "A Statistical Study of Eminent Men." Popular Science Monthly 62:359-77.

_____. 1890. "Mental Tests and Measurements." Mind 15:373-80.

Cattell, Raymond B. 1941. Abilities: Their Structure, Growth, and Action. Boston: Houghton Mifflin.

Chase, Alan. 1977. The Legacy of Malthus. New York: Knopf.

Chomsky, Noam. 1976. "The Fallacy of Richard Herrnstein's IQ." In The IQ Controversy, edited by N. J. Block and Gerald Dworkin, pp. 285-98. New York: Random House.

Cicourel, Aaron, et al. 1974. Language Use and School Performance. New York: Academic Press.

Cicourel, Aaron, and John I. Kutsuse. 1963. The Educational Decision-Makers. New York: Bobbs-Merrill.

Cohen, Rosalie. 1969. "Conceptual Styles, Culture Conflict, and Non-Verbal Tests of Intelligence." American Anthropologist 71:828-56.

_____. 1968. "The Relation between Socio-Cultural Styles and Orientation to School Requirements." Sociology of Education 41: 201-20.

Cohen, Rosalie, Gerd Fraenkel, and John Brewer. 1968. "The Language of the Hard-Core Poor: Implications for Culture Conflict." Sociological Quarterly, Winter, pp. 19-28.

Cole, Michael, and Sylvia Scribner. 1974. Culture and Thought. New York: John Wiley.

Coleman, James, et al. 1966. "Equality of Educational Opportunity." Washington, D.C.: Department of Health, Education and Welfare, U.S. Government Printing Office.

Coleman, William. 1970. "Bateson and Chromosomes: Conservative Thought in Science." Centaurus 15:228-314.

Colman, A. M. 1972. "'Scientific' Racism and the Evidence on Race and Intelligence." Race 14 (October): 137-53.

Cooper, G. D., M. York, P. G. Daston, and H. B. Adams. 1967. "The Porteus Test and Various Measures of Intelligence with Southern Negro Adolescents." American Journal of Mental Deficiency 71:787-92.

Cooper, R., and J. Zubek. 1958. "Effects of Enriched and Restricted Environments on the Learning Ability of Bright and Dull Rats." Canadian Journal of Psychology 12:159-64.

Cowan, Ruth Schwartz. 1972a. "Francis Galton's Contribution to Genetics." Journal of the History of Biology 5:380-412.

_____. 1972b. "Francis Galton's Statistical Ideas: The Influence of Eugenics." Isis 63:509-28.

_____. 1968. "Sir Francis Galton and the Continuity of Germ Plasm: A Biological Idea with Political Roots." Actes XIIe Congres International d'Histoire des Sciences (Paris), pp. 181-86.

Crane, Diana. 1972. Invisible Colleges. Chicago: University of Chicago Press.

Cronbach, Lee J. 1975. "Five Decades of Controversy over Mental Testing." American Psychologist 30 (January): 1-14.

_____. 1969a. Essentials of Psychological Testing. 3d ed. New York: Harper & Row.

_____. 1969b. "Heredity, Environment, and Educational Policy." Harvard Educational Review 39 (Spring): 338-47.

Daniels, J., and V. Houghton. 1972. "Jensen, Eysenck and the Eclipse of the Galton Paradigm." In Race and Intelligence, edited by Ken Richardson, David Spears, and Martin Richards, pp. 68-80. Baltimore: Penguin.

Davis, Kingley, and Wilbert E. Moore. 1945. "Some Principles of Stratification." American Sociological Review 10 (April): 242-49.

Deakin, Michael A. B. 1976. "On Urbach's Analysis of the 'IQ Debate.'" British Journal for the Philosophy of Science 27 (March): 60-65.

Deutsch, Martin. 1969. "Happenings on the Way Back from the Forum: Social Science, IQ, and Race Revisited." Harvard Educational Review 39 (Summer): 523-54.

Dever, R. B. 1970. "Comments on the Jensen Paper." Unpublished. Bloomington: University of Indiana.

Dewey, John. 1910. How We Think. Boston: D. C. Heath.

Dobzhansky, Theodosius. 1962. Mankind Evolving. New Haven, Conn.: Yale University Press.

Dobzhansky, Theodosius, and B. Spassky. 1944. "Genetics of Natural Populations. XI. Manifestations of Genetic Variants in Drosophila Pseudoobscura in Different Environments." Genetics 29:270-90.

Dollard, John. 1949. Caste and Class in a Southern Town. New York: Doubleday.

Douglas, Jack D. 1971. "The Rhetoric of Science and the Origins of Statistical Social Thought: The Case of Durkheim's Suicide." In The Phenomenon of Sociology, edited by Edward A. Tiryakian, pp. 44-57. New York: Appleton-Century-Crofts.

Douvan, E. 1956. "Social Status and Success Striving." Journal of Abnormal and Social Psychology 52 (March): 219-23.

Doyle, Kenneth O., Jr. 1974. "Theory and Practice of Ability Testing in Ancient Greece." Journal of the History of the Behavioral Sciences 10 (April): 202-12.

Dubois, P. H. 1966. "A Test-Dominated Society: China, 1115 B.C.-1905 A.D." In Testing Problems in Perspective, edited by Anne Anastasi, pp. 29-36. Washington, D.C.: American Council on Education.

Dumont, R. V., and Murray L. Wax. 1969. "Cherokee School Society and the Intercultural Classroom." Human Organization 28:217-26.

Duncan, Otis Dudley. 1968. "Ability and Achievement." Eugenics Quarterly 15 (March): 1-11.

Duncan, Otis Dudley, D. L. Featherman, and Beverly Duncan. 1968. "Socioeconomic Background and Occupational Achievement: Extensions of a Basic Model." Mimeographed. Washington, D.C.: U.S. Office of Education, Bureau of Research.

Dunn, L. C. 1965. A Short History of Genetics. New York: McGraw-Hill.

Dworkin, Gerald. 1974. "Two Views on IQs." American Psychologist 29:465-67.

Ebbinghaus, H. 1897. "Uber eine neue Methode zur Prufung geistiger Fahigkeiten und ihr Anwendung bei Schulkinder." Zeitschrift fur angewandte Psychologie 13:401-59.

Eckberg, Douglas Lee, and Lester Hill, Jr. 1976. "The Paradigm Concept and Sociology." Paper presented at the annual meeting of the Southwestern Sociological Association, Dallas. Mimeographed.

Eckberg, Douglas Lee, and David R. Roth. 1977. "Standardization versus Authenticity: Conflict in the Role of IQ Tester." Research Report no. 2. Spencer Foundation Grant no. B-229. University of Texas at Austin. Mimeographed.

Edelman, Murray. 1977. Political Language. New York: Academic Press.

Edwards, Richard C. 1977. "Personal Traits and 'Success' in Schooling and Work." Educational and Psychological Measurement 37 (Spring): 125-38.

Eisenberg, Leon. 1966. "Clinical Considerations in the Psychiatric Evaluation of Intelligence." In Psychopathology of Mental Development, edited by Joseph Zubin and George A. Jervis, pp. 502-13. New York: Grune and Stratton.

Elkins, Stanley. 1963. Slavery. New York: Grosset and Dunlap.

Elson, Ruth M. 1975. "Racial Teachings in the 19th Century Schools." In The American Experience in Education, edited by John Barnard and David Burner, pp. 59-68. New York: Franklin Watts.

Elton, Charles F., and Linda R. Shevel. 1969. "Who Is Talented?" ACT Research Report no. 31. Iowa City: American College Testing Program.

Esquirol, J. E. D. 1838. "Des maladies mentales considerees sous les rapports médical, hygiénique, et médico-légal." Paris: Bailliere.

Evans, Glen T. 1969. "Intelligence, Transfer and Problem Solving." In On Intelligence, edited by W. B. Dockrell, pp. 191-231. London: Methuen.

Evans, Ross A. 1974. "Psychology's White Face." In The New Assault on Equality, edited by Alan Gartner, Colin Greer, and Frank Riessman, pp. 102-13. New York: Harper & Row.

Eyferth, K. 1961. "Leistungen verschiedener Gruppen von Beastzungkindern in Hamburg-Wechsler Intelligentztest für Kindern (HAWIK)." Archiv für die gesamte Psychologie 113:222-41.

_____. 1959. "Eine Untersuching der Neger-Mischlingskinder in Wesdeutschland." Vita Humana 2:102-14.

Eyferth, K., U. Brandt, and W. Havel. 1960. Farbige Kinder in Deutschland. Munich: Juventa Verlag.

Eysenck, Hans J. 1971. The IQ Argument. New York: Library Press.

_____. 1962. Know Your Own IQ. Baltimore: Penguin.

Farrall, Lyndsay Andrew. 1975. "Controversy and Conflict in Science: A Cast Study—The English Biometric School and Mendel's Laws." Social Studies of Science 5 (August): 269-301.

_____. 1970. "The Origins and Growth of the English Eugenics Movement, 1865-1925." Ph.D. dissertation, Indiana University. Ann Arbor, Mich.: University Microfilms.

Feagin, Joe R. 1978. Racial and Ethnic Relations. Englewood Cliffs, N.J.: Prentice-Hall.

Feagin, Joe R., and Clairece Booher Feagin. 1978. Discrimination American Style. Englewood Cliffs, N.J.: Prentice-Hall.

Fehr, F. S. 1969. "Critique of Hereditarian Accounts of 'Intelligence' and Contrary Findings: A Reply to Jensen." Harvard Educational Review 39 (Summer): 571-80.

Feinberg, Walter. 1978. "IQ Tests, Intelligence, and the Distribution of Knowledge." Unpublished. Urbana: University of Illinois.

Feldman, M. W., and R. C. Lewontin. 1975. "The Heritability Hang-up." Science 190 (December): 1163-68.

Fernald, Walter E. 1924. "Thirty Years' Progress in the Care of the Feebleminded." Presidential Address, American Association for the Study of the Feeble-Minded.

Fisher, R. A. 1951. "Limits to Intensive Production in Animals." British Agricultural Bulletin 4:217-18.

_____. 1918. "The Correlation between Relatives on the Supposition of Mendelian Inheritance." Transactions of the Royal Society of Edinburgh 52:399-433.

Fjellman, J. 1971. "The Myth of Primitive Mentality." Ph.D. dissertation, Stanford University. Ann Arbor: University Microfilms.

Flaugher, Ronald L. 1974. "The New Definitions of Test Fairness in Selection: Developments and Implications." Educational Researcher 3 (October): 13-16.

Frederickson, George M. 1971. The Black Image in the White Mind. New York: Harper & Row.

Freeman, Frank N. 1926. Mental Tests. Boston: Houghton Mifflin.

Freeman, Frank N., Karl J. Holzinger, and Blythe C. Mitchell. 1928. "The Influence of Environment on the Intelligence, School Achievement, and Conduct of Foster Children." In The 27th Yearbook, of the National Society for the Study of Education, pt. 1, pp. 102-217.

French, J. W. 1951. "The Description of Aptitude and Achievement Tests in Terms of Rotated Factors." Psychometric Monographs no. 5.

Friedrichs, R. W. 1973. "The Impact of Social Factors upon Scientific Judgment: The 'Jensen Thesis' as Appraised by Members of the American Psychological Association." Journal of Negro Education, vol. 42 (Fall).

Frost, Joe L., and G. Thomas Rowland. 1971. Compensatory Programming: The Acid Test of Education. Dubuque, Iowa: Wm. C. Brown.

Gall, F. J., and J. G. Spurzheim. 1809. Recherches sur le systeme nerveux. Paris: Schoell.

Galton, Francis. 1892. Hereditary Genius. 2d ed., 1962. Cleveland: World.

_____. 1890. "Remarks." Mind 15:380-81.

_____. 1889. Natural Inheritance. London: Macmillan.

_____. 1883. Inquiries into Human Faculty and Its Development. London: Macmillan.

_____. 1874. English Men of Science. London: Macmillan.

_____. 1869. Hereditary Genius. New York: Appleton.

_____. 1865. "Hereditary Talent and Character." Macmillan's Magazine 12 (June): 157-66.

Gambrill, Bessie L. 1922. College Achievement and Vocational Efficiency. New York: Columbia University.

Garcia, John. 1977. "Intelligence Testing: Quotients, Quotas, and Quackery." In Chicano Psychology, edited by J. Martinez. San Francisco: Academic Press.

Garfinkel, Harold. 1967. Studies in Ethnomethodology. Englewood Cliffs, N.J.: Prentice-Hall.

Garrett, Henry E. 1960. "Klineberg's Chapter on Race and Psychology: A Review." Mankind Quarterly 1:15-22.

_____. 1955. General Psychology. New York: American Book.

_____. 1945a. "Comparison of Negro and White Recruits on the Army Tests Given in 1917-18." American Journal of Psychology 58: 480-95.

_____. 1945b. "A Note on the Intelligence Scores of Negroes and Whites in 1918." Journal of Abnormal and Social Psychology 40:344-46.

Garth, Thomas Russell. 1934. "The Problem of Race Psychology: A General Statement." Journal of Negro Education 3 (July): 319.

_____. 1931. Race Psychology: A Study of Racial Mental Differences. New York: McGraw-Hill.

Getzels, J. W., and P. W. Jackson. 1962. Creativity and Intelligence. New York: Wiley.

_____. 1959. "The Meaning of Giftedness: An Examination of an Expanding Concept." Phi Delta Kappan 40 (November): 75-78.

Ghiselli, E. E. 1966. The Validity of Occupational Aptitude Tests. New York: Wiley.

Gilbert, J. A. 1894. "Researches on the Mental and Physiological Development of School Children." Studies from the Yale Psychological Laboratory 2:40-100.

Gillie, Oliver. 1976. "Crucial Data Was Faked by Eminent Psychologist." Sunday Times (London), October 24, 1976, pp. 1-2.

Gilmer, B., J. O. Miller, and S. W. Gray. 1970. "Intervention with Mothers and Young Children: Study of Intra-Family Effects." Mimeographed. Nashville: Demonstration and Research Center for Early Education.

Ginsburg, Herbert. 1972. The Myth of the Deprived Child. Englewood Cliffs, N.J.: Prentice-Hall.

Gobineau, Arthur de. 1970. Gobineau: Selected Political Writings, edited by Michael D. Biddiss. New York: Harper & Row.

Goddard, H. H. 1928. "Feeblemindedness: A Question and Definition." Journal of Psycho-Asthenics 33:219-27.

_____. 1926. Feeble-mindedness: Its Causes and Consequences. New York: Macmillan.

_____. 1920. Human Efficiency and Levels of Intelligence. Princeton, N.J.: Princeton University Press.

_____. 1917. "Mental Tests and the Immigrant." Journal of Delinquency 2 (September): 271.

_____. 1913. "The Binet Tests in Relation to Immigration." Journal of Psycho-Asthenics 18 (December): 109-10.

Goldberger, Arthur S. 1976. "On Jensen's Method for Twins." Discussion Paper 340-76, Institute for Research on Poverty, University of Wisconsin-Madison.

_____. 1974a. "Mysteries of the Meritocracy." Discussion Paper 225-74, Institute for Research on Poverty, University of Wisconsin-Madison.

_____. 1974b. "Professor Jensen, Meet Miss Burks." Discussion Paper 242-74, Institute for Research on Poverty, University of Wisconsin-Madison.

Goldberger, Arthur S., and Richard C. Lewontin. 1976. "Jensen's Twin Fantasy." Discussion Paper 341-76, Institute for Research on Poverty, University of Wisconsin-Madison.

Goodenough, Florence. 1940. "Some Special Problems of Nature-Nurture Research." In The 39th Yearbook, of the National Society for the Study of Education, pt. 1, pp. 367-84.

Goodenough, Florence, and Dale B. Harris. 1950. "Studies in the Psychology of Children's Drawings, 1928-1949." Psychological Bulletin 47 (September): 369-433.

Gossett, Thomas F. 1963. Race: The History of an Idea in America. Dallas: SMU Press.

Gough, H. G. 1965. "Misplaced Emphasis in Admissions." Journal of College Student Personnel 6:130-35.

_____. 1961. "Techniques for Identifying the Creative Research Scientist." In The Creative Person, edited by Frank Barron, pp. III-1—III-27. Berkeley: University of California, Institute for Personality Assessment and Research.

_____. 1953. "A Non-Intellectual Intelligence Test." Journal of Consulting Psychology 17:242-46.

Gough, H. G., W. B. Hall, and R. E. Harris. 1963. "Admissions Procedures as Forecasters of Performance in Medical Training." Journal of Medical Education 38:983-88.

Gould, Stephen J. 1978. "Morton's Ranking of Races by Cranial Capacity." Science 200 (May 5): 503-9.

Grant, Madison. 1916. The Passing of the Great Race. New York: Scribner.

Greenfield, Patricia M. 1971. "Goal as Environmental Variable in the Development of Intelligence." In Intelligence: Genetic and Environmental Influences, edited by Robert Cancro, pp. 252-61. New York: Grune and Stratton.

Griliches, Zvi, and William Mason. 1972. "Education, Income and Ability." Journal of Political Economy 80, pt. 2 (May/June): S74-S103.

Guicciardi, G., and G. C. Ferrari. 1896. "I testi mentali per l'esame degli alienati." Revista sperimentale di freniatnia 22:297-314.

Guilford, Jay Paul. 1968. Intelligence, Creativity, and Their Educational Implications. San Diego, Calif.: Robert R. Knapp.

_____. 1967. The Nature of Human Intelligence. New York: McGraw-Hill.

_____. 1964. "Zero Intercorrelations among Tests of Intellectual Abilities." Psychological Bulletin 61:401-5.

_____. 1963. "Intellectual Resources and Their Values as Seen by Scientists." In Intelligence: Genetic and Environmental Influences, edited by Robert Cancro, pp. 252-61. New York: Wiley.

Haggard, E. A. 1954. "Social Status and Intelligence." Genetic Psychology Monographs 49 (May): 141-86.

Haldane, J. B. S. 1946. "The Interaction of Nature and Nurture." Annals of Eugenics 13:197-206.

Haller, John S. 1971. Outcasts from Evolution. New York: McGraw-Hill.

Haller, Mark H. 1968. "Social Science and Genetics: A Historical Perspective." In Genetics, edited by David C. Glass, pp. 215-25. New York: Rockefeller University Press and Russell Sage Foundation.

_____. 1963. Eugenics: Hereditarian Attitudes in American Thought. New Brunswick, N.J.: Rutgers University Press.

Halsey, A. H. 1968. "Biology and Sociology: A Reconciliation." In Genetics, edited by David C. Glass, pp. 210-14. New York: Rockefeller University Press and Russell Sage Foundation.

Hamblin, R. L. 1974. "Social Attitudes: Magnitude Measurement and Theory." In Measurement in the Social Sciences, edited by Hubert Blalock, pp. 61-120. Chicago: Aldine.

Handlin, Oscar. 1957. Race and Nationality in American Life. New York: Doubleday.

Harlow, Harry F., and Mary K. Harlow. 1962. "The Mind of Man." In Yearbook of Science and Technology. New York: McGraw-Hill.

Harmon, Lindsey R. 1963. "The Development of a Criterion of Scientific Competence." In Scientific Creativity, edited by Calvin W. Taylor and Frank Barron, pp. 44-52. New York: Wiley.

Harrington, Gordon M. 1975. "Intelligence Tests May Favor the Majority Groups in a Population." Nature 258:708-9.

Harris, Marvin. 1968. The Rise of Anthropological Theory. New York: Crowell.

Harwood, Jonathan. 1977. "The Race-Intelligence Controversy: A Sociological Approach II-External Factors." Social Studies of Science 7 (February): 1-30.

_____. 1976. "The Race-Intelligence Controversy: A Sociological Approach I-External Factors." Social Studies of Science 6 (August-November): 369-94.

Haught, B. F. 1922. "The Interrelation of Some Higher Learning Processes." Psychological Monographs, vol. 30, no. 6.

Hause, John C. 1972. "Earnings Profile: Ability and Schooling."
Journal of Political Economy 80, pt. 2 (May/June): S108-38.

Hegmann, J. P., and J. C. DeFries. 1968. "Open-Field Behavior
in Mice: Genetic Analysis of Repeated Measures." Psycho-
nomic Science 13:27-28.

Helson, Ravenna, and Richard S. Crutchfield. 1970. "Mathematicians:
The Creative Researcher and the Average Ph.D." Journal of
Consulting and Clinical Psychology 34:250-57.

Henmon, V. A. C. 1921. "Intelligence and Its Measurement." Journal of Educational Psychology 12 (April): 195-98.

Herrnstein, Richard J. 1973. IQ in the Meritocracy. Boston: Little, Brown.

_____. 1971. "IQ." The Atlantic Monthly 228 (September): 43-64.

Herskovits, Melville J. 1930. The Anthropometry of the American
Negro. New York: Columbia University Press.

_____. 1928. The American Negro: A Study in Race Crossing. New
York: A. A. Knopf.

_____. 1926. "On the Relation between Negro-White Mixture and
Standing in Intelligence Tests." Pedigogical Seminars and
Journal of Genetic Psychology 33:30-42.

Heyns, Barbara. 1978. "Review Essay on Schooling in Capitalist
America, by Samuel Bowles and Herbert Gintis." American
Journal of Sociology 83 (January): 999-1006.

Higham, John. 1971. "Toward Racism: The History of an Idea."
In Majority and Minority, edited by Norman R. Yetman and C.
Hoy Steele, pp. 230-52. Boston: Allyn and Bacon.

Hirsch, Jerry. 1976. "Behavior-Genetics and Its Biosocial Consequences." In The IQ Controversy, edited by N. J. Block and
Gerald Dworkin, pp. 156-78. New York: Random House.

_____. 1975. "Jensenism: The Bankruptcy of 'Science' without
Scholarship." Educational Theory 25 (Winter): 3-28.

_____. 1967. "Behavior-Genetic, or 'Experimental,' Analysis: The Challenge of Science versus the Lure of Technology." American Psychologist 22 (February): 118-30.

_____. 1963. "Behavior Genetics and Individuality Understood: Behaviorism's Counterfactual Dogma Blinded the Behavioral Sciences to the Significance of Meiosis." Science 142 (December 13): 1436-42.

Hirsch, Jerry, and Atam Vetta. 1977. "The Misconceptions of Behavior Genetics." Unpublished. Urbana: University of Illinois.

Hirsch, Nathaniel D. 1926. "A Study of Natio-Racial Mental Difference." Genetic Psychology Monographs 1:394-97.

Hofstadter, Richard. 1959. Social Darwinism in American Thought. Rev. ed. New York: Braziller.

Hogarth, R. M. 1974. "Monozygotic and Dizygotic Twins Raised Together: Sensitivity of Heritability Estimates." British Journal of Mathematical and Statistical Psychology 27:1-13.

Hogben, Lancelot. 1957. Statistical Theory. London: Allen and Unwin.

_____. 1939. Nature and Nurture. Rev. ed. New York: W. W. Norton.

_____. 1932. Genetic Principles in Medicine and Social Science. New York: Knopf.

_____. 1919. "Modern Heredity and Social Science." Socialist Review 16 (April-June): 147-56.

Holden, Constance. 1973. "R. J. Herrnstein: The Perils of Expounding Meritocracy." Science 181:36-39.

Holland, John L., and James M. Richards, Jr. 1965. "Academic and Non-Academic Achievement: Correlated or Uncorrelated?" ACT Research Report no. 2. Iowa City: American College Testing Program.

Hoyt, Donald P. 1965. "The Relationship between College Grades and Adult Achievement: A Review of the Literature." ACT Research Report no. 7. Iowa City: American College Testing Program.

Hudson, Liam. 1971. "Intelligence, Race, and the Selection of Data."
Race 12 (January): 283-92.

_____. 1960. "Degree Class and Attainment in Scientific Research."
British Journal of Psychology 51:67-73.

Hunt, J. McVicker. 1969. "Has Compensatory Education Failed?
Has It Been Attempted?" Harvard Educational Review 39
(Spring): 278-300.

Hyde, R. W., and R. M. Chisholm. 1944. "Studies in Medical Sociology: III. The Relation of Mental Disorders to Race and Nationality." New England Journal of Medicine 231:612-18.

Jarvik, Lissy F., and L. Erlenmeyer-Kimling. 1966. "Survey of
Familial Correlations in Measured Intellectual Functions." In
Psychopathology of Mental Development, edited by Joseph Zubin
and George Jervis, pp. 447-59. New York: Grune and Stratton.

Jefferson, Thomas. 1955. Notes on the State of Virginia, edited by
William Pedan. Chapel Hill: University of North Carolina Press.

Jencks, Christopher. 1973. "The Effects of Worker Characteristics
on Economic Success: An Inquiry into Nonlinearities, Interactions, and Unmeasured Variables Using the NORC Sample."
Mimeographed. Cambridge, Mass.: Center for Educational
Policy Research.

_____. 1972. Inequality. New York: Harper & Row.

Jensen, Arthur R. 1974. "Kinship Correlations Reported by Sir
Cyril Burt." Behavior Genetics 4:24-25.

_____. 1972. Genetics and Education. New York: Harper & Row.

_____. 1971. "Can We and Should We Study Race Differences?" In
Race and Intelligence, edited by C. Loring Brace, George R.
Gamble, and James T. Bond, pp. 10-31. Anthropological
Studies no. 8. Washington, D.C.: American Anthropological
Association.

_____. 1969a. "How Much Can We Boost IQ and Scholastic Achieve-
ment?" Harvard Educational Review 39 (Winter): 1-123.

_____. 1969b. "Reducing the Heredity-Environment Uncertainty."
Harvard Educational Review 39 (Summer): 449-83.

Johnson, D. , and W. Mihal. 1973. "Performance of Whites and
Blacks in Computerized versus Manual Testing Environments."
American Psychologist 28 (August): 694-99.

Joncich, Geraldine. 1968. The Sane Positivist: A Biography of E.
L. Thorndike. Middletown, Conn.: Wesleyan University Press.

Jordan, Winthrop. 1968. White over Black. Baltimore: Penguin.

Kagan, Jerome. 1974. "What Is Intelligence?" In The New Assault
on Equality, edited by Alan Gartner, Colin Greer, and Frank
Riessman, pp. 114-30. New York: Harper & Row.

Kamin, Leon. 1974. The Science and Politics of IQ. Potomac, Md.:
Lawrence Erlbaum Associates.

Kaplan, Abraham. 1964. The Conduct of Inquiry. San Francisco:
Chandler.

Karier, Clarence. 1976. "Testing for Order and Control in the Cor-
porate Liberal State." In The IQ Controversy, edited by N. J.
Block and Gerald Dworkin, pp. 339-73. New York: Random
House.

_____. 1975. Shaping the American Educational State. New York:
Free Press.

Karnes, M. B. , et al. 1969. "Research and Development Program
on Preschool Disadvantaged Children: Final Report." Washington, D.C.: U.S. Office of Education.

Katz, Irwin, Thomas Henchy, and Harvey Allen. 1968. "Effects of
Race of Tester, Approval-Disapproval, and Need on Negro Children Learning." Journal of Personality and Social Psychology
8 (January): 38-42.

Kelley, E. L. , and L. R. Goldberg. 1959. "Correlates of Later
Performance and Specialization in Psychology." Psychological
Monographs, vol. 73, no. 492.

Kelley, Truman. 1928. Crossroads in the Mind of Man. Stanford,
Calif.: Stanford University Press.

Klineberg, Otto. 1935a. Race Differences. New York: Harper and
Brothers.

_____. 1935b. Negro Intelligence and Selective Migration. New York: Columbia University Press.

_____. 1931. "A Study of Psychological Differences between 'Rational' and National Groups in Europe." Archives of Psychology, no. 132.

Krech, David. 1962. "Cortical Localization of Function." In Psychology in the Making, edited by Leo Postman, pp. 31-72. New York: Knopf.

Kuhn, Thomas S. 1974. "Second Thoughts on Paradigms." In The Structure of Scientific Theories, edited by Frederick Suppe, pp. 459-82. Urbana: University of Illinois Press.

_____. 1970a. "Reflections on My Critics." In Criticism and the Growth of Knowledge, edited by Imre Lakatos and Alan Musgrave, pp. 231-78. Cambridge: At the University Press.

_____. 1970b. The Structure of Scientific Revolutions. Rev. ed. Chicago: University of Chicago Press.

_____. 1968. "History: The History of Science." International Encyclopedia of the Social Sciences. Vol. 14, pp. 74-82.

_____. 1962. The Structure of Scientific Revolutions. Chicago: University of Chicago Press.

_____. 1961. "The Function of Measurement in Modern Physical Science." Isis 52:161-93.

_____. 1957. The Copernican Revolution. Cambridge, Mass.: Harvard University Press.

Labov, William. 1972. Language in the Inner City. Philadelphia: University of Pennsylvania Press.

Labov, William, and C. Robins. 1969. "A Note on the Relation of Reading Failure to Peer-Group Status in Urban Ghettos." The Teachers' College Record 70 (February): 395-405.

Lakatos, Imre. 1970. "Falsification and the Methodology of Scientific Research Programs." In Criticism and the Growth of Knowledge, edited by Imre Lakatos and Alan Musgrave, pp. 91-196. Cambridge: At the University Press.

Lannholm, G. V. 1968. "Review of Studies Employing GRE Scores in Predicting Success in Graduate Study, 1952-67." GRE Special Report no. 68-1. Princeton, N.J.: Educational Testing Service.

Lannholm, G. V., G. L. Marco, and W. B. Schrader. 1968. "Cooperative Studies of Predicting Graduate School Success." GRE Special Report no. 68-3. Princeton, N.J.: Educational Testing Service.

Laughlin, Harry Hamilton. 1922. Eugenical Sterilization in the United States. Rev. ed. New Haven, Conn.: American Eugenics Society.

Layzer, David. 1976. "Science or Superstition? A Physical Scientist Looks at the IQ Controversy." In The IQ Controversy, edited by N. J. Block and Gerald Dworkin, pp. 194-241. New York: Random House.

_____. 1974. "Heritability Analysis of IQ Scores: Science or Numerology?" Science 183 (March 29): 1259-66.

Lee, Everett S. 1951. "Negro Intelligence and Selective Migration: A Philadelphia Test of the Klineberg Hypothesis." American Sociological Review 16:227-33.

Leftwich, Richard H. 1973. The Price System and Resource Allocation. 5th ed. New York: Dryden Press.

Lerner, I. M. 1972. "Polygenic Inheritance and Human Intelligence." Evolutionary Biology 6:399-414.

Lewis, Michael. 1973. "Infant Intelligence Tests: Their Use and Misuse." Human Development 16:108-18.

Lewontin, Richard C. 1976a. "The Analysis of Variance and the Analysis of Causes." In The IQ Controversy, edited by N. J. Block and Gerald Dworkin, pp. 170-93. New York: Random House.

_____. 1976b. "Review of Race Differences in Intelligence, by John C. Loehlin, Gardner Lindzey and J. N. Spuhler." American Journal of Human Genetics 28 (January): 92-97.

_____. 1970a. "Race and Intelligence." Bulletin of the Atomic Scientists 26 (March): 2-8.

_____. 1970b. "Further Remarks on Race and Intelligence." Bulletin of the Atomic Scientists 26 (May): 23-25.

Lieberman, Leonard. 1968. "The Debate over Race: A Study in the Sociology of Knowledge." Phylon, Summer, pp. 127-41.

Lieberman, Leonard, and Larry T. Reynolds. 1975. "The Debate over Race Revisited: An Empirical Investigation." Paper presented at the annual meeting of the American Sociological Association, San Francisco. Mimeographed.

Linn, R. L. 1974. "Unsquared Genetic Correlations." Psychological Bulletin 81 (March): 203-6.

Loehlin, John C., Gardner Lindzey, and J. N. Spuhler. 1975. Race Differences in Intelligence. San Francisco: Freeman.

Loehlin, John C., Steven G. Vandenberg, and R. T. Osborne. 1973. "Blood Group Genes and Negro-White Ability Difference." Behavior Genetics 3:263-70.

Loevinger, Jane. 1943. "On the Proportional Contributions of Differences in Nature and Nurture to Differences in Intelligence." Psychological Bulletin 40 (December): 725-56.

Lord, Frederick, and Melvin R. Novick. 1968. Statistical Theories of Mental Test Scores. Reading, Mass.: Addison-Wesley.

Lovejoy, Arthur O. 1942. The Great Chain of Being. New York: Harper & Row.

Ludmerer, Kenneth M. 1972. Genetics and American Society. Baltimore: Johns Hopkins Press.

Lyman, Stanford M. 1974. Chinese Americans. New York: Random House.

Lyons, Charles M. 1975. To Wash an Aethiop White. New York: Teachers' College Press.

McCall, R. B., M. I. Appelbaum, and P. S. Hogarty. 1973. "Developmental Changes in Mental Performance." Child Development Monographs 38, no. 3, pp. 1-84.

McClelland, David C. 1974. "Testing for Competence Rather than for 'Intelligence.'" In The New Assault on Equality, edited by

Alan Gartner, Colin Greer, and Frank Riessman, pp. 163-97. New York: Harper & Row.

McClelland, David C., A. L. Baldwin, Urie Bronfenbrenner, and F. L. Strodtbeck. 1958. Talent and Society. Princeton, N.J.: Van Nostrand.

McGaugh, J. L., R. D. Jennings, and C. W. Thompson. 1962. "Effects of Distribution of Practice on the Maze Learning Descendants of the Tryon Maze-Bright and Maze-Dull Strains." Psychological Reports 10 (February): 147-50.

McGuire, Terry, and Jerry Hirsch. 1977. "General Intelligence (g) and Heritability (H^2, h^2)." In The Structuring of Experience, edited by F. Weizmann and I. C. Uzgiris, chap. 2. New York: Plenum Press.

MacKenzie, Brian. 1976. "Darwinism and Positivism as Methodological Influences on the Development of Psychology." Journal of the History of the Behavioral Sciences 12 (October): 330-37.

MacKenzie, Donald. 1976. "Eugenics in Britain." Social Studies of Science 6 (September): 499-532.

_____. 1974. "Social Factors in the Emergence of Modern Statistics." Paper presented at the Conference on the History of Statistics, Harvard University. Mimeographed.

MacKenzie, Donald, and S. B. Barnes. 1974. "Biometrician versus Mendelian: A Controversy and Its Explanation." Edinburgh: Science Studies Unit, University of Edinburgh. Mimeographed.

MacKinnon, Donald W. 1968. "Selecting Students with Creative Potential." In The Creative College Student: An Unmet Challenge, edited by Paul Heist, pp. 101-16. San Francisco: Jossey-Bass.

_____. 1962. "The Nature and Nurture of Creative Talent." American Psychologist 17 (July): 484-95.

McKusick, V. A. 1966. Mendelian Inheritance in Man: Catalogs of Autosomal Dominant, Recessive, and X-Linked Phenotypes. Baltimore: Johns Hopkins Press.

McNemar, Quinn. 1964. "Lost: Our Intelligence? Why?" American Psychologist 19:871-72.

Mannheim, Karl. 1953. Essays in Sociology and Social Psychology. London: Routledge and Kegan Paul.

Manuel, Frank E. 1963. The New World of Henri St. Simon. Notre Dame, Ind.: University of Notre Dame Press.

Marks, Russell. 1975. "Race and Immigration: The Politics of Intelligence Testing." In Shaping the American Educational State, edited by Clarence Karier, pp. 316-42. New York: Free Press.

Marston, A. R. 1971. "It is Time to Reconsider the Graduate Record Examination." American Psychologist 26:653-55.

Masterman, Margaret. 1970. "The Nature of a Paradigm." In Criticism and the Growth of Knowledge, edited by Imre Lakatos and Alan Musgrave, pp. 59-90. Cambridge: At the University Press.

Mead, Margaret. 1926. "The Methodology of Racial Testing: Its Significance for Sociology." American Journal of Sociology 32 (March): 658.

Medawar, P. B. 1977. "Unnatural Science." The New York Review of Books 24 (February): 13-18.

Mednick, Martha. 1963. "Research Creativity in Psychology Graduate Students." Journal of Consulting Psychology 27:265-66.

Meer, B., and M. I. Stein. 1955. "Measures of Intelligence and Creativity." Journal of Psychology 39 (January): 117-26.

Mercer, Jane R. 1973. Labelling the Mentally Retarded. Berkeley: University of California Press.

Miller, J. K., and D. Levine. 1973. "Correlations between genetically Matched Groups versus Reliability Theory." Psychological Bulletin 79 (February): 142-44.

Montagu, Ashley. 1963. Race, Science and Humanity. Princeton, N.J.: Van Nostrand.

Moran, P. A. P. 1973. "A Note on Heritability and the Correlation between Relatives." Annals of Human Genetics 37:217.

Morton, N. E. 1974. "Analysis of Family Resemblance I: Introduction." American Journal of Human Genetics 26 (May): 318-30.

Muller, Herman J. 1933. "The Dominance of Economics over Eugenics." Scientific Monthly 37:40-47.

Nagel, Ernest. 1961. The Structure of Science. New York: Harcourt, Brace and World.

National Society for the Study of Education. 1940. The 39th Yearbook. Intelligence: Its Nature and Nurture. Part I: Comparative and Critical Expositions. Part II: Original Studies and Experiments. Bloomington, Ill.: Public Schools.

_____. 1928. The 27th Yearbook: Nature and Nurture. Part I: Their Influence upon Intelligence. Part II: Their Influence upon Achievement. Bloomington, Ill.: Public Schools.

Newman, R. W., Frank N. Freeman, and K. J. Holzinger. 1937. Twins: A Study of Heredity and Environment. Chicago: University of Chicago Press.

Oehrn, A. 1895. "Experimentelle Studien zur Individualpsychologie." Psychologischen Arbeiten 1:95-152.

Osborn, Frederick. 1951. Preface to Eugenics. New York: Harper Brothers.

Osofsky, Gilbert. 1969. Puttin' on Old Massa. New York: Harper & Row.

Ossowski, Stanislaw. 1963. Class Structure in the Social Consciousness. Translated by Sheila Patterson. New York: Free Press.

Overton, W. F. 1973. "On the Assumptive Base of the Nature-Nurture Controversy: Additive versus Interactive Conceptions." Human Development 16:74-89.

Page, Ellis B. 1972. "Comment on Behavior and Heredity." American Psychologist 27 (July): 660-61.

Parloff, Morris B., Lois-Ellin Datta, Marianne Klemen, and Joseph H. Handlon. 1968. "Personality Characteristics which Differentiate Creative Male Adolescents and Adults." Journal of Personality 36:528-52.

Parsons, Talcott. 1968. The Structure of Social Action. New York: Free Press.

Pastore, Nicholas. 1949. The Nature-Nurture Controversy. New York: King's Crown Press.

Paynter, Edward L. 1971. "Value Premises in Race Research: The Evolution of Environmentalism." In Race, Change and Urban Society, edited by Peter Orleans and William Russell, Jr., pp. 25-50. Urban Affairs Annual Reviews, vol. 5. Beverly Hills, Calif.: Sage.

Pearson, Karl. 1912. The Problem of Practical Eugenics. London: Dulau.

_____. 1900. The Grammar of Science. 2d ed. London: Adam and Charles Back.

Persell, Caroline Hodges. 1977. Education and Inequality. New York: Free Press.

Peterson, Joseph. 1934. "Basic Considerations in the Methodology of Racial Testing." Journal of Negro Education 3:403-10.

_____. 1925. Early Conceptions and Tests of Intelligence. New York: World.

_____. 1923. "The Comparative Abilities of White and Negro Children." Comparative Psychology Monographs 1.

_____. 1922. "Intelligence and Learning." Psychological Review 29:366-89.

_____. 1921. "Intelligence and Its Measurement." Journal of Educational Psychology 12 (April): 198-201.

Pettigrew, Thomas F. 1964. A Profile of the American Negro. Princeton, N.J.: Van Nostrand.

Pickens, Donald K. 1969. Eugenics and the Progressives. Nashville, Tenn.: Vanderbilt University Press.

Polanyi, Michael. 1966. The Tacit Dimension. New York: Doubleday.

Poston, Dudley, L., Jr., and David Alvirez. 1973. "On the Cost of Being a Mexican American Worker." Social Science Quarterly 54 (March): 697-709.

Poston, Dudley L., Jr., David Alvirez, and Marta Tienda. 1976. "Earnings.Differences between Anglo and Mexican American Male Workers in 1960 and 1970: Changes in the 'Cost' of Being Mexican American." Social Science Quarterly 57 (December): 618-31.

Pressey, S. L. 1921. "Intelligence and Its Measurement." Journal of Educational Psychology 12 (March): 144-47.

Price, D. J. Des. 1963. Little Science, Big Science. New York: Columbia University Press.

Price, P. B., Calvin W. Taylor, C. W. Richardson, and T. L. Jacobson. 1964. "Measurement of Physicians' Performance." Journal of Medical Education 39:203-11.

Provine, William B. 1973. "Geneticists and the Biology of Race Crossing." Science 182 (February 23): 790-96.

Purvin, George. 1974. "Intro to Herrnstein 101." In The New Assault on Equality, edited by Alan Gartner, Colin Greer, and Frank Riessman, pp. 131-62. New York: Harper & Row.

Pyle, William Henry. 1921. The Psychology of Learning. Baltimore: Warwick and York.

Quarles, Benjamin. 1961. The Negro in the American Revolution. New York: W. W. Norton.

Quetelet, Lambert Adolphe Jacques. 1842. A Treatise on Man and the Development of His Faculties. Edinburgh: William and Robert Chambers. Reprint. Gainesville, Fla.: Scholars Facsimiles and Reprints, 1969.

Rao, D. C., N. E. Morton, and S. Yee. 1974. "Analysis of Family Resemblance II: A Linear Model for Family Correlation." American Journal of Human Genetics 26:311-59.

Reeves, Joan Wynn. 1967. "Binet, Alfred." In The Encyclopedia of Philosophy, edited by Paul Edwards, vol. I, pp. 308-9. New York: Macmillan and Free Press.

Richards, J. M., J. L. Holland, and S. W. Lutz. 1967. "Prediction of Student Accomplishment in College." Journal of Educational Psychology 58:343-55.

Richards, James M., Jr., Calvin W. Taylor, and Phillip B. Price.
    1962. "The Prediction of Medical Intern Performance." Jour-
    nal of Applied Psychology 46 (April): 142-46.

Riegel, Klaus F. 1973. "An Epitaph for a Paradigm: Introduction
    for a Symposium." Human Development 16:1-7.

_____. 1972. "Influence of Economic and Political Ideologies on the
    Development of Developmental Psychology." Psychological
    Bulletin 78:129-41.

Riessman, Frank. 1974. "The Hidden IQ." In The New Assault on
    Equality, edited by Alan Gartner, Colin Greer, and Frank Riess-
    man, pp. 206-23. New York: Harper & Row.

Rist, Ray C. 1970. "Student Social Class and Teacher Expectations:
    The Self-Fulfilling Prophecy in Ghetto Conditions." Harvard
    Educational Review 40 (August): 411-51.

Roe, Anne. 1963. "Personal Problems and Science." In Scientific
    Creativity, edited by Calvin W. Taylor and Frank Barron, pp.
    132-38. New York: Wiley.

_____. 1953a. "A Psychological Study of Eminent Psychologists and
    Anthropologists and a Comparison with Biological and Physical
    Scientists." Psychological Monographs 67, no. 352:1-55.

_____. 1953b. The Making of a Scientist. New York: Dodd, Mead.

Rogers, Daniel C. 1969. "Private Rates of Return to Education in
    the United States: A Case Study." Yale Economic Essays 9
    (Spring): 88-134.

Rose, Hilary, and Steven Rose. 1974. "'Do Not Adjust Your Mind,
    There Is a Fault in Reality': Ideology in the Neurobiological
    Sciences." In Social Processes in Scientific Development,
    edited by Richard Whitley, pp. 148-71. London: Routledge and
    Kegan Paul.

Rosenberg, Charles E. 1967. "Factors in the Development of Ge-
    netics in the United States: Some Suggestions." Journal of the
    History of Medicine 22 (January): 27-46.

_____. 1966. "Science and American Social Thought." In Science
    and Society in the United States, edited by D. Van Tassell and
    M. G. Hall, pp. 137-84. New York: Dorsey.

_____. 1964. "The Adams Act: Politics and the Cause of Scientific Research." Agricultural History 38:3-12.

_____. 1961. "Charles Benedict Davenport and the Beginnings of Human Genetics." Bulletin of the History of Medicine 35 (May/June): 266-76.

Rosenthal, Robert, and Lenore Jacobson. 1968. Pygmalion in the Classroom. New York: Holt, Rinehart and Winston.

Roth, David R. 1976. "Reconsidering the Distinction between Verbal and Non-Verbal IQ Tests: A Sociological Perspective." Research Paper no. 1. Spencer Foundation Grant no. B-229. University of Texas at Austin. Mimeographed.

_____. 1974. "Intelligence Testing as a Social Activity." In Language Use and School Performance, edited by Aaron V. Cicourel et al., pp. 143-217. San Francisco: Academic Press.

Royce, J. R. 1950. "The Factorial Analysis of Animal Behavior." Psychological Bulletin 47:235-59.

Ruml, B. 1921. "Intelligence and Its Measurement." Journal of Educational Psychology 12 (March): 143-44.

Ryan, William. 1971. Blaming the Victim. New York: Pantheon.

Sahlins, Marshall. 1976. The Use and Abuse of Biology. Ann Arbor: University of Michigan Press.

Samuda, Ronald J. 1975. "Cultural Discrimination through Testing." In Majority and Minority, edited by Norman R. Yetman and C. Hoy Steele, pp. 490-505. Boston: Allyn and Bacon.

Sarason, Seymour B., and Thomas Gladwin. 1958. "Psychological Cultural Problems in Mental Subnormality: A Review of Research." Genetic Psychology Monographs 57 (February): 3-289.

Scarr-Salapatek, Sandra. 1971a. "Unknowns in the IQ Equation." Science 174 (December 17): 1223-28.

_____. 1971b. "Race, Social Class, and IQ." Science 174 (December 24): 1285-95.

Schegloff, E. A. 1972. "Notes on a Conversational Practice: Formulating Place." In Language and Social Context, edited by Pier Paolo, pp. 95-135. Baltimore: Penguin.

Schieffelin, Barbara, and Gladys Schwesinger. 1930. Mental Traits and Heredity. New York: Galton Press.

Schwartz, Michael, and J. Schwartz. 1974. "Evidence against a Genetical Component to Performance on IQ Tests." Nature 248:84-85.

Seagoe, May V. 1975. Terman and the Gifted. Los Alamos, Calif.: William Kaufman.

Searle, L. V. 1949. "The Organization of Hereditary Maze-Brightness and Maze-Dullness." Genetic Psychology Monographs 39: 279-325.

Seashore, Carl E. 1899. Some Psychological Statistics. Iowa City: University of Iowa Studies.

Seguin, E. 1866. Idiocy: Its Treatment by the Physiological Method. Reprint. New York: Bureau of Publications, Teachers' College, Columbia University, 1907.

Semler, Ira, and Ira Iscoe. 1966. "Structure of Intelligence in Negro and White Children." Journal of Educational Psychology 57: 326-36.

Sharp, Stella E. 1899. "Individual Psychology: A Study in Psychological Method." American Journal of Psychology 10:329-91.

Sherwood, J. J., and M. Nataupsky. 1968. "Predicting the Conclusions of Negro-White Intelligence Research from Biographical Characteristics of the Investigator." Journal of Personality and Social Psychology 8 (January): 53-58.

Shields, J. 1962. Monozygotic Twins. London. Oxford University Press.

Shockley, William. 1972. "Dysgenics, Geneticity, Raceology: A Challenge to the Intellectual Responsibility of Educators." Phi Delta Kappan 53 (January, Special Supplement): 297-307.

Shuey, Audrey M. 1966. The Testing of Negro Intelligence. 2d ed. New York: Social Science Press.

Shwayder, David S. 1965. The Stratification of Behavior. London: Routledge and Kegan Paul.

Skeels, H. M. 1966. "Adult Status of Children with Contrasting Early Life Experiences: A Follow-up Study." Child Development Monographs, vol. 31, Serial no. 105.

Skodak, M., and H. M. Skeels. 1949. "A Final Follow-up Study of 100 Adopted Children. Journal of Genetic Psychology 75:85-125.

Smith, Gene M. 1967. "Usefulness of Peer Ratings of Personality in Educational Research." Educational and Psychological Measurement 27 (Winter): 967-84.

Smith, Richard T. 1965. "A Comparison of Socioenvironmental Factors in Monozygotic and Dizygotic Twins, Testing an Assumption." In Methods and Goals in Human Behavior-Genetics, edited by Steven Vandenberg, pp. 45-61. New York: Academic Press.

Smith, S. 1942. "Language and Non-Verbal Test Performance of Racial Groups in Honolulu before and after a Fourteen-Year Interval." Journal of General Psychology 26:51-93.

Sokal, Michael Mark. 1972. "The Education and Psychological Career of James McKeen Cattell, 1860-1904." Ph.D. dissertation, Case-Western Reserve University. Ann Arbor: University Microfilms.

Sorokin, Pitirim A. 1956. Fads and Foibles in Modern Sociology and Related Sciences. Chicago: Henry Regnery.

Spearman, Charles E. 1927. The Abilities of Man. New York: Macmillan.

_____. 1914. "The Heredity of Abilities." Eugenics Review 6:219-37.

_____. 1904a. "General Intelligence Objectively Determined and Measured." American Journal of Psychology 15:201-93.

_____. 1904b. "Note on the First German Congress for Experimental Psychology." American Journal of Psychology 15:447-48.

Spencer, Herbert. 1899. The Principles of Psychology. 3d ed. New York: D. Appleton.

_____. 1898. The Principles of Sociology. 3d ed. New York: D. Appleton.

Stanton, William. 1960. The Leopard's Spots. Chicago: University of Chicago Press.

Stern, William. 1904. The Psychological Methods of Testing Intelligence. Baltimore: Warwick and York.

Stocking, George Ward, Jr. 1968. Race, Culture, and Evolution. New York: Collier-Macmillan.

_____. 1960. "American Social Scientists and Race Theory, 1890-1915." Ph.D. dissertation, University of Pennsylvania. Ann Arbor: University Microfilms.

Stoddard, George D. 1943. The Meaning of Intelligence. New York: Macmillan.

_____. 1940. "Introduction." In The 39th Yearbook, of the National Society for the Study of Education, pt. 1, pp. 3-7.

Stoddard, George D., and Beth L. Wellman. 1940. "Environment and the IQ." In The 39th Yearbook, of the National Society for the Study of Education, pt. 1, pp. 405-42.

Sturtevant, A. H. 1965. A History of Genetics. New York: Harper & Row.

Tanser, H. A. 1941. "Intelligence of Negroes of Mixed Blood in Canada." Journal of Negro Education 10:650-52.

_____. 1939. The Settlement of Negroes in Kent County, Ontario, and A Study of the Mental Capacity of Their Descendants. Chatham, Ont.: Shepherd.

Tarter, Donald. 1970. "Attitude: The Mental Myth." The American Sociologist 5:276-78.

Taylor, Calvin W., and John L. Holland. 1962. "Development and Application of Tests of Creativity." Review of Educational Research 32 (February): 91-102.

Taylor, Calvin W., W. R. Smith, and B. Ghiselin. 1963. "The Creative and Other Contributions of One Sample of Research

Scientists." In Scientific Creativity, edited by Calvin W. Taylor and Frank Barron, pp. 53-76. New York: Wiley.

Taylor, Donald W. 1963. "Variables Related to Creativity and Productivity among Men in Two Research Laboratories." In Scientific Creativity, edited by Calvin W. Taylor and Frank Barron, pp. 228-50. New York: Wiley.

Terman, Lewis Madison. 1954. "The Discovery and Encouragement of Exceptional Talent." American Psychologist 9:221-38.

_____. 1940. "Personal Reaction to the Yearbook as a Whole." In The 39th Yearbook, of the National Society for the Study of Education, pt. 1, pp. 460-67.

_____. 1928. "General Introduction to the 1928 Yearbook." In The 27th Yearbook, of the National Society for the Study of Education, pt. 1, pp. ix-xv.

_____. 1922. "The Great Conspiracy: The Impulse Imperious of Intelligence Testers, Psychoanalyzed and Exposed by Mr. Lippmann." New Republic 33:116-20.

_____. 1921. "Intelligence and Its Measurement." Journal of Educational Psychology 12 (March): 127-33.

_____. 1917. "Feeble-Minded Children in the Public Schools of California." School and Society 5:161-65.

_____. 1916. The Measurement of Intelligence. Boston: Houghton Mifflin.

_____. 1906. "Genius and Stupidity: A Study of the Intellectual Processes of Seven 'Bright' and Seven 'Stupid' Boys." Pedagogical Seminars 13:307-73.

Terman, Lewis Madison, and Maud A. Merrill. 1937. Measuring Intelligence: A Guide to the Administration of the New Revised Stanford-Binet Tests of Intelligence. Boston: Houghton Mifflin.

Thompson, Charles H. 1934. "The Conclusions of Scientists Relating to Racial Differences." Journal of Negro Education 3 (July): 494-512.

Thomson, G. H. 1951. The Factorial Analysis of Human Ability. 5th ed. London: University of London Press.

Thorndike, Edward Lee. 1940. Human Nature and the Social Order. New York: Macmillan.

_____. 1925. The Measurement of Intelligence. New York: Bureau of Publications, Teachers' College, Columbia University.

_____. 1921. "Intelligence and Its Measurement." Journal of Educational Psychology 12 (March): 124-27.

_____. 1920. "Intelligence and Its Uses." Harpers 140:227-35.

_____. 1905. "Measurement of Twins." Journal of Philosophy, Psychology, and Scientific Methodology 2:547-53.

Thorndike, Edward Lee, E. O. Bregman, M. V. Cobb, and Ella Woodward. 1927. The Measurement of Intelligence. New York: Teachers' College Press.

Thorndike, Edward Lee, Elsie O. Bregman, Irving Lorge, Zaida F. Metcalfe, Eleanor Robinson, and Ella Woodward. 1934. The Prediction of Vocational Success. New York: Commonwealth Fund.

Thorndike, Robert Ladd, and Elizabeth Hagen. 1959. 10,000 Careers. New York: Wiley.

Thurstone, L. L. 1938. "Primary Mental Abilities." Psychometric Monographs, no. 1.

_____. 1934. "The Vectors of Mind." Psychological Review 41:1-32.

_____. 1933. The Theory of Multiple Factors. Ann Arbor: Edwards Brothers.

_____. 1921. "Intelligence and Its Measurement." Journal of Educational Psychology 12 (April): 201-7.

Tillyard, E. M. W. 1944. The Elizabethan World Picture. New York: Random House.

Tobias, Philip V. 1970. "Brain Size, Grey Matter and Race—Fact or Fiction?" American Journal of Physical Anthropology 32 (January): 3-25.

Tomilin, M. I., and C. P. Stone. 1934. "Intercorrelations of Measures of Learning Ability in the Albino Rat." Journal of Comparative Psychology 17 (February): 73-88.

Torrance, E. Paul. 1963. "Explorations in Creative Thinking in the Early School Years: A Progress Report." In Scientific Creativity, edited by Calvin W. Taylor and Frank Barron, pp. 173-83. New York: Wiley.

Trabue, M. R. 1922. "Some Pitfalls in the Administrative Use of Intelligence Tests." Journal of Educational Research 6 (June): 1-11.

Tryon, Robert Choate. 1940. "Genetic Differences in Maze-Learning Ability in Rats." In The 39th Yearbook, of the National Society for the Study of Education, pt. 1, pp. 110-19.

_____. 1935. "A Theory of Psychological Components—An Alternative to 'Mathematical' Factors." Psychological Review 42: 425-54.

_____. 1932a. "Multiple Factors versus Two Factors as Determinants of Ability." Psychological Review 39:324-51.

_____. 1932b. "So-Called Group Factors as Determinants of Abilities." Psychological Review 39 (September): 403-39.

_____. 1929. "The Genetics of Learning Ability in Rats: Preliminary Report." University of California Publications in Psychology 4:71-89.

Tuddenham, Read D. 1962. "The Nature and Measurement of Intelligence." In Psychology in the Making, edited by Leo Postman, pp. 469-525. New York: Knopf.

_____. 1948. "Soldier Intelligence in World Wars I and II." American Psychologist 3:54-56.

Tupes, E., and M. Shaycoft. 1964. "Normative Distributions of AQE Aptitude Indexes for High School Age Boys." Technical Document Report PRL-TDR-64-17. Lackland Air Force Base, San Antonio, Texas.

Urbach, Peter. 1974. "Progress and Degeneration in the IQ Debate." British Journal for the Philosophy of Science 25:99-135, 235-39.

Vandenberg, Steven G. 1968a. "Primary Mental Abilities or General Intelligence? Evidence from Twin Studies." In Genetic and Environmental Influences on Behavior, edited by J. M. Thoday and A. S. Parkes, pp. 146-60. New York: Plenum Press.

_____. 1968b. "The Nature and Nurture of Intelligence." In Genetics, edited by David C. Glass, p. 22. New York: Rockefeller University Press and Russell Sage Foundation.

_____. 1967. "Hereditary Factors in Psychological Variables in Man, with a Special Emphasis on Cognition." In Genetic Diversity and Human Behavior, edited by J. N. Spuhler, pp. 89-98. Chicago: Aldine.

_____. 1965. "Multivariate Analysis of Twin Differences." In Methods and Goals in Human Behavior Genetics, edited by Steven G. Vandenberg, pp. 29-40. New York: Academic Press.

Varon, Edith J. 1935. "The Development of Alfred Binet's Psychology." Psychological Monographs, vol. 46, no. 207.

Vernon, Phillip E. 1969. "Intelligence." In On Intelligence, edited by W. B. Dockrell, pp. 99-117. London: Methuen.

Vetta, Atam. 1974. "Ethnic Difference in Intelligence: Does It Exist?" Bulletin of the British Psychological Society 27:398-402.

Wade, Nicholas. 1976. "IQ and Heredity: Suspicion of Fraud Beclouds Classic Experiment." Science 194 (November 26): 916-19.

Wallach, Michael A. 1976. "Tests Tell Us Little about Talent." American Scientist 64 (January/February): 57-63.

_____. 1971. "Intelligence Tests, Academic Achievement, and Creativity." Impact of Science on Society 12 (October-December): 333-45.

Wallach, Michael A., and C. W. Wing, Jr. 1969. The Talented Student: A Validation of the Creativity-Intelligence Distinction. New York: Holt, Rinehart and Winston.

Waller, Jerome H. 1971. "Achievement and Social Mobility: Relations among IQ Score, Education, and Occupation in Two Generations." Social Biology 18 (September): 252-59.

Wallin, J. E. Wallace. 1916. "Who Is Feeble-Minded?" Journal of Criminal Law and Criminology, January.

Warburton, F. T. Fitzpatrick, J. Ward, and M. Ritchie. 1972. "Some Problems in the Construction of Individual Intelligence Tests." In Readings in Human Intelligence, edited by H. J. Butcher and D. E. Lomax. London: Methuen.

Weber, Max. 1946. From Max Weber. New York: Oxford University Press.

Wechsler, David. 1971. "Intelligence: Definition, Theory and the IQ." In Intelligence: Genetic and Environmental Influences, edited by Robert Cancro, pp. 50-58. New York: Grune and Stratton.

_____. 1958. Measurement and Appraisal of Adult Intelligence. 4th ed. Baltimore: Williams and Wilkins.

_____. 1949. Wechsler Intelligence Scale for Children. Administrative Manual. New York: The Psychological Corp.

Weiss, R. D. 1970. "The Effect of Education on the Earnings of Blacks and Whites." Review of Economics and Statistics 52 (May): 150-59.

Wellman, Beth L. 1940. "Personal Reaction to the Yearbook." In The 39th Yearbook, of the National Society for the Study of Education, pt. 1, pp. 468-71.

Wellman, David. 1968. "The Wrong Way to Find Jobs for Negroes." TransAction, April, pp. 9-18.

Wheeler, L. R. 1942. "A Comparative Study of the Intelligence of East Tennessee Mountain Children." Journal of Educational Psychology 33:321-34.

Whimbey, Arthur. 1976. "You Can Learn to Raise Your IQ Score." Psychology Today, January, pp. 27-29, 84-85.

Whipple, Guy M. 1940. "Editor's Preface." In The 39th Yearbook, of the National Society for the Study of Education, pt. 1, pp. xvii-xviii.

_____. 1928. "Editor's Preface." In The 27th Yearbook, of the National Society for the Study of Education, pt. 1, pp. viii-ix.

Willerman, Lee, A. F. Naylor, and N. C. Myrianthopoulos. 1974. "Intellectual Development of Children from Interracial Matings: Performance in Infancy and at 4 Years." Behavior Genetics 4 (March): 83-90.

_____. 1970. "Intellectual Development of Children from Interracial Matings." Science 170:1329-31.

Williams, Roger John. 1969. Biochemical Individuality. Austin: University of Texas Press.

Wilson, Kenneth, and Alejandro Portes. 1975. "The Educational Attainment Process: Results from a National Sample." American Journal of Sociology 81 (September): 343-63.

Wing, Cliff W., Jr., and Michael A. Wallach. 1971. College Admissions and the Psychology of Talent. New York: Holt, Rinehart and Winston.

Wissler, Clark. 1923. Man and Culture. New York: Crowell.

_____. 1920. "Opportunities for Coordination in Anthropological and Psychological Research." American Anthropologist 22:1-12.

_____. 1901. "The Correlation of Mental and Physical Traits." Psychological Monographs, vol. 3, no. 16.

Witty, Paul, and M. D. Jenkins. 1936. "Intra-Race Testing and Negro Intelligence." Journal of Psychology 1:179-92.

Wolf, Theta H. 1973. Alfred Binet. Chicago: University of Chicago Press.

Woodrow, Herbert. 1921. "Intelligence and Its Measurement." Journal of Educational Psychology 12 (April): 207-10.

Wright, Sewell. 1931. "Statistical Methods in Biology." Journal of the American Statistical Association 26 (March, Supplement): 155-63.

Yerkes, Robert M., ed. 1921. Psychological Examining in the United States Army. Washington, D.C.: U.S. Government Printing Office.

_____. 1917. "The Binet versus the Point Scale Method of Measuring Intelligence." Journal of Applied Psychology 1:111-22.

Yerkes, Robert M., and Josephine Curtis Foster. 1923. A Point Scale for Measuring Mental Ability. Baltimore: Warwick and York.

Yoder, Dale. 1928. "Present Status of the Question of Racial Differences." Journal of Educational Psychology 19:463-70.

INDEX

ABOUT THE AUTHOR

DOUGLAS LEE ECKBERG is assistant professor of sociology at the University of Tulsa. In 1978-79 he was assistant professor at Texas Christian University. Until 1978, he served as instructor in sociology at Austin Community College, Austin, and as assistant instructor in sociology at the University of Texas at Austin. He was also holder of the W. H. Webb Chair Fellowship in History and Ideas and was a Fellow of the Graduate School at the University of Texas at Austin.

Dr. Eckberg has written widely in the field of sociology. His work has appeared in The American Sociologist, Contemporary Sociology, and the American Sociological Review.

Dr. Eckberg holds a B.A. degree in psychology from the University of Texas at Austin, an A.M. degree in sociology from the University of Missouri-Columbia, and a Ph.D. in sociology from the University of Texas at Austin.